CUBA
THE MORNING AFTER

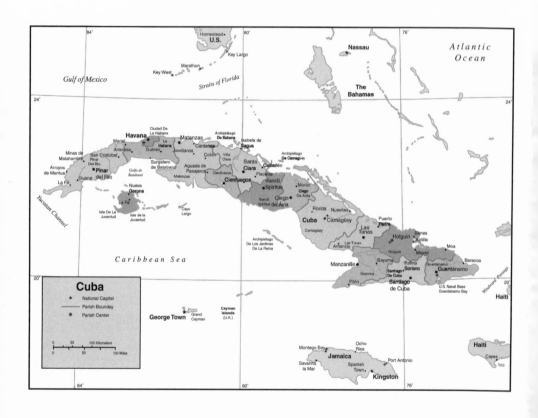

Atlantic
Ocean

Gulf of Mexico

Nassau

The
Bahamas

24°

24°

Homestead
U.S.

Key Largo

Key West   Marathon

Straits of Florida

Ciudad De
La Habana

Havana

Matanzas

Archipiélago
De Sabana

Isabela de
Sagua

Mariel

La
Habana

Cárdenas

Jovellanos

Artemisa

Guines

Santa
Clara

Archipiélago
De Camagüey

Colón

Villa
Clara

Caibarién

Minas de
Malahambre

San Cristobal

Pinar
Del Rio

Surgidero
de Batabanó

Aguada de
Pasajeros

Cienfuegos

Placetas

Arroyos
de Mantua

Pinar
del Rio

Golfo de
Batabanó

Matanzas

Cienfuegos

Sancti
Spiritus

Guane

Guane

La Fé

Nueva
Gerona

Sancti
Spiritus de Ávia

Olego

Morón

Ciego
De Ávila

La Fé

Isla De La
Juventud

Isle de la
Juventud

Cayo
Largo

Florida

Cuba

Camagüey

Nuevitas

Yucatan Channel

Caribbean Sea

Camagüey

Archipiélago
De Los Jardines
De La Reina

Las
Tunas

Puerto
Padre

Bánes

Holguín

Antilla

Amancio

Las Tunas

Holguín

Moa

Mayari

Baracoa

Manzanillo

Bayamo

Palma
Soriano

Guantánamo

Guantánamo

Gibara

Santiago
De Cuba

U.S. Naval Base
Guantánamo Bay

Windward Passage

Pilón

Santiago
de Cuba

Haiti

20°

20°

Cuba

★ National Capital

— Parish Boundry

⊙ Parish Center

0   50   100 Kilometers

0   50   100 Miles

George Town   Grand
Cayman

Cayman
Islands
(U.K.)

Haiti

Cayes

Montego Bay

Ocho
Rios

Port Antonio

Jamaica

Savanna
la Mar

Spanish
Town

Kingston

84°

80°

76°

CUBA
THE MORNING AFTER

Confronting Castro's Legacy

Mark Falcoff

The AEI Press

Publisher for the American Enterprise Institute

WASHINGTON, D.C.

2003

Available in the United States from the AEI Press, c/o Client Distribution Services, 193 Edwards Drive, Jackson, TN 38301. To order, call toll free: 1-800-343-4499. Distributed outside the United States by arrangement with Eurospan, 3 Henrietta Street, London WC2E 8LU, England.

Library of Congress Cataloging-in-Publication Data

Falcoff, Mark.
    Cuba the morning after : confronting Castro's legacy /
Mark Falcoff.
        p. cm.
    Includes bibliographical references and index.
    ISBN 0-8447-4175-2 (cloth: alk. paper)
    1. Cuba—Economic conditions—1990- 2. Cuba—Social conditions.
    3. Cuba—Relations—United States. 4. United States—Relations—Cuba.
    I. Title.

    HC152.5.F35 2003
    303.48'27291073—dc21

                                                                2003038514

3 5 7 9 10 8 6 4

Printed in the United States of America

For Les Gelb

Contents

Acknowledgments

The author wishes to express his deepest appreciation to the Lynde and Harry Bradley Foundation, the Smith Richardson Foundation, and the Tinker Foundation for the generous support that made this study possible.

He also acknowledges the indispensable support of five extraordinary research assistants—Dean Schaffer, Christopher Weld, Stephen Joyce, Román Martínez, and Lauren Di Cecio. A tip of the hat to James Knowles, who penetrated the mysteries of both software and economics to produce the charts in chapter 2, and to Ralph Galliano for generating the data on which they are based. In addition, the author thanks his editor, Juyne Linger, for her perspicacious and diligent preparation of the manuscript for publication.

Above all, thanks to David Rockefeller and Peter G. Peterson, who co-chaired a Council on Foreign Relations delegation that visited Cuba in February 2001, for inviting the author to come along.

Introduction

As its title announces, this is a book about Cuba's future. But it is also a book about the future of U.S.-Cuban relations.

It could hardly be otherwise. In spite of a forty-year period with no formal diplomatic relations, the United States and Cuba have never ceased to be close to one another—not simply geographically but in terms of their broader political imaginations as well. No Latin American country arouses the level of interest that Cuba perennially evokes; one need only visit any bookstore or library in the United States to establish this fact. And no American or foreign visitor to Cuba can come away from the island without being struck by how firmly Cubans of all classes and political ideologies have their gaze fixed across the Florida straits. Acting as a bridge of sorts is a large, relatively affluent, and politically well-organized exile community centered in southern Florida, hostile to the regime that governs its homeland, but intensely involved with the island and its people in myriad other ways.

Standing between the two countries lies something called "the revolution"—a shorthand term for the events that followed the triumph of a movement led by Fidel Castro, and Cuba's transformation into a tropical Communist state and member of the Soviet community of nations. Although that larger community no longer exists, Cuba's Communist state remains—as does its progenitor. More convinced than ever that his version of Marxist socialism will ultimately prevail, Fidel Castro continues to wait for the collapse of both the capitalist system and the United States of America.

Meanwhile, his adversaries on the other side of the water—not just the expatriate Cuban community but its allies in the U.S. political class—await the collapse or disappearance of the Castro regime and its replacement by something more nearly resembling the "bourgeois" democracies of El Salvador, Uruguay,

Chile, or Costa Rica. Indeed, much of U.S. policy, particularly since the end of the Cold War, has been predicated on Castro's Cuba losing its lease on life, its extinction but a matter of time. Meanwhile, a series of laws that hinder normal trade and travel relations between the two countries—the so-called "embargo"— remain in place. So far both sides have been disappointed: neither capitalism nor Castroism has yet disappeared from the map.

Underpinning this book is the presumption that sooner rather than later, relations between the two countries are bound to resume, though under circumstances yet unclear. At that point the United States will confront a Cuba very different from the one with which it broke relations more than four decades ago. This new Cuba—new, at any rate, to the United States—will pose a whole range of problems, many of them far more nettlesome and complex than the enforcement of a trade embargo or the marshaling of support for resolutions at the various international organizations. Much of this book is dedicated to teasing those problems out from the shadows of imminence, where they presently lurk, ignored in the pressure of current events and necessities.

More than a decade has passed since the collapse of the Soviet empire, and with it, the loss to Cuba of an entire network of advantageous trade and political and intelligence assets worldwide. Since 1991, Cuba has been living in what President Fidel Castro calls a "Special Period in Time of Peace," which is to say, one in which the country has known greater privations than ever before in its history. The collapse of the Soviet Union has deprived the island of an economic subsidy amounting to roughly $6 billion a year. Ironically, the disappearance of a strategic logic to hostility between Cuba and the United States has only deepened the antagonism between them. At the same time, however, the links between the two countries—both human and economic—have grown stronger than ever before. Cubans now depend heavily on remittances from their American cousins and on tourism—much of it from the United States, and most of that from Cuban expatriates returning to see their families.

Meanwhile, both sides nourish long-standing grudges. The United States, on behalf of nearly 6,000 certified claimants whose property was expropriated by the revolution, brandishes a bill running into several billions of dollars. For its part, the Cuban government demands not merely the unilateral lifting of the trade embargo, but literally hundreds of billions of dollars in "reparations" for economic damage allegedly inflicted by the same.

As this book tries to show, however, the issue of expropriated property is far less serious than the loss of Cuba's capacity to earn a living wage in today's world economy. This is due partly to the collapse of its sugar economy, for more than a century its principal source of income, and partly to the structural inability of tourism—even massive tourism—to replace it. While a drastic reform of its economy may render Cuba at least able to feed its 11.2 million residents—a task that far exceeds its current capacity—it will probably never again be an important participant in the world agricultural economy.

While history takes its own time resolving its conundrums, hundreds of thousands, perhaps even millions of Cubans dream of emigrating to the United States, just as legions of their compatriots have done almost without interruption since 1960. Many Cuban émigrés have prospered in their new lives, and even those who have not are enjoying a far higher standard of living than they would have if they had remained at home. A special entry regime for Cubans set up during the Cold War continues, somewhat anomalously, partly to inhibit a "migration crisis"—that is, the unrestrained release of thousands to make their way to the United States as best they can, as occurred in 1980 and again in 1994—and partly because of inertia and vested domestic political interests.

Although the Castro government officially (and loudly) objects to special treatment for Cuban entrants, it is probably the principal beneficiary of this policy. The possibility of leaving Cuba for a happier existence across the Straits of Florida has acted as a stabilizing political influence; many who would protest the policies of the Castro government simply opt out and queue up for an exit visa. Once relations between the two countries have been normalized, it seems unlikely that Cuba will continue to enjoy this safety valve. Surely Cuba will not "deserve" special treatment more than Mexico, Haiti, the Dominican Republic, or Cuba's other island neighbors. But will the absence of special treatment for its émigrés compromise Cuba's basic stability? If so, what policies and attitudes should the United States pursue? These issues have disturbing implications for the island's political future, a point explored at some length in the final chapter.

This book also takes issue directly with two underlying assumptions that drive both U.S. Cuban policy and opposition to it. First, many assume that once the Castro regime is gone and full diplomatic and trade relations resume, the island will experience rapid economic reconstruction thanks to the existence of a large, affluent, and able exile community based in southern Florida. This would be a logical (and happy) outcome were it not for the fact that Cuba today in no way resembles the country most of these expatriates left twenty, thirty, much less forty years ago. Everything—political culture, habits of work, expectations, even notions of national identity and everyday speech—is completely different and cannot be transformed overnight. Both Cuban "nations"—the one on the island and the one in exile—have lived different histories since 1959, cherish different memories, and worship, so to speak, at the altar of different gods. It goes without saying that the diaspora has enjoyed a far more constructive and wholesome experience than the one endured by those who remained at home, but the bottom line remains the same.

It is reasonable to assume that some expatriates will return to do business in Cuba; some already have, through third parties or third countries, and many more are preparing to do so. But to assume that the reconstruction of Cuba can simply be farmed out to the Miami diaspora is a fantasy that the United States would be best advised to abandon. The future relationship of Miami and Havana is bound to be far more complex and problematic than that, even assuming a political transformation that is likely to be nowhere near as far-reaching as many (myself included) would wish.

The book also challenges a second underlying assumption—that lifting the embargo will rescue Castro's revolution and make socialism finally "work" in Cuba. This is the aspiration of the international left and those in the American cultural community who currently control our institutions of higher education and much of our print and electronic media; it finds resonance among important congressional Democrats and their staffs.

The reality is quite the contrary. The normalization of relations will have the important side effect of trivializing the Cuban drama, stripping the country of its adversarial mystique—arguably its only remaining asset after a forty-year detour through suffocating authoritarianism and harebrained economic experimentation. The eventual and inevitable disappearance of Fidel Castro—a figure of ineffable (if somewhat inexplicable) glamour to Western journalists, celebrities, and politicians—will also deprive Cuba of much of its global prestige and influence. The sight of his successors, whoever they might be, welcoming American investors will probably do the rest. Indeed, there are signs that the opening to European and Latin American investment and the priority given to foreign tourism—and the consequent introduction of new economic and racial inequalities—have already begun to tarnish Cuba's prestige among what might be called the solidarity community.

Ironically, the U.S.-Cuban passion play is drawing to a close at the very moment that a new generation of leaders in Latin American countries far larger and more significant geopolitically than Cuba has arisen to reject the United States as a hemispheric leader, and more important, to question market-driven solutions to economic problems. The wisest among them would do well to consider the experience of Cuba and thereby spare themselves and their people Cuba's harsh reckoning, which, along with normalization of relations with the United States, may be remarkably close at hand.

1

The Shadow of the Past

The Search for Utopia

The late sociologist Lowry Nelson, one of the first American academics to devote serious attention to Cuba, wrote that "all revolutions are matters of controversy: their achievements and even their justifications are debated for generations after they happen."[1] The debates over the French, Russian, and Chinese revolutions fill whole libraries, so perhaps it is not surprising that the argument over what happened in Cuba—and why—dwarfs all the literature on other attempts at radical social reconstruction in the Western Hemisphere. This is surely not for lack of competition, since more than half a dozen countries—Mexico, Bolivia, Argentina, Guatemala, Chile, Peru, and Nicaragua—have in their own way undertaken revolutionary or semi-revolutionary excursions during the twentieth century.

Cuba, however, is in a class by itself, both because of the extremes to which the Castro regime has gone to abolish private property, suppress individual economic initiative, and block independent political expression, and because of the degree to which it has framed these efforts as part of a larger design to directly confront and humiliate the United States. In effect, in no other country in the hemisphere has there been so consistent, so thorough, and so ruthless an attempt to create utopia.

Such experiments in any country exact enormous costs from its population and require elaborate rationalizations. These are typically sought by rewriting its history to depict the old regime in the darkest possible tones. By way of contrast, antirevolutionary or counterrevolutionary emigrations have tended to produce a literature that idealizes the pre-revolutionary order. Both these generalizations hold true for the country that is the subject of this book.

5

History as Melodrama

On January 8, 1959, Fidel Castro and his bearded revolutionaries entered Havana on the heels of the fleeing dictator Fulgencio Batista. At the time most Americans could barely identify the location of the island, and probably not more than several dozen could discourse authoritatively on the peculiarities of its social and political system. Since then, however, Castro's revolution and its supposed antecedents have become part and parcel of the collective imagination of journalists, politicians, intellectuals, and artists around the world. Paradoxically—or perhaps, not so paradoxically—in spite of its historic antagonism toward Castro and all his works, the United States has become one of the principal producers and consumers of Cuba's revolutionary historiography.

The most emblematic example is Robert Redford's film *Havana,* which appeared in theaters in 1990, roughly the same time that the Castro regime was plunging into the worst economic crisis in its history, thanks to the collapse of its longtime Soviet ally and patron. The action of the film takes place between Christmas 1958 and New Year's Day 1959, which is to say, in the final week of the Batista regime. Almost half the action occurs in various luxury hotels, where Robert Redford, who plays a professional gambler, is moving about trying to find the perfect poker game. Quite by accident, he becomes involved with a beautiful woman on the ferry over from Key West; she turns out to be the wife of an anti-Batista activist from an old society family. When her husband is apparently killed by Batista's secret police—the dreaded SIM—she becomes involved romantically with Redford, who in spite of a determination to remain apolitical is gradually sucked into the triumphant movement of noble, Che Guevara-like peasant revolutionaries.

Throughout the film, the Cuban capital is represented as little more than an opulent gambling den-cum-bordello, a decadent façade behind which there languishes a people mired in misery and want. As the upper-class revolutionary tells Redford, "Children in the country die of TB, and those that don't die, when they get hungry, you know, they come to Havana and sell themselves. Some of us are trying to change that." By way of contrast, the characters in the film that represent or support the old regime make no apologies about their own crass motivations. The actor playing U.S. gambling kingpin Meyer Lansky loudly complains that Batista is not effectively using the army that "we [the United States] gave him," and warns that if Batista fails to suppress the revolutionaries, "we'll send him back to selling beans" [presumably where Washington found him]. One club owner, likening Havana to Shanghai, laments, "but then the Communists came in; I lost a fortune." The head of the secret police blurts out to Redford, "These people want to bring down everything you're here for—the food, the f—-ing, the gambling, the shows. . . . [T]hey think this is all for the government to decide." The film ends conveniently with the triumph of the revolution, whose fruits, the audience is left to surmise, can hardly be as rotten as those of the regime it replaced.[2]

Is Redford's version of Cuban history simply a piece of Hollywood eccentricity? Not at all. It merely dramatizes notions held very strongly and for many years by the American mainstream. Here, for example, is Arthur Schlesinger, Jr., Harvard historian and former White House aide to President Kennedy, recalling a trip to the Cuban capital in 1950:

> I was enchanted by Havana—and appalled at the way that lovely city was being debased into a giant casino and brothel for American businessmen over for a big weekend from Miami. My fellow countrymen reeled through the streets, picking up fourteen-year-old Cuban girls and tossing coins to make men scramble in the gutter. One wondered how any Cuban—on the basis of this evidence—could regard the United States with anything but hatred.[3]

The same theme recurs in the television documentary series on the Cold War produced by Cable News Network (CNN) in 1998. "Throughout the 1940s and '50s," the narrator explains, "the Caribbean island of Cuba had been America's playground: beaches, booze, and casinos. Havana had it all."[4] But then, he adds in an ominous undertone, "Cuba's land and industry were almost entirely owned by American corporations." Veteran newscaster Walter Cronkite is summoned to recite this useful glissando: "We considered it part of the United States practically, just a wonderful little country that was of no danger to anybody. As a matter of fact," he adds, "it was a rather important economic asset to the United States."[5]

Most remarkable of all (in light of his personal rivalry with Fidel Castro and the elaborate efforts he made to get rid of him) is the statement President

John F. Kennedy is supposed to have made to French journalist Jean Daniel a few days before Kennedy's assassination:

> I believe there is no country in the world, including all the African regions, including any and all countries under colonial domination, where economic colonization, humiliation and exploitation were worse than Cuba, in part owing to my country's policies during the Batista regime. . . . I will go even further: to some extent it is as though Batista was the incarnation of a number of sins on the part of the United States. Now we shall have to pay for those sins.[6]

Perhaps President Kennedy never really said these words, but as far as many American and European intellectuals are concerned, he might as well have done so, since this point of view has become the received liberal wisdom on the subject of pre-revolutionary Cuba, and by indirection, the politically correct justification for forty years of Communist rule.

Cuba's *Sonderweg*

Some of these statements about Cuba are true or partly true, some were true at one point in the twentieth century but not by 1958, some are flatly untrue, while others—such as the army the U.S. supposedly "gave" to Batista—are grotesque falsehoods. But the most important affirmation of all—that of President Kennedy—at best describes episodes in the history of the Dominican Republic, Haiti, or Guatemala; it has little or nothing at all to do with Cuba. As a matter of fact, the most striking feature of that island's evolution has been its distinctiveness: it has trod a historical path different from that of other Spanish-American countries, different from its immediate neighbors, and different, too, in its relations with the United States.

Discovered by Christopher Columbus on his second voyage in 1493–1494, Cuba had only recently been settled by Spain when Hernán Cortés and Francisco Pizarro discovered far more valuable territories in Mexico and Peru. Both territories were rich not only in gold and silver, but—in sharp contrast to Cuba—possessed of large, tractable Indian communities that could be conscripted into a disciplined labor force. As a result, for 250 years Cuba remained a mere colonial entrepôt—albeit a very important one. Its capital, Havana, housed a large Spanish military and a naval, clerical, administrative, and customs establishment composed of soldiers, officials, clergy, merchants and adventurers who moved back and forth between the Iberian peninsula, Mexico, and the South American mainland. The port of Havana was also the point where the Spanish treasure fleet assembled each year to await the large naval escort that would accompany it on its return to the imperial countinghouses in Cádiz and Seville.

The permanent Spanish presence on the island was so large, in fact, that almost alone among Spain's American principalities, Cuba did not rebel against colonial rule during the second and third decades of the nineteenth century. When the last Spanish forces were compelled to quit the American mainland in 1824, Cuba, along with Puerto Rico and the Philippines, became the final remnants of what had once been a vast overseas empire. More to the point, for its loyalty and constancy, Cuba won the appellation "the ever-faithful isle."

The Spanish hold on the island was both strengthened and weakened by three developments beginning in the final half of the eighteenth century. The first was the temporary capture of Havana by the British (1762–1763), which gave the city's inhabitants a taste of the goods denied them by a restrictive trade regime. After the British withdrawal under the Treaty of Paris (1763), the authorities in Madrid felt compelled to gradually loosen those barriers, conceding to Havana the status of a free port and abandoning duties on machinery for the production of sugar and tobacco. They even allowed foreign merchants to settle and buy property in the city. Therein lay the seeds of future sentiment for separation.

But the second and third developments had the effect of neutralizing the first, at least in the short term. Throughout the late eighteenth century, West Indian sugar production declined sharply due to soil erosion and the exhaustion of the relatively limited amount of flat, arable land in Jamaica and other British Caribbean islands. At the same time, a revolution erupted in nearby St. Domingue (Haiti). The uprising, which began as a movement of the colony's tiny white population asserting its rights under the French constitution of 1793, quickly spun out of control, unleashing African or African-descended slaves against their masters and destroying the most economically productive plantation economy in the Caribbean.

The immediate effect of this social upheaval—the most radical in the history of the Americas until the Castro revolution of 1959—was to take the world's largest sugar supplier out of the market altogether, dramatically increasing the world price of the product and providing an incentive for the fullest development of Cuba's own agro-industrial potential. This turn of events was bolstered by the emigration from Haiti of many French planters, who brought to Cuba not merely their knowledge of the sugar industry and more arcane aspects of its technology, but also tales of pillage and murder by a slave population on the rampage. These stories, which surely lost nothing in the telling, were so horrifying as to encourage Cuba's white population increasingly to take shelter in the Spanish connection as the island's own African labor force grew to meet the needs of the expanding sugar economy. Spain's garrison—40,000 strong as early as the 1820s—remained the best and ultimately the only insurance against "another Haiti," and as such underpinned colonial interests on the island for another three to four decades.

By 1860, Cuba was producing a sugar harvest of 450,000 tons a year, virtually a quarter of the world's production. The relationship between the institution of slavery and the island's loyalty to the Spanish crown was so firmly intertwined that the first movements favoring Cuban separation from the mother country were driven by Spain's decision in 1820—under heavy British pressure—to end the trade altogether. Again, however, unlike their counterparts in Latin American countries, Cuban Creole elites did not in the first instance aim at independence, but rather annexation to the United States, which presumably would provide more reliable protection for the institution of slavery. These aspirations meshed with those of politicians and intellectuals in the southern United States who were always seeking to bring additional slave territories into the Union. A case in point is the unsuccessful conspiracy of Narciso López, a renegade Spanish general, hatched in 1850 in collusion with Mississippi and Louisiana slave owners. As López himself put it before being betrayed, captured, and garroted, "The star of Cuba . . . will emerge beautiful and shining on being admitted with glory into the splendid North American constellation whence destiny leads it."[7]

American interest in acquiring Cuba was long-standing and not limited to slavocrats or their confederates on the island, as Cuban historians never tire of reminding us. It dates back to the first years of the United States as a republic, if not indeed before. This interest arose from a variety of geopolitical considerations, the most central of which was the fear that Spain, a weakened and declining power, would be unable to defend the island against more vital European forces represented by England and France. Even worse, in the eyes of American statesmen, was the possibility that Spain might transfer Cuba to England or France through a diplomatic settlement. As Daniel Webster put it in a speech on the floor of the U.S. House of Representatives in 1843, "The real question is whether the possession of Cuba by a great maritime power of Europe would seriously endanger our own immediate security, or our essential interest." Webster pointed out in passing that American trade with the island, even at that early date, exceeded that of U.S. trade with France and its dependencies. Webster added,

> But this is but one part of the case and not the most important. Cuba . . . is placed in the mouth of the Mississippi. Its occupation by a strong maritime power would be felt, in the first moment of hostility, as far up the Mississippi and the Missouri as our population extends. It is the commanding point of the Gulf of Mexico. See, too, how it lies in the very line of our coast wise traffic; interposed in the very highway between New York and New Orleans. . . .[8]

Throughout the first half of the nineteenth century there was much talk in high places in Washington and elsewhere about the desirability and even inevitability of Cuba's eventual annexation to the United States. The most famous remark of all was that of John Quincy Adams, who in 1823 likened the island to "an apple severed by the tempest from its native gravitation. . . , [inevitably moving] towards the North American Union."[9] It is also true, however, that from the early 1820s to the mid-1840s, successive American administrations consistently supported Spanish control of Cuba, and what is more, cooperated with Spain in putting down Cuban internal revolts. If the United States could not acquire the island for itself, then to the extent to which Spain appeared marginally capable of maintaining its power there, the United States preferred the status quo to any alternative.

During the 1850s, the proposed purchase of Cuba from Spain was one of the devices by which American politicians sought to temper regional conflict within the United States. The assumption was that the southern states would be less inclined to conspire at secession if they were offered the prospect of Cuba tilting the internal balance of free versus slave territories in their favor. To this end, Presidents James K. Polk, Franklin Pierce, and James Buchanan each in turn approached Madrid, though ultimately to no avail. In less than a decade, three developments—the emergence of the Republican party in the late 1850s, a new force committed to stanching the entry of new slave territories into the Union; the U.S. Civil War (1861–1865); and the abolition of slavery in the United States in 1863—removed the principal incentive to annexation. For its part, Spain officially terminated the slave trade throughout its territories in 1866. Meanwhile, a sustained expansion of the sugar industry had attracted sufficient emigrants from Spain to significantly "whiten" the Cuban population.

In the first half of the nineteenth century, Cuban secessionists, real and potential, were driven by the fear that Spain could not adequately protect the institution of slavery; in the second half, they were actuated by a resentment of high taxes and an arrogant colonial bureaucracy. A steady demographic increase in the number of "Creoles" (that is, Cubans of recent Spanish origin) necessarily raised serious questions about why the island was governed in a manner so distinct from that of the provinces of metropolitan Spain. Anti-Spanish sentiment was also fed by the island's growing lack of economic complementarity with the mother country. For its part, Spain—torn by internal conflict and weighed down by its own economic and cultural backwardness—was increasingly incapable of providing either the technology or the markets needed to meet the emerging challenge of American and European beet sugar; nor could it supply most of the consumer goods that the prosperous Creole aristocracy wished to buy. These grievances congealed around a reform movement in the mid-1860s which, failing to achieve minimal satisfaction, exploded into an armed insurrection, the so-called Ten Years' War (1868–1878).

During its early phase, the rebellion was confined to the eastern provinces of Santiago and Holguín; even so, Spain found it necessary to dispatch 100,000 troops to reassert its control. The conflict assumed a form and style that would be repeated in subsequent Cuban civil wars—a ragtag rebel army; few set piece battles; long periods of stalemate; unsettled political conditions in the metropolis; and a counterinsurgency campaign continually undermined by bad weather, disease, ignorance of local conditions, and lack of local support on one hand and by bureaucratic corruption and political favoritism on the other.

To break the stalemate, the rebels decided to carry the war to the western provinces of Matanzas, Havana, and Pinar del Río, where the richest sugar lands and most modern mills were located. The logic of the insurgents was dictated by the assumption that if the source of Cuba's wealth could be effectively destroyed, the Spaniards would abandon the island as economically useless. A helpful side effect would be to throw thousands of field and mill hands out of work, many of them black or mulatto, freeing them to join the rebels. While this tactic did not in fact convince the Spanish to abandon Cuba—at enormous human and financial cost, the mother country finally crushed the insurgency in 1878—it did have the unanticipated effect of financially destroying the Cuban landed aristocracy and opening the way for American interests to purchase its ruined properties, including one whose principal stockholder had been the Queen Mother of Spain.

The seventeen-year period between the end of the Ten Years' War and the beginning of the Second Cuban War of Independence (1895–1898) was marked by three major developments. The first was the failure of Spaniards and Cubans to find a satisfactory "autonomist" solution that would have given the island something similar to the dominion status enjoyed by Canada in the British Empire. The second was the definitive displacement of Spain by the United States as Cuba's economic metropolis and the increasing presence of Cuban political dissidents in major American cities, particularly New York. And the third was the formation and growing influence of a new independence movement, the Cuban Revolutionary Party, led by a remarkable journalist, poet and essayist José Martí.

A precocious political activist whose earliest efforts earned him a prison sentence in Spain, Martí went on to study at Zaragoza, worked as a journalist in Mexico, and taught in Guatemala, eventually settling in New York. There he became the correspondent for leading Latin American newspapers, most notably the Argentine flagship daily *La Nación*. Though deeply patriotic, Martí was also very much a Hispanic-American internationalist, and he had widespread connections throughout the Caribbean basin. He both admired and feared the United States, and sought to preempt both Cuban annexationists and American imperialists by forming an effective independence movement that would have both civil and military components. His Cuban Revolutionary Party, funded largely by the tithes of Cuban workers in

New York, Key West, and other centers of expatriation, eventually drove other contenders from the field and became, perforce, the effective expression of anti-Spanish sentiment both on the island itself and among the Cuban diaspora in the United States.

Martí was less successful in the military sphere. In gross violation of U.S. neutrality, he and his confederates laboriously assembled the ships and weaponry for three separate expeditions at a remote port near Jacksonville, Florida, in January 1895. Several days before its scheduled departure, U.S. officials seized the lot, forcing Martí to reassemble what forces and weaponry he could in the Dominican Republic, home of one of his principal military commanders, General Máximo Gómez.

None of these actions went unnoticed by the Spanish authorities; as a result, when small groups rose in arms in a number of Cuban cities in February, they were easily thwarted. Inevitably, eastern Cuba once again became the epicenter of the rebellion, and, as in the Ten Years' War, what had begun as an attempted *coup de main* was transformed into a protracted conflict. Martí himself was an early casualty, killed shortly after disembarking in May 1895. By the end of the war, most of his important confederates had also perished. Consequently, at the time of the establishment of the Cuban republic in 1901, the only plausible political class to lead the new nation, apart from a handful of civilians from aristocratic (but ruined) planter families, were second-line "generals" and "colonels" recruited from the ragtag army of liberation. For generations thereafter, Cuban intellectuals and historians speculated on how different things might have been "if Martí had lived." The question is unanswerable, but surely one individual, no matter how gifted, could not have fully shaped and controlled the direction of the country once the Spanish link was severed.

The Second Cuban War of Independence (1895–1898) was even more violent and destructive than the first. The Cuban patriots repeated the scorched-earth tactics of the Ten Years' War, and by early 1896, some of the country's richest zones had been laid waste by the rebels. In desperation, Madrid replaced the Spanish commander, General Arsenio Martínez Campos, with an even tougher general, Valeriano Weyler, with instructions to fight to the "last man and the last peseta."

General Weyler set about pacifying Cuba by emptying the countryside of the population that had supported the insurgents. Entire peasant communities were rounded up into relocation centers *(reconcentrados),* a move that seriously disrupted Cuban agriculture and created drastic food shortages. Moreover, the poor quality of Spanish military administration made this tactic, which was already harsh, inhumane as well, with perhaps more people dying in the *reconcentrados* from lack of proper sanitation than from inadequate nutrition. This was, in fact, the first time in modern Western warfare that civilians had been treated in this fashion, and it provoked widespread international protest which representatives of the patriot cause in the United States and elsewhere were quick to exploit. A series of events in Spain, including the assassination of Weyler's patron, Prime Minister Antonio Cánovas del Castillo, led to Weyler's recall and replacement by General Ramón Blanco, whose brief was to proclaim Cuba's autonomy and attempt to divide the island's political community by luring a number of Creoles to serve in a dominion-style administration.

Was this a sign of Spanish recognition of imminent military defeat? Cuban historians have often said so, some even to the point of arguing that the United States intervened in the war purposely to forestall the unconditional (and inevitable) victory of patriot arms. At best this is idle speculation. Though the Cubans had won some important tactical victories in 1897, Spain had not been defeated, and its willingness to subsequently take on the United States—a far stronger opponent and under circumstances that could only be regarded as suicidal—suggest that it would have continued the war regardless of cost. This interpretation is buttressed by the subsequent history of Spain's colonial wars in North Africa in the early twentieth century, a record marked by intransigence in the service of a lost cause bordering on pure irrationality.

What is beyond dispute is that the spectacle of the *reconcentrados* and the high human cost that the war exacted from the Cuban people transformed the war into a domestic political issue in the United States and created a constituency for U.S. aid to the insurgents, if not indeed for outright intervention. In no way did this sentiment respond to economic pressures. American business interests in Cuba had traditionally been on the side of the Spanish, partly because the colonial government conscientiously paid indemnities to those whose properties had been damaged by the insurgents, and partly because the U.S. business community did not relish the prospect of a patriot government of improvised soldiers, former field workers, or unemployed journalists, lawyers, and journeymen, many of them black or of mixed race. As a result, during the second administration of President Grover Cleveland (1893–1897), U.S. neutrality effectively favored continued Spanish rule.

By the time that President William McKinley took office in March 1897, the situation was changing. Both Congress and elements of the press were urging recognition of Cuban belligerency. Their calls—actuated by humanitarian sentiment, anti-Spanish and anti-Catholic feeling, a desire to sell newspapers, or merely a yen for excitement—converged with those of Assistant Navy Secretary Theodore Roosevelt, who in the age of expanding sea power was suddenly discovering the geopolitical centrality of the island. At the same time, to the extent that Spain was seen as unable to hold the island, many, including some U.S. business interests, preferred to see it annexed to the United States.

For his part, President McKinley urged patience and restraint upon his countrymen. He even suggested that the autonomist solution be given a chance to work. However, rising political unrest in Havana led the U.S. consul-general to urge the dispatch of the U.S. warship *Maine* from its base in Key West. The ultimate purpose of this "friendly visit," as it was called, has never been made quite clear. Whatever it was, the ultimate effect was to drive the United States to war. On February 15, 1898, the ship mysteriously exploded in Havana harbor, killing 260 of its crew.[10] The event itself electrified opinion in the United States and led Washington to deliver an ultimatum to Madrid: the colonial authorities were to offer to the Cuban patriots an immediate, unconditional truce. The Spanish were of a mind to satisfy Washington, but the rebels were not so easily persuaded. As a result, Madrid could find no way to meet the demands of the United States. On April 16, the U.S. Congress approved a joint resolution that both asserted the right of the Cuban people to independence and disavowed any intention to exercise "sovereignty, jurisdiction, or control over said island . . . and asserts its determination . . . to leave the government and control of the island to its people." On the other hand, no effort was made to recognize or deal with the insurgent government-in-arms, and U.S. forces assigned their patriot counterparts secondary tasks which, again according to Cuban historians and others as well, provided the margin of difference for victory in the only crucial land battle of the war, fought at Santiago de Cuba. Even so, the Cuban forces were not allowed to participate in the surrender ceremonies or even to enter the city when it fell to American forces in July 1898.

Spain's brief war with the United States was an unmitigated disaster for Madrid. In addition to the loss of its entire fleet—destroyed in a single engagement with the U.S. Navy outside of Santiago Bay—Madrid was forced by the Treaty of Paris (December 1898) to surrender not only Cuba but its two other remaining island dependencies, Puerto Rico and the Philippines. While the United States immediately began to organize the latter two as U.S. territories, Cuba was temporarily occupied by American troops and placed under a U.S. military government. Most galling of all, no Cuban was a party to the discussions in Paris that brought an end to the struggle for which so many patriots had given their lives. It was an oversight that no Cuban, even those otherwise well disposed toward the United States, has ever been able to forgive.

As in all of the crucial encounters between the United States and Cuba, the record of the U.S. military government (1898–1901) is the subject of acute historical controversy. Unquestionably, General Leonard Wood, the supreme U.S. authority on the island, took a dim view of the Cubans' capacity for self-government and acted—as one might well expect of the generalíssimo of any occupying army—with arrogance and insensitivity. On the other hand, the accomplishments of his administration were many. In addition to organizing the orderly demobilization of the Cuban patriot army, which might otherwise have degenerated into a series of armed robber bands, Wood oversaw a significant improvement in public health, including the eradication of yellow fever; development of the island's communication network; and establishment of the country's first system of public schools.

Although much of the country's productive capacity had been destroyed during the war, the economy was almost instantly revitalized by the massive entry of American capital, which invested not only in sugar, but railways, utilities, tobacco, minerals, and other resources. No doubt many of these investors were encouraged to risk their money in the expectation that the island would remain a permanent U.S. dependency—and this in spite of repeated assurances to the contrary by the occupation authorities. In point of fact, Article 4 of the joint resolution that led the United States to enter the war against Spain, the so-called Teller Amendment, specifically disclaimed any U.S. intention to annex the island. Whatever temptations might have existed to contravene this pledge, the revolt of disappointed patriots under General Emilio Aguinaldo in the Philippines—an insurgency that cost the United States millions of dollars and many years to extinguish—undoubtedly acted as a persuasive counterexample.

Yet the United States did not intend to walk away from Cuba altogether. The Cuban constitutional convention convened by General Wood in 1900 had produced a document that the occupying authorities found unsatisfactory. To consummate the withdrawal of the American authorities, the delegates were forced to incorporate into the charter a piece of legislation that had already found its way into an Army appropriation bill in the United States—the so-called Platt Amendment, which reserved for the United States the right to intervene in Cuba in the event that, in its own estimation, "life, liberty or property" were in peril. The effect was to truncate the country's sovereignty as an independent republic; indeed, until the United States unilaterally repealed the amendment in 1934, most Europeans regarded Cuba as a protectorate of the United States rather than an independent country in its own right.

The Years of Protectorate, 1901–1934

Cuba thus came into the community of Latin American nations in a fashion very different from that of Mexico, Peru, Argentina, or even Guatemala or El Salvador. Again, the circumstances, however unsatisfactory from the point of view of Cuban patriots, were not wholly negative. A U.S.-Cuban Reciprocity Treaty (1903) afforded Cuban sugar preferential treatment in the American market in exchange for reduced duties on American imports. No doubt this document was drafted with greater solicitude to American sugar interests on the island than to the interests of the Cuban people, but the effect was nonetheless favorable to the population as a whole because it encouraged significant investment in a country that had been utterly devastated by years of continuous war. Some Cubans (and others) have complained bitterly that the price Cuba paid for its place in the American market was too high. On one hand, they have argued, it saddled the country with a monoculture from which there was no easy escape, making the entire society dependent upon the perpetually oscillating world price of sugar. On the other, they point out, the treaty essentially liberated U.S. exporters from the need to compete with European or Japanese competitors.[11]

Both charges are true and yet probably ultimately irrelevant. Given the conditions in Cuba at the end of the Second War of Independence, no other source of income was likely to generate economic recovery as rapidly and completely as sugar (and to some extent, tobacco). And while the United States undoubtedly enjoyed a serious commercial advantage in the Cuban market, given geographical proximity and established consumer habits, it was unlikely that, all things being equal, the island would have recurred massively to other suppliers. The case of nearby Mexico, where no such treaty restrictions existed, but where the pattern of imports was roughly similar in the same time period, makes this clear.

The end of the war with Spain produced one unexpected and certainly ironic consequence—namely, the emigration of more Spaniards to the island between 1898 and 1920 than during the entire 400 years that Cuba had been a Spanish colony. "The percentage of Spaniards among the island's population," historian Alistair Hennessy has noted, "climbed from 8.2 percent in 1899 to 11.1 in 1907, 14 in 1919, and 15.8 in 1931." Cuba, he adds, "along with Argentina and Uruguay, is predominantly an immigrant country, but it is uniquely a country of *Spanish* immigrants."[12] Most of these migrants were poor, often arriving with little more than their personal baggage, and they tended to go into the retail trade or agriculture. Close-knit and clannish, often bonding in associations based on common provincial origins in Spain, they eventually created a society within a society, complete with social clubs, mutual lending associations, schools, and clinics. With larger business enterprises controlled by Americans or their Cuban affiliates, and smaller and middle-sized operations in the hands of Spaniards, the only real occupation open to many ambitious Cubans, apart from the military, was politics.

In this regard, it is difficult to say whether Cuba was so very different from other Latin American countries. It is true that the existence of the Platt Amendment with its ever-present threat of U.S. intervention acted as a permanently destabilizing force in the nation's civic life. While Cuban historians, intellectuals, and politicians tend to ascribe to the United States an active desire to dominate Cuban politics that far exceeds the case, there is no doubt that the Platt Amendment acted as a kind of sword of Damocles suspended over the country's institutions, depriving them of the most elementary credibility.

But that was not all. The Platt Amendment also acted as a goad to political unrest as disappointed office seekers, typically defeated in rigged elections, were tempted to create precisely those kinds of situations that would justify, even require, U.S. military intervention. This is precisely what occurred in 1906, when Cuba's first president, Tomás Estrada Palma (1901–1906), decided to run for reelection. When his defeated opponents rose up to challenge the outcome, Estrada Palma called for troops from the United States. When President Theodore Roosevelt refused to oblige, the Cuban president and his entire cabinet resigned, leaving the United States with little choice but to assume control of the island, which it did until new elections were held three years later. The experience of this second occupation (1906–1909) was sufficiently problematic for the United States to lead it to resist such traps in the future, but it was far from disillusioning for cynical Cuban politicians, who continued to denounce the Platt Amendment and at the same time speculate on its possibilities to destroy their opponents.

A second effort, this time centered on indirect control, was likewise unsuccessful. After the collapse of world sugar markets in the early 1920s, the island's financial situation became precarious and Washington was sufficiently concerned to dispatch General Enoch H. Crowder as ambassador, charged with straightening out the country's tangled economic affairs. A veteran Indian fighter rather than a practiced diplomat, Crowder arrived on a battleship that became his headquarters during his entire mission. His chief Cuban interlocutor, President Alfredo Zayas, was a clever scoundrel, adept at manipulating both Americans and his hapless countrymen. At first acceding to Crowder's demands, Zayas appointed an "honest cabinet," reduced the government budget, and purged the administration of corrupt officials. But the Cuban president was also capable of draping his own insincerity and self-seeking with the flag of injured patriotism. He eventually found the courage to reverse the reforms urged upon him by Crowder, defying the American envoy to right the situation with the only recourse that remained to him— the deployment of American troops. Once again the United States discovered that the Platt Amendment was as much a burden as a weapon.

The third episode of U.S. intervention was even more disastrous from the perspective of both countries. Zayas's successor, Gerardo Machado, was a veteran of the Second War of Independence and a tough and experienced politician. After an auspicious start at cleaning up corruption, he eventually succumbed to the temptations of power, overturning existing institutions and becoming a virtual dictator. The result was a widespread movement of civic resistance that incorporated students, workers, and members of the urban middle class. By the time the United States became fully cognizant of the extent of the resistance, the anti-Machado forces had seized the initiative.

An effort at mediation by U.S. Ambassador Harry Guggenheim came to naught; a change of administration in Washington in March 1933 led to the dispatch of Ambassador Sumner Welles, a career diplomat and personal friend of President Franklin D. Roosevelt, to secure Machado's resignation. This Welles did by brandishing the threat of U.S. military intervention. Once Machado was gone, Welles set about assembling a government to his own taste; he seemed genuinely surprised when it collapsed within a matter of hours thanks to an unusual alliance of students and noncommissioned officers in the Cuban army who had seized control from their superiors. The revolutionaries installed a new administration under Dr. Ramón Grau San Martín, a physiologist and university professor who enjoyed widespread support from all of the elements that had mobilized against Machado.

Deeply offended, Welles convinced Washington not to recognize the new government, all the while endlessly lobbying for effective U.S. military intervention.[13] While President Roosevelt was not persuaded to send American troops to the island, he did not recognize Grau's administration. Meanwhile, Welles connived with Sergeant (later Colonel) Fulgencio Batista to separate the military component from the student-soldier coalition upon which the government rested. Batista, leader of the sergeant's rebellion, had no difficulty seeing where his advantage lay, and once he abandoned Grau, the latter's fate was sealed. A new government more to Welles' liking was installed; on the envoy's recommendation, Washington promptly extended diplomatic recognition; and Batista, now self-promoted to colonel and head of the Cuban army, became the power behind the throne until winning election to the presidency in his own right in 1940.

Welles' role in Cuba provoked sharp criticism in both the United States and Latin America, and no doubt played an important role in bringing about a revision of U.S. policy toward the region.[14] First came the unilateral abrogation of the Platt Amendment in 1934, then the acceptance of the doctrine of absolute nonintervention at the Sixth Pan American Conference held in Buenos Aires in 1936. In effect, the United States adopted the Estrada Doctrine, which holds that states rather than governments are the proper objects of diplomatic recognition. The effect, at least insofar as Latin America was concerned, was to remove any element of moral or political judgment in the establishment of relations between the United States and other governments. Latin American politicians, journalists, and intellectuals professed to be pleased, as did American liberal critics of U.S. foreign policy. All of these groups imagined that the United States, having finally converted diplomatic recognition into a neutral tool of statecraft rather than an instrument of policy, was finally eschewing intervention in the affairs of other countries. At the time none grasped the point that recognition, like nonrecognition, could serve sinister purposes just as easily as it could satisfy high principle. Nonrecognition could undermine a liberal reformer like Grau San Martín, but the automatic acceptance of any government in control of forces on the ground could also serve the interests of unpopular dictators, as the subsequent histories of the Dominican Republic, Nicaragua, Haiti, and Cuba itself would demonstrate.

The Batista Years, 1934–1958

This explains in large measure why, after 1934, U.S. political concerns with Cuban internal politics were minimal. The country remained a good customer and a good ally under the puppet presidents installed by Batista (1934–1940), under Batista himself (1940–1944), and under his opponents, Ramón Grau San Martín (finally elected 1944–1948) and Carlos Prío (1948–1952). If Washington seemed remarkably unconcerned with the corruption, jobbery, and violence that afflicted Cuban politics, it also displayed a marked indifference to the course of economic and social policy. This made it possible for Cuba to become in many ways one of the most advanced countries in Latin America, with policies in land tenure, education, health, and labor rights that elsewhere in the region might well have aroused a strong negative reaction in the United States. Indeed, more than one American businessman in the 1950s was heard to describe Cuba as a country that had already experienced an undesirable social revolution, one more profound than that of Mexico, Bolivia, or even Argentina under General Juan Perón.

Because so much of Cuba's revolutionary historiography depends upon blackening the figure of General Fulgencio Batista, it is perhaps useful to say a few words about him here. In reality there were two Batistas—one before 1952 and one after. The Batista of the 1930s and 1940s was a nimble and imaginative politician who thought of himself as somewhat left of center; during his early days of power and influence, he sponsored or supported legislation that transformed Cuba into a country where the government played a crucial role in determining economic outcomes and which possessed a large and expensive social safety net. In that sense, Batista's Cuba came to more nearly resemble postrevolutionary Mexico than, say, Nicaragua under Anastasio Somoza or the Dominican Republic under Generalissimo Rafael Trujillo, two regimes with which it has been frequently and somewhat carelessly compared. (Any perusal of the more "progressive" American periodicals of the time—say, the *New Republic, PM,* or the *Nation*—will turn up some surprisingly favorable comments about the man and his regime.)

In an attempt to trump the populist Auténtico Party, whose outstanding figures were Grau and Prío, Batista established lines to the Popular Socialist party, as the Cuban Communists were called, and in fact during his first presidency (1940–1944), two of its members held ministerial portfolios, the first such experience anywhere in Latin America. For their part, Grau and Prío responded by becoming firm anti-Communists, and the rivalry between the two populist poles of Cuban politics was played out for some years in Cuban trade union affairs as well.

The second, "bad" Batista emerged in 1952, when the general seized power on the eve of an election in which his own efforts to stage a political comeback were obviously failing (he was trailing at third place in the polls). Because the coup itself came on the heels of eight years of unprecedented corruption and the cynical manipulation of power by the Auténticos, the initial reaction of the public was somewhat complacent. But as time went on, Batista revealed himself to be far less creative and energetic, and also less intent upon winning popular support, than during his first term of power.

Moreover, sugar prices were in a slump, and many of Cuba's economic and social indicators were in temporary decline. To revitalize the sluggish Cuban economy, Batista even toyed with dismantling some of the social legislation that made it prohibitively expensive to hire new workers or close unprofitable enterprises. In the best of times this innovation would have exacted a very high political cost, but in the context of a regime that lacked basic political legitimacy, it acquired explosive possibilities.

And, like all dictators, Batista was faced with a succession crisis—one that he resolved, as dictators so often do—by continually postponing his scheduled departure from office. When challenged, he became ever more violent and cruel, depending increasingly on police methods to remain in power. These in turn provoked the formation of an opposition which was also prepared to use violence, including one attempt to assassinate the dictator in 1957 which very nearly succeeded.

In short, even if Fidel Castro had never existed, the Batista government would eventually have collapsed from lack of popular support. By the time the United States took full cognizance of what was going on in Cuba, the best it could do was to link its demands with those of the civic opposition—to pressure Batista to leave office in an orderly manner by ceding power to a freely elected successor. The dictator's steadfast refusal to cooperate with either Cuba's traditional democratic forces or the U.S. Embassy eventually brought down the entire apparatus of "bourgeois" politics, and opened the way to power to a leader who has transformed the island beyond all recognition.[15]

Cuba in 1958

The exceptionalism that shaped Cuba's development from the early nineteenth century was still present in 1958, indeed surviving in some ways in exaggerated relief. For one thing, Cuba was and remained the most "Spanish" of Latin American countries, with a large "white" middle class of relatively recent (post-colonial) origin, including a new complement of refugees from Franco Spain. The Iberian influence was present in food preferences, family customs, entertainment (jai-alai and cockfighting), private education, and the affairs of the Catholic church, as well as in a peculiarly corporatist approach to social welfare. Paradoxically, at the same time it was also far and away the Latin American country most strongly influenced by the United States—whether measured in consumer preferences (automobiles, electrical appliances, interior décor, clothes), entertainment (Hollywood films, American music, baseball), tourism (more Cubans visited the United States in 1958 than Americans visited Cuba), graduate education, or business practices. As one character in Redford's *Havana* blurts out, "We Cubans want to be just like you Americans."

Of course, this was, on the face of it, impossible. Cuba was not the United States and could not be: it was a Spanish-speaking tropical island largely dependent upon agriculture. While its standard of living was considerably higher than that of most Latin American countries, including nearby Mexico, it was not to these places that Cuba compared itself. The demonstrated incapacity of the country's leaders to fully replicate a model so nearby, so well-known, and so ardently desired was in and of itself a permanently perturbing element in Cuban politics and to some extent remains so to the present day.[16]

As for the United States, it cast a shadow over the island far larger than it knew. For most Americans, the earlier episodes of U.S.-Cuban relations either were forgotten or had never been perceived in the first place; for many Cuban intellectuals and politicians, those events constituted a kind of open wound which they made sure was never cauterized. Whatever was wrong with Cuba could be traced either to the U.S. treatment of the patriot forces in the war of 1898, the Platt Amendment, the two U.S. occupations, the meddling of General Crowder or Sumner Welles, or the allegedly inadequate price paid for sugar versus the intolerably high price paid for American imports—or all these things combined. Even the persistence of the Batista regime in its final phase was attributed to concrete U.S. preferences rather than indifference or neglect; the failure of Washington to convince the dictator to retire was seen as proof of American duplicity rather than evidence that even hegemony had its limits.

On an official level, the bilateral relationship moved along smoothly under most governments after 1901. Cuban resentment of the United States, however, remained an important subtheme which could never be eased except by altering the terms of a geopolitical relationship that was inevitably unequal and could never be made otherwise. The United States could arguably have acted with greater wisdom or discretion at many points along

THE UNITED STATES AND FULGENCIO BATISTA

To this very day, American journalists habitually refer to the Batista dictatorship as "U.S.-supported," as if diplomatic recognition and normal relations constituted a concrete political statement. To be sure, *Cubans*—both those favorable to and those opposed to the Batista regime—found it convenient to broadcast this version. But others, including Americans, have accepted their views a bit too uncritically. Actually, by the time the Batista dictatorship entered its terminal phase in early 1958, the United States mission in Havana was working tirelessly to provide it with an expeditious exit. Unfortunately for the Batista regime, the Cuban dictator of the day had no particular interest in Washington's scenario for his country.

Another Latin American case provides an interesting contrast: no one has ever talked about the "British-supported" or "French-supported" Pinochet dictatorship in Chile (1973–1989), even though both countries, along with the Federal Republic of Germany, took advantage of a U.S. arms embargo (1976–1989) to sell Chile their warplanes, naval bottoms, even riot-control gear, not to mention the tendering of private loans from banks, slots in service institutes, and other aspects of a correct and even cordial relationship.

the way—for example, by allowing the 1933 "revolutionary" events to run their course rather than purposely truncating Grau's government. Yet nothing could be done about either the geographical proximity of the two countries or the radical asymmetry of their power and wealth. And it was the latter—not any particular action on the part of Washington—that gnawed away at Cuban self-esteem.

In this, Cuba was not alone in Latin America. But unlike Mexico or Venezuela, the relationship with the United States had always been more intimate, for good and for ill. Indeed, as in the case of Panama, the only other republic to which Cuba could be compared in this regard, the history of the two countries is virtually inseparable. This situation presented no great problem for the United States, a large, wealthy, and powerful country whose citizens are famously ignorant of foreign countries or their histories. But it constituted a very large problem for Cuba, which has always had to struggle to assert its own identity. Because the United States was so important to the island, Cuban citizens often imagined that the reverse was true, which ultimately turned out to be nearly so, though not in the ways that most Cubans imagined or hoped.

Apart from the intimate relationship with the United States, Cuba was unique in another regard—namely, its dependence on the production of a single crop, sugar. To be sure, there were other monocultures in the Caribbean basin and Central America, but none as heavily capitalized, as technologically advanced, and as well-connected to major markets as that of Cuba. Again, the cause of this was the island's relationship to the United States. Cuba was an early recipient of massive U.S. investment in its basic industry, and thanks to two reciprocity treaties—one in 1903, the other ratified in 1934—it was assured a privileged place in the American market. By 1958, roughly a quarter of all U.S. sugar imports were reserved for purchase from Cuba. As noted, reciprocity was originally intended as a favor to American investors capable of hiring the expensive legal talent necessary to coax it out of the U.S. Congress, but a significant side effect was to produce far higher living standards in Cuba than in otherwise similar countries nearby. Moreover, by the 1950s, American capital was withdrawing from the sugar industry, which in fact was becoming increasingly "Cubanized."

Unfortunately, there was nothing that Cuba—or, for that matter, the United States—could do about occasional fluctuations in the price of sugar and their inevitable impact on the island's fortunes as a society, including its basic social indicators. Throughout the twentieth century, there were periods of boom and bust in the world sugar markets, with high points coinciding with periods of war-induced scarcity (1914–1919, 1940–1945, 1950–1951), followed by sharp dips when the bubble burst. The recovery of European agriculture after World War II was particularly devastating to Cuban producers, a challenge that was doubly difficult because the peculiar land tenure arrangements and labor laws put in place during the late 1930s made it difficult to modernize production.[17] By the 1950s, sugar had ceased to be the motor of economic growth in Cuba, yet its importance still outweighed all other alternatives.[18]

This is not to say that there was no economic diversification at all. In the final decade before Castro's assumption of power, sugar still represented 80 percent of export earnings, but it was slowly falling as a percentage of national income. Meanwhile, the production of other crops—rice, coffee, potatoes, corn, beans, and pineapples—increased markedly. A dramatic rise in the number of poultry farms made Cuba self-sufficient in both chicken meat and eggs. The country's stock of cattle was being constantly improved and had grown more than eleven-fold since the end of the Second War of Independence, reaching 5.5 million head in the late 1950s, which was four times the per capita average for the United States. Between 1940 and 1956, the number of pigs more than quadrupled and the number of sheep tripled. Light manufacturing—particularly shoes, textiles, fibers, and several sugar-industry derivatives such as paper and boxes pressed from bagasse—also increased. In addition, Cuba produced cement, flour, chemicals for fertilizers, and feed for cattle and poultry. Finally, the country's mineral deposits were beginning to be exploited more aggressively. Some of this was due to foreign investment, but much of it drew on local capital markets. Indeed, by 1955, bank deposits had reached an all-time high of 815 million pesos, and Cubans controlled 60 percent of the banking sector.[19]

It is certainly arguable that these parallel economic activities, so often ignored or minimized by Cuban and foreign commentators, would never have effectively counteracted the dominant weight of sugar in the economy. But to say that the country had exhausted the expansive potential of its developmental model by the time the Batista regime entered its death agonies does not establish that a radical social revolution was the inevitable or even the most desirable outcome—except for those who believe it is a worthy objective on its own terms.[20] Nor does it prove that there was something particularly malevolent about U.S. involvement in the development and marketing of Cuba's principal product. As one observer has trenchantly remarked, "Development in the wrong direction is not identical with the absence of any development," and "it is very doubtful whether Cuba would have reached even the relative prosperity which it did in fact achieve had it not been for large American investments."[21] Subsequent events have demonstrated beyond all doubt that such a revolution could not resolve the problem of Cuba's place in the international economic system, which remains today perhaps its biggest challenge for the future.

With all its problems, the most important of which was political, Cuba in 1958 remained one of the more advanced and successful Latin American societies. The revolutionary version of pre-Castro history has been so widely diffused in the American and European media during the last four decades that such an assertion seems preposterous on its face. It is not, however, an opinion confined to disaffected Cuban exiles or Anglo-Saxon conservatives. No less an authority than veteran Communist Party chieftain Aníbal Escalante is on record as avowing that "Cuba was not one of the countries with the lowest standard of living of the masses in Latin America, but on the contrary one of those with the highest standard of living." If misery and want alone were the causes of revolution, he added, then the "first great patriotic, democratic and socialist revolution of the continent . . . should have been first produced in Haiti, Colombia, or even Chile, countries of greater poverty for the masses than the Cuba of 1952 or 1958."[22]

Indeed, at the time of Castro's formal embrace of Marxism-Leninism, memories of the pre-revolutionary dispensation were so fresh that an entirely new theory had to be hatched by Ernesto "Che" Guevara to explain the anomaly of a social revolution developing in a country of this sort—a theory satisfying perhaps to foreign romantics but surely not to any serious student of Marxist theory, or for that matter, of Cuban development.[23]

The raw statistics repose in sources published before 1959 and therefore cannot be denied or altered after the fact, at least outside of Cuba. They establish that in the indices employed at the time to judge economic and social development, the island ranked near the very top of twenty countries in Latin America, just behind Argentina and Uruguay. It had the *highest* percentage of its population in the money economy. It was fifth in per capita income (1956–1959); third in the percentage of the population not employed in agriculture; either third or fourth in life expectancy; second in per capita consumption of oil and fourth in per capita use of electrical energy; first in railroad mileage in proportion to size; second in per capita ownership of cars; second in number of telephones per inhabitant; third in per capita ownership of refrigerators; third in ownership of radios per inhabitant (270 radio stations); and *first* in possession of television sets per inhabitant (six TV channels).

Cuba's literacy rate of 76.4 percent was then fourth highest in Latin America, behind middle-class Argentina, Uruguay, and Chile. It was third in the per capita consumption of newsprint (58 dailies, 129 magazines) and third in the percentage of student-age population enrolled in universities. It had a hospital bed for every 300 inhabitants (Mexico at the time had one for every 875 inhabitants). It was fifth in the hemisphere (including the United States and Canada) in the daily per capita consumption of calories (2,730) and third in Latin America in per capita consumption of meat. Fully 44 percent of its population was covered by social legislation (health insurance, pensions, unemployment benefits), a share that exceeded every other Latin American country and even the United States! Globally, Cuba's per capita income compared favorably with some of the poorer European countries, including Italy, Spain, Portugal, Hungary, Poland, Bulgaria, Romania, and Greece.[24]

Because so much has been written about Cuba's advances in health services under Castro, it is perhaps useful to cast a momentary glance at the island's medical system under the old regime. The favorable social indicators in 1958—infant mortality, expected lifespan, incidence of communicable diseases, and so forth—could hardly have been accomplished in the absence of a serious and fairly modern health delivery infrastructure. In point of fact, Cuba then ranked eleventh *in the world* in number of physicians per inhabitant, and in that one respect was ahead of every other country in Latin America, including Argentina and Uruguay. Important regional differences within Cuba were largely urban versus rural rather than the metropolis versus the provinces. For example, while Havana had a disproportionate share of all medical services—doctors, clinics, hospital beds—it is also true that Matanzas had more doctors than all of Sweden; Las Villas and Camagüey had more than Chile, Poland, or Venezuela; Pinar del Río and Oriente more than Puerto Rico, Mexico, Colombia, or Costa Rica. Physicians in private practice charged fees, but many doctors were employed on salary by the widespread mutual associations, many of them established by Spanish immigrants or trade union federations. There were also many private clinics and hospitals that offered the full range of services for $2.50 a month. The 1,300-bed Calixto García Hospital in Havana provided services free to indigent patients.[25] Cubans did not enjoy universal coverage, since many rural dwellers resided outside the range of these services; still, the pre-Castro medical system was remarkable for the time and place.

None of this is intended to suggest that Cuba was some sort of paradise in 1958, merely that, far from being the hellhole depicted by the Castro regime and its foreign admirers and apologists, it was well ahead of most Latin American nations. It was still, however, a Latin American republic and as such suffered from the characteristic deficiencies of these societies.

In the first place, it was a country where foreign economic interests, largely from the United States, still controlled some of the most visible major enterprises—electric power, telephones, the big oil refineries, parts of the mining industry (especially nickel and manganese), tire production, three cement factories, and some of the larger banks. In 1958, U.S. portfolio investment in Cuba amounted to about $3 billion, a remarkably large sum for such a small country. (The one area in which U.S. control decreased dramatically was in plantation agriculture, where U.S.-owned acreage dropped from 5.7 million acres in 1933 to a mere 1.9 million in 1958.)[26] Whether foreign ownership of those important sectors of the economy was a good or bad thing for Cuba was wholly a matter of opinion, but at the time, many Cubans, like the citizens of other Latin American countries, could easily be mobilized against it.

Second, although Cuba's indices of economic and social development on a per capita basis were impressive, they represented only part of the story. Because they were calculated by dividing the country's total wealth by the number of inhabitants, these indices revealed nothing about the distribution of goods and services. Cuba had the largest middle class in Latin America in proportion to population—perhaps as much as a quarter to a fifth of all Cubans could be described as "well off." At the same time, however, among Cuba's working population of 2.2 million (53 percent of the population over the age of fourteen were in the labor force), 16.4 percent were chronically unemployed, 6.1 percent were underemployed, and 7 percent worked for their families without remuneration. Moreover, 60 percent of those who worked forty hours a week or more earned less than the minimum wage of seventy-five pesos a month. In effect, by the most optimistic calculations slightly less than 40 percent of all working Cubans received more than the bare minimum wage.[27]

Roughly half the population of Cuba lived in cities, which was a very large proportion for Latin America at that time. Demography established the fundamental parameters of income distribution, with the top half of the pyramid allocated to urban workers, the bottom to the rural labor force. The latter was further divided between those employed most or all of the year, and those hired on a seasonal basis. Many seasonal laborers worked only during the sugar harvest, which is to say, four months a year. The living conditions of the latter were probably not much different from those of the degraded peasantries of the Dominican Republic or Central America, perpetually in debt to local traders and continuously exploited by middlemen. Although some protective legislation for land workers was passed during Batista's first period of power—a curious kind of land reform that will be discussed in chapter 2—in many parts of the country, especially the mountains, the laws had little impact. Likewise, many basic services such as health and education did not reach very far down the rural social pyramid. One might best summarize an extremely complex situation by saying that by the late 1940s, urban Cuba had come to more nearly resemble a southern European country (with a living standard as high as or higher than France, Spain, Portugal, Greece, or even parts of Italy), while rural Cuba replicated the conditions of other plantation societies of the circum-Caribbean.[28]

Third, though surprisingly dense, Cuban civil society was fragile and curiously immature. The church and the army, which gave ballast to the social structure in other Latin American societies, were weak, the former having been on the wrong side of the wars of independence, the latter a recent creation (or re-creation) of Batista and his confederates. The emerging landholding, banking, or industrial classes had one foot (psychologically and culturally) in either the Spain from which their fathers or grandfathers had emigrated, or the United States, where many of them had been trained. Politics was seen as essentially the pursuit of booty, and although there were mass parties, they were essentially cooperatives for the distribution of patronage. Political life was characterized, in the words of one historian, by *"personalismo,* corruption and cynicism."* While the United States had not taken an active part in Cuban politics for many years, just because it had once done so, it was perceived by many as maintaining an invisible veto power that presumably made it ultimately responsible for the failures and deficiencies of Cuban society. Above all, the intellectual classes—in Cuba as in other Latin American countries rather more important than in the United States or even much of Western Europe—were deeply disaffected with the established order.[29]

These are somber considerations, but—even taken together with the inequalities and deficiencies of Cuban society—they do not point in the direction of any particular historical outcome.[30] Rather, the Cuban revolution was the product of a specific political crisis; the country's social and economic shortcomings were simply conscripted on a highly selective basis after the fact to provide the rationale for an outcome that was determined by concrete choices rather than impersonal social forces.

Past and Present Compared

Perhaps the most important of those choices was the decision to radically alter the country's developmental model to one that was far more "inclusive."[31] In effect, in Cuba today there are no marginal classes, as there were in the Cuba of 1958, in the sense that no one remains beyond the reach of government services or—what amounts to the same thing—free of government discipline. Given the totalitarian logic of the regime, it could hardly be otherwise. Some Cubans profess to greatly prefer the difference. "I lived under capitalism," a 53-year-old Cuban woman told an American journalist not long ago. "I suffered. When I was 11, I started cleaning floors in private homes. I could not go to school. . . . Things were hard." Now, however, "we are another people. There is less diversion, but we have other things. We have a roof. We have security. We have schools for our children."[32]

This sunny view of the revolution and its accomplishments is shared by a surprisingly wide range of Western politicians, intellectuals, journalists, and cultural figures. The "undeniable advances" of Cuba under Castro—particularly in the areas of health and education—are, in fact, conceded even by those who otherwise profess to be troubled by the regime's harsh political texture. And their views are ratified periodically by apparently unimpeachable sources. For example, a United Nations report released in 1997 placed Cuba second best among developing nations, scoring higher than Singapore or Chile, on a new "human poverty index." The report arrived at its findings by measuring poverty not by income but by a blend of five indicators: literacy, life expectancy, percentage of malnourished children, and access to health care and safe water. "On that basis," one news magazine reported, "Cuba has managed to maintain basic services and improve living standards for the poor, even though its economy has shrunk by a third since losing Soviet financial support in 1989."[33]

"Cuba's Infant Death Rate Drops Again" reported a headline in the *New York Times* on December 28, 1999. Already one of the lowest in the world, the story recounted, infant mortality in Cuba fell further in 1999, to about 6.5 deaths per thousand births, "down from a rate of 7.1 per thousand the previous year and 11 per thousand a decade ago." The article went on to explain, "Free health service for all, a rarity in Latin America, has been one of the main features of President Fidel Castro's government since he seized power in 1959."

On July 18, 1998, the *Economist* reported that Cuba's 98 percent rate of immunization of children against measles exceeded that of Canada, Israel, New Zealand, Venezuela, and—in a special note of *schadenfreude*—the United States. "Prosperity is no guarantee of success," the *Economist* lectured its readers. "Political will and organized campaigns make a difference. America fails to immunise 11 percent of its under-ones against measles, whereas much poorer Cuba, which emphasizes vaccination, misses only 2 percent."

Another United Nations document released in 1999 ranked Cuba at 58 among 174 countries in its "human development index," which is based on survival rate at birth, adult literacy rate, gross enrollment in the first three grades of primary school, real GDP per capita, life expectancy, and educational opportunities. This index placed Cuba at the top of the Latin American range, ahead of Colombia (57), Mexico (50), Panama (49), Venezuela (48), Costa Rica (45), Uruguay (40), Argentina (39) and Chile (34).[34] Cuba likewise ranked surprisingly high (5) in its "human poverty in developing country" index for 1997, bested in Latin America only by Uruguay (3) and Costa Rica (4). This finding was based on indicators such as adult illiteracy, undernourished children, population without access to safe water, and percentage of the population below the poverty line.[35] Cuba's high score seems all the more remarkable since for some years now it has not provided some of the basic statistical information, such as real GDP per capita, on which such considerations are partly based.[36]

The same UN document gives Cuba an excellent rating (21) on something it calls "gender empowerment"—a ranking higher than any Latin

American country and also higher than major European nations such as France (36), Italy (26), and Spain (22), and major Asian powerhouses such as Japan (38).[37] This assessment reflects indicators such as the number of seats in parliament held by women; the percentage of administrators and managers who are female; the percentage of women who are professional and technical workers; and women's real GDP per capita.[38] Whether such things are as important to the vast majority of Cuban women as the ready availability of basic foodstuffs or articles of daily use is left for others to surmise.

These remarkably favorable findings on contemporary Cuba seem strangely incompatible with other available indicators, particularly those that measure the country's overall economic performance. According to data culled from a confidential report from the Central Bank and leaked to the foreign press along with two studies carried out for or by Western diplomatic missions in Havana, the island's foreign debt and commercial deficit hit records in 1998. Only tourism and remittances from émigrés abroad—variously estimated at between $400 million and $800 million—prevented Cuba from sinking into a "sea of budget deficits, [due to] a fall in the prices of export products, and a decline in foreign investment." In the same year, the economy grew at 1.2 percent, according to official figures—this, after falling 35 to 40 percent in 1989–1990 as a result of the collapse of the Soviet Union, from whom the island historically received roughly $6 billion a year in subsidies.[39] Economic growth rates for 1999 and 2000 were far better—6.2 percent and 5.6 percent, respectively—but in the latter year, the country's GDP was still roughly a fifth below its 1989 level. When population growth is taken into account, Cubans were probably subsisting on the same level in 2001 as they were in 1986.[40]

Moreover, other countries to which Cuba has been historically compared have not stood still during the past forty years—a point that Cuba's admirers never seem to take into account. The 1960 *Statistical Yearbook of the United Nations* ranked Cuba third among eleven Latin American nations in per capita daily caloric consumption; today, according to the United Nations Food and Agriculture Organization, it ranks last, even worse than Honduras. Its record of infant mortality in 1957 (32 per 1,000 live births) was the thirteenth lowest in the world—ahead of France, Belgium, West Germany, Japan, Austria, Italy, Spain, and Portugal, all of which have subsequently passed Cuba. It remains the most advanced country in Latin America in this

CUBA'S EXTERNAL DEBT

Cuba's external debt as of 2001 was just short of $11 billion. Roughly 75 percent had already matured; in 1986, the island declared a unilateral moratorium on its foreign obligations and has yet to reach an agreement with the Paris Club. Nor has any payment been made since 1990 on the debt owed to the Russian Federation or Cuba's former partners in the Council of Mutual Economic Assistance (CMEA). Such defaults have undoubtedly improved the country's momentary liquidity, though raised the spread on interest payments to new money to intolerable heights; the sugar harvest, for example, has been financed in recent years on short-term loans from European banks whose rates could only be called usurious. Even so, in 2001 Cuba defaulted on short-term debts to France, Spain, and South Africa, among others. [See "Debt Defaults Hurt Cuba's Credit Rating," *Miami Herald,* April 8, 2002.]

measure, but its world ranking has fallen from 13 to 24. Cuba ranked fourth among Latin American countries in literacy in 1953, but Panama, which ranked just behind it at that time, has matched its improvement in percentage terms, as have Costa Rica and Chile.[41] All of this, of course, omits any consideration of the quality of Cuban education, which is burdened by heavy doses of ideology.

In the area of food production, Cuba's performance has been particularly disastrous. Since 1989 there has been a drop in every major crop except fresh vegetables, tubers, and corn, which recovered in 1998. Even so, by 2000 (the last year for which figures are available), output in per capita terms was stagnant or slightly lower. In other areas, production was dramatically lower than in 1989: milk production was off 48 percent; eggs, off 37 percent; rice—the staple of the Cuban diet—off 13 percent; citrus fruits, off 6 percent.[42] In 1956, Cuba's consumption of beef was among the highest in the world (62.5 kilograms per capita per year, 97.7 in Havana); since then beef has virtually disappeared from Cuban tables.[43] This is not surprising since the size of the livestock population plummeted from 6.8 million (0.83 head per capita) in 1967 to 4.4 million (0.39 head per capita) in 1999.[44] At the same time, imports of food, which typically came from East bloc countries, has dropped by nearly half.

During the 1954–1957 period, Cuba's per capita consumption of calories stood at 2,730 per day—slightly behind Argentina and Uruguay. In 1996, that figure had fallen to 1,906 per day—about the same level as Haiti and Bolivia, two of the hungriest populations in Latin America. While food resources were unquestionably distributed in a more equitable fashion before 1990 than elsewhere in Latin America, the legalization of the dollar in 1993 has produced the worst of both worlds—growing inequality combined with increasing scarcities. Not surprisingly, a disturbing increase in the incidence of meningitis, polyneuritis, and malnutrition has occurred since the early 1990s, while the body weight of Cuban adults has fallen by an average of 15 to 20 pounds.[45] Meanwhile, the country's vaunted medical system is being reoriented toward serving foreign "health tourists" who can pay for their services in dollars.

These grim statistics suggest that, in the best of cases, whatever the Cuban revolution may have accomplished before 1989 is in the process of being swept away by a major geopolitical shift—that is, the disappearance of the Soviet Union and its associated states in Eastern Europe. The importance of this event can hardly be underestimated, since Cuba's relationship with Moscow was utterly unlike that of any other member of the Soviet family of nations. For more than thirty-five years, the Kremlin treated Cuba as a favored client rather than—as in the case of East Germany, Poland, or Czechoslovakia—a colony to be pillaged for raw materials and industrial goods. Whether in the form of preferential prices for Cuban sugar (sometimes at many times the world market price) or subsidized energy or foodstuffs, it was the generosity of the Soviet Union—not the genius of Fidel Castro—that made Cuba "work." Indeed, it would be surprising if it had not "worked": for more than three decades, the Soviets transferred to the island the rough equivalent of ten Marshall Plans (in 1947 constant dollars).

Even so, it is useful to recall just what "working" meant. Rationing of food and clothing, in place since 1961, was universal and while everyone dressed shabbily and ate poorly, no one went naked or hungry. Education was often

EDUCATION IN CUBA, CIRCA 1973:
LIFE IN A RURAL BOARDING SCHOOL

" Like inmates of an immense jail, millions of young Cubans were roused each morning from their beds at 6 a.m. with slogans and revolutionary songs, or news broadcasts announcing our uninterrupted victories over Yankee imperialism or regaling us with statistics of huge agricultural harvests obtained by our socialist economic system (which for some inexplicable reason never arrived to fill our empty stomachs). We hungrily devoured whatever they gave us for breakfast—sometimes almost nothing—followed by meetings at which we were harangued about socialism and the luminous communist future. From there it was off to the classrooms or the fields in morning or afternoon shifts according to the school year. For four hours a day we bent over furrows planted with vegetation that probably derived even fewer nutrients from the sterile soil than we ourselves received, working under the implacable Caribbean sun or rain, sometimes even thunder and lightning. To which we added five hours in the classroom, where they regaled us with detailed accounts on how the world was in chaos, a true inferno of exploitation of man by man, until the day—luminous for all humanity!—that Soviet communism was born, making possible the advent of the most illuminating of all events in the history of humanity—Fidel Castro and the Cuban revolution.

"We returned to the classrooms between six and eight in the evening to do our homework, after which we had about an hour and a half of free time. At ten in the evening it was 'lights out' in the dormitory. Almost before we knew it we were awakened by loudspeakers at full blast, broadcasting the voice of Silvio Rodríguez or a radio program recounting the huge catches hauled in by a fishing cooperative.

"To miss agricultural work or classes, to commit any act of mischief or to fail to complete a task could be penalized by taking away our weekend passes to see our families. But worse still, to question in any form the regime that was imposed upon us was the worst of offenses. To express any idea not aligned one hundred percent with the magnanimous ideals of the Revolution was a dangerous sign of IDEOLOGICAL DEVIATIONISM and would forever after disfigure the course of our adult lives. The hideous specter of a blotted copybook would hang over us wherever we went." [Andrés Jorge, "Olvidar Sandino," *Encuentro de la Cultura Cubana* (Winter 2001–2002).]

mediocre in quality and distorted by ideological bias, but at the most elementary levels it was available to all children without distinction. (At higher levels, students were required to pass political tests for entry.) Medical services, including complicated surgical procedures, were offered without charge to all citizens, though their quality remains a matter of controversy.[46] Infant mortality dropped but was influenced by one of the world's highest abortion rates.[47] Meanwhile, Cuba's suicide rate ranks among the top five in the world and first in the entire Latin American region.[48]

In effect, the most significant accomplishment of the Cuban revolution was to eliminate the class differences that existed in the old society. As elsewhere in the former socialist world, changes that leveled society down did not come without price. In the Cuban case, however, Castro's extreme ideological rigidity has probably exacted a higher price from his people than elsewhere. Journalist David Rieff explains that "while the regime [has] demonstrated considerable imagination in redividing the economic pie, it has never been able to make the pie bigger. . . . The economic record of Cuba is one of unbroken failure."[49] While some Soviet aid was put to useful purposes, much of it was allocated to an oversized security apparatus (until quite recently the second largest army in Latin America after Brazil); foreign adventures; or the dictator's own harebrained schemes, which included squandering millions of dollars on research on interferon and establishing a massive program of cross-breeding Holstein and Brahman cattle.

The choice of a Soviet model of economic organization also led to the adoption of a deeply repressive political system. On this point there is a virtual international consensus, not only on the part of the United Nations Commission on Human Rights, but also among respected nongovernmental organizations. A case in point is Human Rights Watch, which in its most recent report characterized the Cuban political scene as one dominated by "the denial of basic civil and political rights" as a matter of state policy. It called attention to the punishment of dissent "with heavy prison terms, threats of prosecution, harassment, or exile," and severe restrictions on "the exercise of fundamental human rights of expression, association and assembly. The conditions in Cuba's prisons," it added, "are inhuman, and political prisoners suffer additional degrading treatment and torture." In recent years, moreover, "Cuba has added new repressive laws and continued [to prosecute] nonviolent dissidents while shrugging off international appeals for reform."[50] Indeed, the violation of human rights under Castro has been so extensive that the depredations of his predecessor virtually pale into insignificance.

The most serious failure of the Cuban revolution, however, is not the poor selection of its foreign sponsor, but rather, that having found such a sponsor for however limited a period, two entire generations of Cubans have been brought up to expect—as a matter of right—a standard of living that the island cannot possibly produce without massive and continuous outside assistance or a radical reordering of its economic system, or quite possibly both.[51]

With all of the changes Cuba has experienced during the past four decades, some things have remained much the same. One of its principal limitations in 1958—vulnerability to periodic fluctuations in the world price of sugar—remains in force. Another has been its perennial shortage of energy supplies. Still another has been the need since the early 1990s to depend on tourism for foreign exchange. Yet another has been the persistent and provocative counterexample of the United States nearby. All of these things have been immensely complicated by the departure over time of more than a million of Cuba's most talented and useful citizens; the emergence of a large, prosperous, politically powerful exile community with revanchist agendas; the destruction of incentives to normal economic activity; the division of families and destruction of trust among ordinary citizens; and the quickening transformation of a typically ambivalent relationship with the United States into an all-out ideological war. At the same time, what in 1958 was a fragile and immature civil society has been completely shattered. These are the legacies of Cuba's past, both remote and immediate, which must be surmounted if the country is to preserve its viability as a nation state—with or without Castro and under communism, capitalism, fascism, or some system yet to be devised.

2

Sugar

A Blessing and a Curse

"Without sugar, there is no nation"—such was the memorable dictum of José Manuel Casanova, president of the Cuban Sugar Mill Owners Association in the 1940s. Whether one celebrated or deplored the fact, none could deny it. No other product has so acutely defined Cuba's evolution as a society or symbolized both its possibilities and its peculiar frustration. It was sugar that converted the island from an administrative and shipping center of the Spanish mainland empire in South America to an economic powerhouse in its own right; sugar dictated the introduction of hundreds of thousands of African slaves in the nineteenth century; and sugar ultimately linked Cuba to the wider world of commerce, and very particularly to that of the United States, which was until 1960 its principal customer for the product and the banker for its harvest.

A few statistics plucked more or less at random underscore just how important that crop was on the eve of the Castro revolution.[1] In the forty years prior to the overthrow of Fulgencio Batista, sugar accounted for fully 82 percent of the island's hard currency earnings, and in the final decade of the *ancien régime*, represented from a quarter to a third of the national income. After 1930, sugar accounted for 30 percent of Cuba's gross national product. If one focused exclusively on the countryside, the crop loomed larger still: two-thirds of all agricultural incomes were based on it; nearly half the irrigated areas of the island grew cane, which covered over a quarter of the total land mass of the country. Indeed, half of Cuba's electrical power generating capacity was diverted to sugar processing. Some 500,000 workers were employed in the industry at harvest time: four-fifths of them were cane cutters and the rest worked in the mills. This labor force constituted virtually a third of the country's wage earners.

As historian Hugh Thomas points out, "When sugar prices were good, no other enterprise in Cuba was so rewarding. When they were bad, most other activities suffered at the same time."[2] The ebb and flow of sugar futures on the markets of London and New York were of enormous moment to the country; in effect, nothing its politicians, bankers, economists—even the most clever or gifted among them—could conjure up could compete with a variation of a cent or two in the price of a pound of sugar, a number determined far from the island by an unholy combination of impersonal market forces and rigid purchasing agreements.

Although the world sugar market had been expanding steadily since the end of the nineteenth century and continued to do so throughout the twentieth, by the time of the Castro revolution in 1959, the production of sugar in Cuba had leveled off, with no immediate prospects for improvement. This was because, among other things, at least eight important sugar-importing countries had begun to produce it on their own, largely from beets. In the final decade before Castro's assumption of power, the number of nations (apart from Cuba) whose sugar harvests exceeded a million tons a year rose from five to twelve. Meanwhile, in the United States, Cuba's traditional and most important customer, beet production during that decade rose by two-thirds; domestic cane production, in those days mainly from Louisiana, increased markedly; and Puerto Rico, another cane producer, obtained a permanent increase in its own U.S. market quota. To some extent, the impact of these menacing developments was temporarily masked by international crises—the Korean conflict of 1950–1953 and the Suez crisis in 1956—which produced sharp, if transitory, upturns in sugar prices.

Although Cuba has always been particularly well endowed by nature and geography to be a major sugar producer, it has never been able to capitalize fully on its bounty. This is because sugar, probably more than any other widely traded agricultural product, has been consistently sheltered from the full effect of market forces by preferential trading arrangements. At the time of the Castro revolution, international commerce in sugar was controlled by four major powers: the United States, France, Great Britain, and the Soviet Union. Beyond their writ, a mere fifth of the world's total production was priced in accordance with real supply and demand.

Moreover, in the 1950s Cuba was slowly but perceptibly losing its share of that fifth. At the London Conference in 1953, the major consuming countries assigned Cuba an export quota of 2.25 million tons. Worse still, in 1958 the Geneva Conference approved a five-year agreement that fixed Cuba's share of the free market at 2.4 million tons a year, which was numerically larger but little more than what by then was a third of that market. Meanwhile, the price of sugar in the free market was slowly dropping in relation to other essential goods that Cuba needed to import. In one frequently quoted study produced in 1955, the National Bank of Cuba estimated that, for the country to enjoy in 1965 the standard of living it had in 1947, sugar production would have to exceed 9 million tons and be valued at nearly $800 million— which in the event proved impossible, and probably would have been so even if Cuba had remained part of the Western economic system rather than opting for absorption into the Soviet community of nations.

For Cuba, of course, the really important market for its sugar was not the free market or purchasers in Europe or Asia, but the United States, whose hegemonic position was based on geographical propinquity; heavy investment in the Cuban industry, particularly after 1898; and, after 1934, by a sugar quota which American growers in Cuba and their allies in the business community had wrenched from the U.S. Congress.[3] Under the Jones-Costigan Act, the Secretary of Agriculture was authorized each year to anticipate the sugar consumption requirements of the United States and assign a preferred supplier a stipulated percentage. Quotas were based on a rather depressed period in international commerce—the three-year period from 1931 to 1934; as a result, Cuba ended up with a rather smaller percentage than would have been the case if an earlier triennium had been used as a reference. Even so, the assignment to Cuba of 28 percent of the American market was not negligible, inasmuch as it provided an assured "floor" and to some extent buffered Cuba from the worst effects of those years when the product was in drastic oversupply. It also made available a large quantity of hard currency on a continuing basis; while the actual amounts were unpredictable, they were nevertheless sufficient to underpin one of the most advanced economies and living standards in Latin America. Moreover, even though the quota was established largely as a favor to U.S. landowners in Cuba, by the 1940s Americans were withdrawing from ownership of the industry. The new Cuban sugar producers were thus "grandfathered" into a preferential situation with virtually no change in U.S. legislation.

To be sure, Cubans critical of their own society and its relations with the United States saw no reason to be grateful for the quota—far from it. Ernesto Guevara, Fidel Castro's first minister of industries, though himself an Argentine rather than a Cuban, nonetheless spoke for many of his adopted countrymen—by no means all of them from the left—when he claimed that "the U.S. quota system meant stagnation for our sugar production; during the last years the Cuban productive capacity was rarely utilized to the full, but the preferential treatment given to Cuban sugar by the quota also meant that no other export crops could compete with it on an economic basis." Guevara professed to perceive behind the quota a deeply sinister design, not only to protect the U.S. domestic sugar industry, "but also make possible the unrestricted introduction into our country of American manufactured goods," since the sugar treaties signed with Washington gave the United States a 20 percent preference over most favored nation (MFN) tariffs, making it "impossible for another country to compete with U.S. goods."[4]

Guevara's point was valid as far as it went—that is to say, both domestic and foreign U.S. economic agendas lay behind the concession,[5] but it is also true that without the quota Cuba would have been hard pressed to fight off the growing pressures of domestic U.S. producers and the competition from other countries. Further, not only did the quota permit Cuba to export a significant share of its production to the United States, but it did so at the highly protected prices of the U.S. market, which represented an implicit subsidy to the Cuban economy.[6]

Moreover, some of Cuba's limitations as a sugar producer lay within the sociological peculiarities of its own society. Since the 1930s, social peace in the countryside had been purchased by two pieces of Cuban legislation: the Sugar Stabilization Act (1931), which created a government agency to regulate the amount of sugar to be produced each year, apportioning the harvest to different mills; and the Sugar Coordination Law (1937), which gave tenants (*colonos*) on the sugar estates what amounted to permanent tenure as long as they delivered a specified minimum amount of cane to the mills from which they "rented" their land. The growing strength of the rural labor movement led to additional legislation in the 1940s forbidding such techno-logical improvements as fertilization or fumigation from the air or the intro-duction of labor-saving machinery. As a result, at the time of the Castro revolution no new mill had been built for thirty years. Finally, with outdated equipment and a highly uneconomic system of land tenure, the yield per acre was considerably less than in many other sugar-producing countries.[7]

It is significant that no Cuban politician, no matter how far left of center, ever really addressed these issues. Indeed, at the beginning of his career as a conven-tional reformist politician, Fidel Castro had even promised further advantages to the tenant class, which, despite the connotation of rural poverty associated with the term, already constituted one of the most privileged recipients of gov-ernment entitlement in the old Cuba. More typical were the views of out-and-out radicals (and Marxist technocrats like Guevara) who regarded sugar as a kind of "yoke of imperialism" to be cast off at the earliest possible moment in favor of agricultural diversification or even the construction of heavy industry *à la Staline*. The revolutionary aim, both before and after 1959, was to build "new roads, to rework the nickel mines, to grow tomatoes or avocados, to become self-sufficient in steel, to sell cigars to China: anything to avoid the production of sugar on the existing scale, much less an increased one."[8]

Agriculture under Socialism, 1960–1963

It is hardly surprising that sugar was relegated to a minor role in Cuban agri-culture during the first years of the Castro revolution. In any event, the land reform policies of the new government were dictated not so much by consid-erations of agricultural productivity or even social justice as by a desire to break the economic and political back of the local landowning class and also to elim-inate highly visible and deeply symbolic American companies, such as United Fruit, that were still proprietors in Cuba. The sudden turn away from sugar would probably have occurred even in the absence of the Eisenhower adminis-tration's decision late in 1960 to suspend the Cuban quota—a response both to punitive nationalization of American property and to the obvious and grow-ing tilt of the new regime toward the Soviet bloc.[9]

During the early days of the revolution, agriculture in general was treated as an unwanted stepchild in favor of an all-out push for "accelerated industrialization" under the leadership of the ubiquitous Ernesto Guevara. The notion underpinning this campaign was, as historian Theodore Draper tartly observes, "childishly simple. Its aim was the substitution of homemade goods for those previously imported from the United States. Its method was the physical transplantation across half the globe of dozens of factories in the shortest possible time. Its financial basis was long-term credits or outright gifts from the Communist world."[10]

In his capacity as minister of industries, Guevara entertained fantasies of Cuba producing tractors, trucks, internal combustion engines, even automobiles and jet planes. In due course, however, it became clear that many raw materials on which the factories relied cost Cuba almost as much to import or produce as it would cost to buy the finished goods, and that there were in fact sound geo-economic reasons why the island had so long devoted itself to large-scale agriculture. At the end of the day, the question became how far the Soviets would go toward paying for Cuban industrialization; by 1964, it was obvious that the outer limits of Moscow's philanthropy had been reached. Perhaps not coincidentally, at about the same time, Guevara himself disappeared from the Cuban political scene.

Until then, however, a deliberate effort was made to reduce the island's sugar production. Fully a quarter of the area under cane cultivation was cleared between 1958 and 1963. In 1962, for example, nine sugar mills with a grinding capacity of 15,000 tons a day were dismantled altogether. Sugar land was cleared for rice, cotton, tubers, fruits and vegetables, even for pasture. Not surprisingly, the 1963 harvest (3.9 million tons) was less than half that of 1961.

This radical shift in direction was facilitated by a thoroughgoing transformation of the land tenure system. Private property in agriculture virtually ceased to exist; rural properties, large and small—including the lands formerly occupied by *colonos*—were confiscated by the state. Initially declared to be cooperatives, they were quickly transformed into state farms on the Soviet model. The impact on productivity was felt almost immediately. According to French agronomist René Dumont, a leftist sympathizer who visited the island several times during this period, between 1958 and 1963, "The productivity of an agricultural work day had decreased by about half. In 1963 the harvests were probably only 75 percent of those in 1960, whereas the number of work days had been rising rapidly. Though unemployment had disappeared, production had not benefited."

By 1963, Dumont found the situation "almost catastrophic." While he agreed with the overall objective of diversifying Cuban agriculture, the new land reform agency proved monumentally incapable of fulfilling its mission. State farms "received successive and contradictory orders from various offices. . . . Some areas were never sown at all in 1963, after being plowed four times for four different crops."[11] He went on to report that each state farm "had too much land, in too many regrouped plots. Each produced from twenty to thirty-five different crops, often very badly." Alternatives to sugar such as "cotton, kenaf (fiber), peanuts, sunflowers, and most fruits and vegetables had been more or less unknown to both workers and technicians, who were usually familiar with sugar cane and sometimes a little stock farming, but the monthly INRA (land reform agency) pamphlet was concerned with propaganda rather than instruction."[12]

The Return to Sugar, 1963–1989

Almost overnight, new crops were dropped unceremoniously in a rush to maximize sugar production.[13] The driving concept was initially still the same—to transform Cuba into an industrial nation, but now sugar was assigned a key role in producing the necessary foreign exchange to purchase capital imports. The first five-year plan (1965–1970) envisaged a major increase in investment, a substantial expansion of cultivated area, the planting of improved varieties, improvement of irrigation, and—here, a new touch—the mechanization of harvesting, largely with newly imported Soviet or Soviet-bloc machinery. The crowning objective of the plan was to produce a record-breaking 10-million-ton harvest in 1970, followed by annual production increases during the subsequent five years, ultimately reaching 12 million tons by 1975. Despite the mobilization of the entire society toward the production of 10 million tons, including the lengthening of the harvest season, the 1970 production of 8 million tons fell well short of the five-year plan's objective. During this period, moreover, pursuit of the plan inflicted additional opportunity costs on the society through the massive and often arbitrary diversion of labor, transportation, energy, and other inputs.

By the time Cuba formally entered the Soviet Council of Mutual Economic Assistance (CMEA) in 1972, all hope of financing heavy industry through sugar exports had been abandoned, and Cuba resumed its traditional role as a sugar producer, this time within the so-called socialist division of labor. Ironically, in its new incarnation as a member of the Soviet family of nations, Cuba's economy was far more tightly tied to the production of a single product than ever before—more so indeed than at any time during the sixty years of American "domination"—but under circumstances that, at least at first glance, seemed somewhat more advantageous to the island. As primary sugar supplier to the bloc, Cuba could count on a large assured market[14] and receive preferential prices, sometimes several times that of the (admittedly semi-fictitious) "world" price. In addition, the island received assistance in the form of credits, as well as technical aid for the improvement of its industry, the development of new byproducts, even the production of harvesting equipment.

Since all of Cuba's transactions with the bloc were carried out in a non-convertible currency—the so-called convertible ruble, which in fact was not convertible at all[15]—it is difficult to measure the relationship for comparative purposes.[16] The Soviet Union bartered for much of its Cuban sugar with oil, allowing Cuba to resell occasional surpluses for hard currency. Just how beneficial all of this was to the island remains a matter of controversy. Bartering meant that Cuba was often deprived of high-quality or even essential goods normally obtainable in the hard-currency market, and Soviet prices for their exports to Cuba may well have been higher than they would have commanded in the open market.[17]

The task of evaluation is further complicated by a drastic change in the methodologies used to compute economic performance after the revolution. Before 1959, Cuba employed the standard Western System of National Accounts (SNA). After joining the bloc, it shifted to the Material Production System (MPS) employed by all centrally planned economies, and from Gross National Product to Global Social Product.[18] Furthermore, Cuban official data are often sketchy or incomplete, so that, as one specialist puts it, "It is not possible to measure with precision changes in the structure of Cuban production even for fairly close years during the revolutionary period."[19]

However one evaluates the relative advantage to Cuba of membership in the CMEA, one point is beyond dispute. In the final decade of the Cuban-Soviet relationship, sugar had become considerably more central to the island's economy than it had been before the revolution. By 1984, some 1.75 million hectares[20] were under cultivation for sugar cane, only slightly below the historic 1982 high of 1.752 million and substantially above any year in the pre-revolutionary period. (For example, the amount of land devoted to sugar cane was 20 percent higher in 1984 than in 1952, the record year for the pre-Castro period.) This constituted roughly *two-thirds* of all the cultivated land in Cuba. From 1975 (the first year for which disaggregated data are available) through 1989, sugar was the largest single recipient of investment, constituting fully one-third of the resources the island devoted to any economic endeavor, and provided a livelihood for 400,000 Cubans and their families—some 15 percent of the total population.[21]

It is a stunning testimony to the structured inefficiencies of Cuba's agricultural policies and practices that in spite of the evident priority assigned to this crop, by the early 1980s the country was no longer able to meet its fixed commitments to some members of the CMEA and actually had to purchase sugar on the world market to resell to its clients ($101 million was spent in this way in 1984, and an additional $100 million in 1985). Indeed, during those years it is at least arguable that the Cuban economy would have registered zero or negative economic growth were it not for the availability of Soviet oil shipments, which permitted the island—not itself a major oil producer—to become an oil re-exporter.[22] At any rate, in 1983, 1984, and 1985—a period of depressed energy prices—oil actually replaced sugar as Cuba's premier hard currency earner.

The dissolution of the Soviet Union and the CMEA, and with both, an end to subsidized inputs such as fertilizer, chemicals, and replacement parts for machinery, further complicated matters by greatly reducing the amount of sugar Cuba has been able to produce. The last harvest (1991–1992) under the old arrangements amounted to 7 million metric tons. After plunging to slightly less than half that amount—3.3 million metric tons in 1994–1995—recent harvests have hovered slightly above the 4-million mark, including the yield for 1999–2000—which at 4.05 million was among the country's six poorest since 1946.[23] The 2000–2001 harvest was reported to be even poorer—3.53 million metric tons, with much of the drop attributed to bad weather. The excuse may be valid as far as it goes, but as one U.S. sugar specialist pointed out, "With its worn equipment, dilapidated transport system, and scant technical resources,

Cuba's sugar industry is . . . susceptible to being thrown off course by minor hiccups."[24] Although one would have thought that Hurricane Michelle would have had an even more devastating effect on the 2001–2002 harvest, Cuban authorities claim a slight increase of 80,000 metric tons over the previous year. Any economic gain, however, was wholly canceled by depressed commodity prices; Cuba received $120 million less for this harvest than the one the year before.[25] New economic protocols between Cuba and the Russian Federation signed on May 14, 1999, have put an end to subsidized oil shipments, which had continued after the demise of the Soviet Union; the effect on the industry over the longer term is not difficult to imagine.[26]

Some Problems of Socialist Production

Why should Cuba fail—even before the demise of the Soviet empire—to fulfill its commitments to sugar consumers, particularly given the enormous resources devoted to the crop for more than three decades? The answer to that question lies at the intersection of technology and politics. Milling costs tend to be roughly the same in all producing countries; the margin of difference (and therefore of competitive advantage) tends to be in the agricultural sector. The bulk size of the sugar cane harvest is evidently one indicator; another, equally crucial factor is the condition of the cane delivered to the mill. A key concept here is "polarization," a technical term that applies to the maturity of the plant. Under ideal conditions, that figure will hover at about 96 degrees, which is to say, the maximum amount of juice that can be squeezed from the cane and converted to sugar through the manufacturing process. During the 1950s, an average of 12.8 percent of all cane delivered to Cuban mills had reached this optimal state. Since then, the proportion of cane reaching the mill in its optimal state has steadily risen in most countries, but during the socialist period in Cuba it has fallen by slightly more than 17 percent. The figure was a mere 10.6 percent for the 1985–1986 crop.[27]

The Cuban industry has also been plagued by serious management problems. Until recently, at least the top executive in every mill was the Communist Party secretary of the plant, with whom all projects and decisions had to be cleared. He was, and perhaps still is, authorized to overrule technicians, even in their own areas of specialized expertise. Some technical positions—chief engineer, fabrication chief, labor chief—have occasionally been filled by people without specialized degrees or training, based on presumed political merit or political connections. In 1985, for example, not one of the twenty-one mills in the province of Matanzas had an experienced, qualified chief engineer. The same problem has plagued the industry at higher levels. In 1993, Juan Herrera, an engineer and competent sugar technologist, was replaced as minister of the sugar industry by Nelson Torres, chief of the Communist Party in the province of Cienfuegos. (Though a civil engineer, Torres had no experience in the industry.) In 1997, Fidel Castro named Division General Ulises Rosales del Toro, a career military officer, to the same post. Rosales is known as an excellent organizer but has no background whatever in agricultural engineering.

Theoretically, at least, Cuba should have no problem on the industrial side. It has experienced a 32 percent increase in installed capacity since 1952. Mechanization has allowed the government to reduce the total factory labor force by 40 percent (though much of the savings has probably been absorbed by bloated personnel in other departments).[28] By one calculation, the country today possesses, at least on paper, the capacity to crush 732,410 metric tons of sugar every day (compared with 555,832 in 1952). Assuming an industrial yield of 10.6 percent, the crop should produce about 8.9 million metric tons in 132 working days. But in 1995–1996, when the grinding season spanned 156.6 days, the actual amount of sugar totaled only 4.5 million metric tons. By way of comparison, Mexico currently produces 5 million metric tons a year with half the number of mills that Cuba has, not to mention Australia, which can make as much or more sugar in a mere three-month period.[29]

In practice, the poor performance of Cuba's sugar mills can be traced largely to qualitative considerations. Some of the equipment in these plants is old and subject to frequent breakdowns, and since 1990 at least a third of Cuba's mills have not functioned in selected harvests, because of either a lack of cane to grind or a lack of spare parts. Thanks to its default on its hard currency debt to Western creditors in 1986, spare parts cannot always be readily obtained. This means that even those mills still in operation are drastically underperforming. In 1997, for example, Cuba's mills were reportedly operating at only 60 to 70 percent of capacity, and only 23 percent of the mills reached their output targets for that year. As a result of a breakdown in the island's transportation system and fuel shortages, much cut cane was left for twenty-nine hours or more in the fields rather than being taken expeditiously to the mills (where it normally should be processed within twelve hours). Such delays make it impossible for the cane to retain a high degree of polarization, and therefore reduce the amount of sugar ultimately extracted from the crushed plant.

These deficiencies also reflect the mediocre performance of an inefficient, demoralized, and poorly paid agricultural workforce. In the pre-revolutionary period, the salaries of Cuban sugar workers were regulated by an escalator clause linked to the U.S. market price of the product. In 1958, the indicator, in U.S. dollars, was just under $.05 per pound FOB Cuban port; as of April 2000, it would have been $6.70 per pound.[30] Since the Castro regime came to power, however, salaries have been frozen at the 1958 level, which has allowed the government to skim off considerable profits at the expense of the labor force. By one calculation, the real minimum wage of Cuban sugar workers (both agricultural and industrial) was *twenty times* higher in 1958 than in 1996, and for mill workers some thirty-one times.[31] "Many months no cooking oil/fat is available. No meat is available through the ration book, although some off quality meat mixed with soybean, inedible to many, is distributed irregularly. After that every individual is on his/her own."[32] Cane cutters often lack shoes and even gloves. Small wonder that the industry has suffered from absenteeism, a lack of discipline, theft, low-level sabotage, and a management that lacks authority.[33]

The collapse of the Soviet Union and the loss of privileged markets to CMEA countries in 1991–1992 forced the Castro regime to reorganize its agricultural sector. In September 1993, about 2,800 state farms representing roughly 42 percent of the country's agricultural land were reorganized into semi-autonomous cooperatives known as Basic Units of Cooperative Production (UBPCs). Under this arrangement, while land title remains with the state, the UBPCs have the right to use the land and make production and resource decisions on their own. State enterprises still provide marketing, technical assistance, production services, and agricultural inputs; and they still purchase most of the outputs.

Insofar as the production of cane is concerned, reform has thus far had a marginal effect. Three years into the new arrangements—that is, in 1996—only 76 of nearly 1,300 cane UBPCs managed to operate in the black; three years after that, despite an increase in world sugar prices, that number had climbed to 475, which is still, of course, considerably less than half.

At this point, it is not at all clear, in fact, that the purpose of Cuba's sugar industry in recent years has been to provide export earnings as in the past. Rather, the highest priority seems to have been to keep the industry going so that the nearly half million workers it employs will not be idle, even if that means that the sector itself barely breaks even. It cannot be surprising that Cuba is an unusually high-cost sugar producer, given the exorbitant interest rates—as high as 20 percent—that European banks now charge to finance the harvest; the generally depressed commodity prices (sugar futures oscillate between five and eight cents a pound, which is where they were in the 1950s, without adjusting for inflation); and the inefficient, backward, and disorganized nature of the industry.[34]

In a desperate attempt to square the circle, in mid-2002 the Cuban government was reported to be on the verge of closing 71 of its 156 mills—nearly half its plant. Redundant workers—about 100,000 people or 2.5 percent of the country's economically active population—were to be "retrained" in other lines of agricultural activity, during which time they would be paid between 60 and 100 percent of their former salaries.[35] Quite apart from the politically charged risks this decision would entail, it is by no means clear that a drastic reduction in plant operation would make the Cuban industry significantly more profitable, because too many countries are already producing and exporting the product.

Changes in the World Sugar Market

The proliferation of sugar-producing and -exporting countries is crucial to understanding the challenges that Cuban sugar faces in the future. At the time of the revolution, the island was the world's largest exporter, a reliable and reasonably efficient producer with an assured place in the world's largest single market. In the forty years since then, the sweetener world has undergone three dramatic transformations that continue to challenge the viability of Cuba's standing in the market.

The first of these is an enormous increase in the number of countries producing sugar, which in 1990 stood at 110, representing every continent and stage of economic development. Even more important, many sugar producers have become important exporters in their own right. The European Union (EU) is a striking example. In the mid-1970s, the EU was still purchasing roughly 7 percent of world production; twenty years later, its own sugar exports (derived from beets) represented 13 percent of the world sugar trade. Another is Australia, which exported 3.8 million metric tons in 1994, pushing ahead of Cuba to second place in world rankings, first, if EU countries are counted separately. Thailand virtually replicated Australia's performance in the same time period, thanks largely to a combination of low labor costs and highly advanced technology imported from Western countries.

The same is true for Brazil, which has emerged as the world's largest sugar producer, exporting a record 7.2 million tons in 1998–1999. This is all the more remarkable in light of the fact that Brazil presently devotes half its cane production to the elaboration of ethanol fuel.[36] It is worth noting as well that because of varied harvest schedules (the country's long north-south axis allows it two growing seasons rather than one), Brazil has the unique technical flexibility to shift significant tonnage of cane between sugar and ethanol production as market incentives dictate, so that the ultimate impact of its industry on the world sweetener market may have yet to be felt.[37]

Although Mexico is still a net importer, largely from the United States, it has sufficient land to expand sugar cane acreage significantly, and yields could be further improved with existing technology. There is considerable reason to expect as much, partly because of recent modifications in the land tenure system and new liberalized foreign investment laws. In addition, as of October 2000, Mexico acquired the right under the North American Free Trade Agreement (NAFTA) to begin selling 276,000 tons of duty-free sugar a year to the United States—a tenfold increase over its previous quota. Moreover, the tariff on any sugar Mexico ships to the United States in excess of the 276,000 tons began to decline in 2001 and is scheduled to terminate altogether by 2008.[38]

The second great change since 1959 has been the large-scale entry into the market of alternative sweeteners. These include saccharine, aspartame, acesulfame-K, cyclamate, and sucralose. Such compounds are often referred to as "high-intensity sweeteners," inasmuch as they contain many times the sweetening effect per unit of weight as sugar (fully 600 times in the case of sucralose). While such substitutes are unlikely to replace sugar as a product

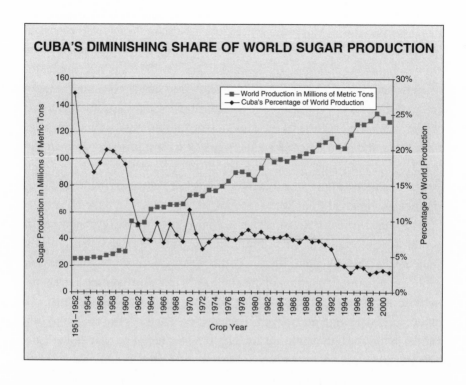

CUBA'S DIMINISHING SHARE OF WORLD SUGAR PRODUCTION

of direct consumption, they lend themselves to widespread industrial use, particularly for soft drinks, and have the potential to replace demand for 8 million tons of sugar worldwide. Moreover, earlier health concerns about saccharin seem to have been unjustified; reports linking it to cancer by the U.S. Food and Drug Administration in the late 1970s have recently been reversed on the basis of research by the U.S. National Institute of Environmental Health.[39]

An even more important challenge comes from high fructose starch sweeteners, derived from wheat or potatoes, but most important of all from corn syrup. The latter—high fructose corn syrup (HFCS)—has been marketed since 1972 and is often used in processing foods where liquid application is appropriate (e.g., baked goods, beverages, jams, and jellies). Beverages alone account for more than 70 percent of HFCS consumption in the United States. Supplies of this product are more reliable and predictable than sugar, and prices less volatile; moreover, HFCS facilities can be operated year round compared with the seasonal three- to five-month operations of beet factories and most sugar mills.[40]

At present the United States is the main producer of HFCS, putting the rough equivalent of 10.4 million tons of sugar on the world market (approximately 8 percent of the total). The growth of its market share is currently constrained by the requirement that a corn crop always be harvested at competitive costs. HFCS production technology is also more complex and more capital intensive than sugar and because HFCS transportation costs are high, requires consumers sufficiently close at hand to use it. Nonetheless, since the mid-1980s, HFCS has become available in crystalline form; this may be the first of a series of technological innovations that will lower costs and make it substantially more competitive with sugar in the future.

The entry of many new producers into the sugar market, combined with the emergence of alternative sweeteners, has over time depressed prices for both cane and beet sugars. To be sure, these prices are, and remain, broadly cyclical, but changes in the structure of the world market tend to keep the price run-up below historic peaks. For one thing, less developed countries (LDCs) account for a much larger (and growing) percentage of world consumption, and with lower incomes, they are more likely to cut back on imports sooner as prices rise. For yet another, both starch-based and low-calorie sweeteners are now more widely accepted as sugar substitutes. The latter are particularly well positioned to take advantage of sugar shortfalls and high prices. Finally, refined beet sugar now accounts for a larger percentage of the trade, and its producers can respond more quickly than cane sugar producers to an occasional rise in prices.[41]

The third change has been the disappearance of the Soviet family of nations, and with it, a large protected market for Cuba dictated partly or wholly by geostrategic considerations. As noted, the subsidized oil-for-sugar barter agreements with the Russian Federation survived the Soviet Union for nearly a decade but have since come to an end. Meanwhile, Cuban access to markets in Poland, the Czech Republic, and Hungary has drastically declined, and with the accession of the former GDR into the German Federal Republic and the European Union, the formerly sizable East German market has been completely lost. If Romania manages to improve its own industry, historically as inefficient as Cuba's (and for many of the same reasons), it will no longer need to import the product; even if it does, Romania might well turn to nearby Ukraine.

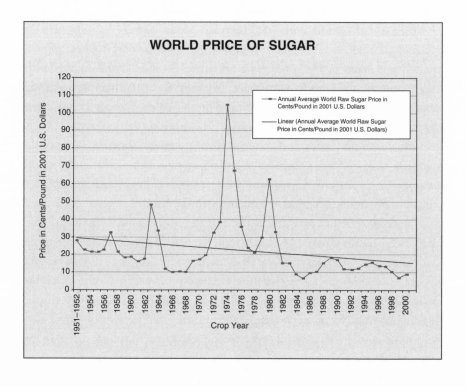

WORLD PRICE OF SUGAR

Throughout the 1990s, Cuba survived on reduced but continuing purchases from the Russian Federation, but also by cobbling together distant and sometimes marginal markets—Vietnam, North Korea, China, and Japan. Only the latter two have been buying substantial quantities—that is, between 300,000 and 900,000 tons a year. China possesses considerable potential for long-term self-sufficiency; however, it is also one of the few countries where artificial sweeteners pose a serious challenge to sugar in the domestic market. Its interest in Cuban sugar would seem to be dictated largely by political considerations, though for how much longer remains to be seen. In Japan, Cuba is likely to face serious competition from Australia and Thailand, which benefit not only from lower production costs but far lower freight rates—sometimes as much as 60 percent lower.

In recent years, the Middle East and North Africa have spoken for slightly more than 10 percent of Cuban exports. Algeria, Syria, and Egypt have taken increasing quantities in the last decade, and Cuba has had some discussion with oil-producing countries such as Libya and Iraq; Cuba has even signed a sugar-for-oil agreement with Iran. These markets have been ranging from between 600,000 to 850,000 metric tons per year, but their long-term outlook is uncertain, partly because of subsidized EU exports to former colonies in the area; the emergence of Turkey as an exporter; and the lifting of sanctions on South Africa, a supplier that enjoys a significant freight advantage in the area.

Within the Western Hemisphere, Cuba has maintained modest market shares in Canada, Peru, Mexico, and Venezuela, and on occasion, in Brazil. These markets are based on sales of raw cane sugar for refining and re-export, but improvements in domestic production levels in Mexico and Venezuela have dampened enthusiasm for the Cuban imports. Canada was taking virtually half of Cuba's regional exports in the early 1990s, but any significant increase would require Canada to deliberately reduce its domestic beet sugar production, a doubtful eventuality. In effect, Cuba's exports to the Western Hemisphere are not likely to exceed 800,000 metric tons in the near future, and in bad years could dip to half that number.

Prospects for Reinsertion in the U.S. Market

Potential sugar exports to countries in the Western Hemisphere are likely to be limited by major changes in the U.S. sugar industry during the last four decades. Cane is now grown not only in Louisiana, but in Florida and Texas, and there are important beet sugar industries in Michigan and California (the latter, because of its unique climatological situation, enjoys two growing seasons). At the same time, the U.S. industry has become remarkably efficient. The 1997–1998 harvest was roughly 7.86 million short tons, up 9 percent from 7.2 million the previous year and only 1 percent below the record of 1994–1995. Part of the increase was due to a new variety of cane introduced in Louisiana, which is producing higher yields per acre; in Florida, the recovery rate was up 10 percent over the previous year. That, together with the growing HFCS industry, has exercised a steady downward pressure on sugar prices.[42]

As noted, roughly a third of U.S. imports were reserved for Cuba in the decades prior to the revolution. After 1960, the Cuban quota (about 2.9 million tons) was distributed among sixteen other countries, most of them in Latin America and the Caribbean. The number of countries has since been increased to forty, all of which must satisfy themselves with meager portions of a greatly reduced overall U.S. import quota—which now stands at slightly more than 1.1 million tons. What are the circumstances under which Cuba could recover all or part of its previous market share?

In the first place, a new U.S. constituency would have to be formed around the proposition that the imperative of an economically stable Cuba far outweighed all other considerations of domestic and foreign economic policy. The ensuing debate would pit the State and Defense Departments, as well as the Immigration and Naturalization Service, the Coast Guard, and the Drug Enforcement Agency against the U.S. domestic sugar lobby, whose campaign contributions, as one journalist has observed, "exceed even those of the much-vaunted dairy lobby."[43] The United States would also have to decide to overrule the interests of longtime suppliers in the circum-Caribbean, including Jamaica, Barbados, and other Windward and Leeward Islands,[44] not to mention the Dominican Republic and the Central American states.

In discussions concerning the future prospects of Cuban sugar in the U.S. market, much has been made of the supposed clout that the Cuban-American community could bring to bear on behalf of its former homeland. While the Miami–New Jersey diaspora has demonstrated considerable capacity to shape the broad political parameters of U.S. Cuban policy over the last two decades, it has never put its influence to the test on an issue affecting so many and such well-placed domestic and foreign economic interests. Moreover, Cuban-Americans have their own agendas, and there is no guarantee that these will be embraced or even respected by whatever regime happens to be in power in Havana at the time relations are normalized. As for the massive foreign investment required to revive the Cuban sugar industry, there is a certain circularity to the dilemma. Without the investment, Cuba can never recover its place in the constellation of major producers. But foreign investors are likely to hold back until they are reassured that political stability has been achieved, clear rules of law have been enacted, unambiguous guidelines for privatization have been defined, and clear titles to properties have been established.

Even assuming that all of these obstacles could be surmounted, to find a place for Cuban sugar in the U.S. market would require Washington to revisit an entire range of credit, marketing, and import policies, many in place for decades. A truly free market option—in which the U.S. would abandon the Sugar Loan Program and its import-quota tariff regime, and thus open the gates to whatever sugar Cuba could produce at an attractive price—is virtually inconceivable. One economist has developed a series of alternative "managed" scenarios that are marginally more plausible. One is that the United States would redesign its import quotas, depriving allotments from countries that are not net exporters and reassigning their deficits to Cuba. Another scenario would eliminate country quotas; the first-tier tariffs would be global rather than country-specific. Refiners could then purchase raw sugar from any foreign source, including Cuba. Another would reduce the current domestic support price to growers, which would lead to a larger demand for imports. Another would have Cuba enter an enlarged NAFTA, becoming a residual supplier to the United States and also a provider of raw sugar which, refined in the United States, could presumably be exported to Mexico as long as that country remained a net importer from the United States. Yet another scenario would establish a Cuban ethanol import program, in which Cuba would develop a fuel alcohol industry based on the construction of distilleries annexed to existing mills.[45] All of these options are theoretically possible, but given the political landscape in Washington, and particularly in the U.S. Congress, none is likely.

Quite apart from the vested interests lined up to preserve the status quo, many of Cuba's sugar lands are still subject to claims by expropriated U.S. investors. A case in point is Borden, the third largest of the nearly 6,000 certified claimants, which has acquired the rights of the former North American Sugar Industries, Cuban-American Mercantile Corporation, and the West India Company. In 1969, the Foreign Claims Settlement Commission found that these properties were worth $109 million, and for compensation purposes assigned a statutory 6 percent simple annual rate of interest to be calculated from the date of confiscation to the date of ultimate settlement. The principal Borden stake in Cuba consists of three of the most modern mills, significantly deteriorated but still functioning, as well as 300,000 acres of land, including some of the best sugar land in Cuba, many hundreds of miles of railroads, port facilities, a sugar refinery, electrical power plants, warehouses, pasture lands, employee housing, assorted mill machinery and equipment, as well as other related real property.[46] Borden's claim in the year 2000, including accumulated interest, amounted to slightly more than $1 billion.[47] It is difficult to imagine Cuba reentering the U.S. sugar market with a product that—in the opinion of certified claimants such as Borden—derives from or represents stolen property, and this is likely to be so even if the explicit barriers established by the Helms-Burton Law are abolished before full normalization of relations.[48]

Alternatives to Sugar

If Cuba can no longer look forward to making a living on sugar, what of other products? Apart from the growing tourism sector, which is discussed at some length in chapter 5, the following sectors are possible alternatives to sugar.

Citrus. After 1959, the revolutionary government designated citrus as having the greatest potential for growth, and much capital and technology were invested in this area. The most important crop was oranges, which in 1992–1993 amounted to 350,000 metric tons. Thirteen percent of this harvest was destined for the foreign market, and another 23 percent was processed into orange juice for export. The remainder (64 percent) was directed to the domestic market.

Grapefruit is a crop with even greater potential. In 1992–1993, Cuba produced 250,000 metric tons, and at that point was the world's third largest producer, after the United States and Israel. The island is also capable of growing limes, sour oranges, and tangerines, but the quality of its harvest is currently too poor to compete in the world market and is consumed almost entirely at home.

After the collapse of the Soviet Union and consequent loss of inputs such as energy, insecticides, and fertilizer, the Cuban citrus culture—like sugar—entered into something of a tailspin. The first indicator was a reduction in the size of the area devoted to citrus crops, which dropped from 355,700 "net tree acres" in 1989 to 238,000 in 1994–1995. As a result, the harvest itself dropped by nearly 40 percent, from 1 million metric tons in 1989 to 620,000 metric tons in 1993.

In an effort to revitalize the citrus industry, the Cuban government was forced to undertake two major economic reforms. The first was the transformation of many collective farms into cooperatives (UBPCs). In the citrus area, each cooperative is managed autonomously insofar as the technical aspects of husbandry are concerned, but even so, UBPCs are obliged to purchase their inputs from the state and sell a portion of their output back to it at fixed prices. Presumably some production incentives are built into these procedures, but they are limited in scope to avoid excessive devolution of economic power. The other is the sudden entry into the Cuban agricultural scene of foreign companies from Israel, Chile, and Greece, working in conjunction with state farms under marketing agreements. It is not possible to chart the full impact of these changes because the Cuban government has been extremely reluctant to publish recent statistics, but unofficial reports suggest that the decline in citrus production has been stanched. On the other hand, no decisive turnaround has yet occurred.[49]

Vegetables. Cuba is also well situated to grow a wide variety of fresh vegetables, and in fact does produce tomatoes, cucumbers, onions, garlic, sweet peppers, melons, cabbage, and a wide variety of other products in smaller quantities. In the late 1980s, its annual vegetable harvest was estimated at 572,000 tons; by 1993, for the same reasons the sugar and citrus harvests decreased, the vegetable harvest had declined by 30 percent. Even in the relatively good old days, however, its productivity was far below what one might expect from acreage devoted to these crops. Between 1975 and 1989, Cuba's tomato production dropped by 20 percent, while Florida's—using half the acreage—increased by 15 percent.

Cuba's production of tuber and root crops (cassava, boniato, malanga, and tropical yams) more than doubled between 1975 and 1981, but from 1982 to 1992, its output remained relatively stable. On the other hand, the actual harvest was again far lower than one would expect given the resources involved. Here, too, a comparison with Florida is useful. In 1989, which is to say, in the waning days of its special relationship with the Soviet Union, Cuba had 131,000 acres devoted to boniato culture and 31,000 acres to malanga. The figures for Florida were 6,000 and 5,100 acres, respectively. Throughout the 1980s, Florida's boniato crop was anywhere from two to four times the size of Cuba's, and although in some years the island's malanga harvest reached the same level as Florida's, it was generally about half as large.

Partly due to the modest reforms associated with land tenure and use since 1993, vegetables are the one area of agricultural production that have registered a dramatic increase in recent years. In one calculation, the island's vegetable harvest was 140 percent higher in 2000 than in 1989.[50] In per capita terms, however, output was either stagnant or slightly lower in 2000 than it was a decade before.[51] Cuba is still far from being in a position to export seasonal vegetables, both because of the modest size of its harvest and the mediocre quality of its products.

Tropical Fruits. Cuba's tropical fruit industry (mango, guava, papaya, pineapple, and coconut) has virtually disappeared. In 1989, it had 220,000 acres under cultivation, including 18,000 acres of papaya and 32,000 acres of pineapple; but by 1992, only 14,000 acres were under cultivation, including 9,800 of papaya and 4,000 of pineapple. The harvest figures tell their own somber story. In 1985, tropical fruit production peaked at 240,000 tons; in 1992, it fell to 68,000 tons. Between 1972 and 1992, mango production dropped 20 percent, guava 35 percent, and papaya fully 50 percent. The one crop that experienced an increase in acreage after the collapse of the Soviet Union was bananas, which expanded from 106,000 acres in 1989 to 140,000 in 1992. In the same period, however, banana yields *declined* by 9 percent (plantains by 20 percent).[52] Figures for more recent years are still unavailable.

Tobacco Products. One agricultural product for which Cuba is justly famous is tobacco, used both to make cigars and furnish fillers for cigarettes. Here the island enjoys a remarkable comparative advantage, since the Vuelta Abajo region of the Pinar del Río possesses the ideal combination of light, soil, humidity, and rainfall to grow the world's finest cigar wrapper leaf.[53] In 1962, smokers in the United States were consuming about 190 million cigars a year, of which 15 million were produced in Cuba (8 percent of the U.S. market). Moreover, almost all the leaf used to roll other premium cigars, produced either in the United States or elsewhere in the Caribbean, came from Cuba.

After the revolution and up to 1989, Cuban cigar exports fell flat, partly due to the U.S. trade embargo but also to a generalized decline in cigar smoking, as well as the entry of new producers into the market. For example, in 1959 the Dominican Republic possessed only an embryonic cigar industry; today, thanks largely to Cuban émigrés, it is one of the world's largest producers of premium hand-rolled cigars, using Cuban seed and producing established Cuban brands such as Cohiba and Montecristo. In 1997, Dominican cigars accounted for nearly half the U.S. market, at a value of $210 million. Other countries in the circum-Caribbean that have entered the cigar market during the last four decades include Honduras, Nicaragua, Jamaica, Costa Rica, and Mexico.

Since 1994, there has been a moderate upsurge in cigar consumption worldwide, and Cuba has responded by training new rollers and expanding its production for export. To this end, it has entered into production agreements with the Spanish firm Tabacalera, S.A., which now advances credit to Cuban producers based on guaranteed deliveries. This, combined with unusual production incentives to workers, has led to a dramatic recovery of the industry. Official Cuban sources claim that current world demand for premium Cuban cigars still exceeds the current level of production. This would seem to be borne out by the export figures, which have increased from $100 million in 1991 to $250 million in 1999. Cigars are currently the fourth largest generator of hard currency in Cuba, exceeded only by tourism, sugar, and nickel.[54] Given the cyclical nature of the market, however, combined with the fact that both Cuba and the Dominican Republic are busily increasing production, it is only a matter of time before demand is satisfied and prices once again decline.

Ironically, the Cuban cigar industry in some ways benefits from the U.S. economic embargo, to the extent that the latter creates artificial scarcities that not only drive up prices but also encourage contraband across Mexican and Canadian borders.[55] Once the embargo is lifted and American companies are in a position to import Cuban leaf, the United States could conceivably become a producer of cigars competitive with those coming from Cuba, as was the case before 1959. Meanwhile, the case of tobacco demonstrates that Cuba can best exploit its comparative advantage in certain products by returning to the old-fashioned system of (capitalist) market and production incentives.[56]

Even after the embargo is lifted, however, the U.S. market potential for Cuban tobacco products may prove far more limited than in the past. In June

2000, the National Cancer Institute, the Surgeon General's office, and the Federal Trade Commission came together to warn consumers that cigar smoking can cause cancers of the mouth and throat, even if the smoker does not inhale; they also announced that cigar smoking can cause lung cancer and heart disease. Indeed, the seven American companies already producing cigars have been ordered to include warnings about significant adverse health risks to cigar use in both their advertising and packaging.[57]

Fisheries. Although not strictly speaking a branch of agriculture, the Cuban fishing industry deserves mention because it constitutes a source of nutrition for the population and it has the potential to become a major source of hard currency.

Prior to 1959, Cuba's commercial fishing industry was purely artisanal, composed of small boats that plied near-shore waters. The yield consisted largely of reef fish, spring lobster, sponge, and a few pelagic fin-fish species. As a reward for strategic alignment, the Soviet Union financed the modernization of the island's port facilities, commercial fishing fleet, and processing sector, at the same time granting it access to relatively cheap fuel. As a result, the Cuban fishing industry reached a level of sophistication virtually unknown in the region, increasing its yield by a factor of ten between 1959 and 1976.

Unfortunately, the new fleet came on stream at roughly the same time that most Latin American nations were effectively imposing a 200-mile limit on their territorial waters. Consequently, Cuban vessels were forced to operate on the high seas, consuming disproportionate amounts of fuel and pursuing low-value species for internal consumption rather than for export. As in all other energy-dependent areas of the Cuban economy, the fisheries industry suffered acutely from the breakup of the Soviet Union, and landings decreased from 230,000 metric tons in 1988 to 90,000 in 1993. As in other areas of the Cuban economy, the Ministry of Fisheries was reformed in 1995 and the industry restructured to allow for greater decentralization of management and greater incentives to enhance production. As a result, the total catch between 1995 and 1999 has increased slightly more than 9 percent, income slightly more than 8 percent, and seafood exports by almost 7 percent.[58] Even so, as of 2000, Cuba's catch was still more than 15 percent below what it had been in 1989.[59]

In any case, the Cuban industry still has a long way to go to become truly world-class. Distant-water trawlers are reportedly tied up in Havana Harbor due to a lack of fuel oil or spare parts; a few are in Canada fishing for hake (though environmental concerns in that country may put an end to that). Cuba's near-coastal fleet, the so-called Flota de Plataforma, continues to haul in a wide variety of high value species, the most important of which is the spring lobster, which together with pink shrimp, reef fish, and fresh tuna could conceivably find important export markets in Florida. (Most of Cuba's lobster is currently exported to Japan or the European Community.) The Florida market is particularly promising in light of the fact that Cuban spring lobster lands normally take place during Florida's closed season, though the entry of Cuban reef fish—particularly snapper and grouper—would probably compete with catches landed by that state's own maritime industry. But before entering the U.S. market, Cuba would have to meet the new quality and safety standards established under the Food and Drug Administration's Hazardous Awareness at Critical Control Points (HACCP) program. At the same time, it would have to find new sources of energy at reasonable prices so that its fleet could market its catch at competitive prices.[60]

Mining. One of the most dramatic developments in the Cuban economy in the post–Cold War period has been the revival of the mining industry. Cuba possesses known reserves of zinc, iron, gold, bauxite, quartz, and phosphorus, but it is particularly well-provisioned with nickel and cobalt, possessing the world's largest and second largest reserves of each, respectively. The country's first nickel processing plant was established in 1943 at Nícaro, in the Oriente region, with U.S. capital and technology. A second plant was opened at Moa Bay, also in the Oriente, in 1960. In 1972, Cuba and the Soviet Union agreed to modernize both plants and construct a third at Pinta Gorda, which was opened in 1986.

A record 46,000 tons of nickel were produced in 1989. With the collapse of the Soviet Union, however, Cuban output plummeted to 27,000 tons in 1994. The prospect of the industry's imminent collapse forced the government to conclude joint ventures with foreign investors, most notably Sherritt International Corporation of Canada, which has improved technology, lowered production costs, increased output, and provided Cuba with full access to first-world markets. As a result, nickel production soared to 72,000 tons by 2000, making Cuba the world's sixth largest producer.

This experience has encouraged other investors to enter the field, and some fifty-five foreign companies are reported to be prospecting, evaluating, or extracting Cuban gold, silver, chromium, magnesium, lead, and zinc, though not yet in significant quantities. One resource—copper—was no longer produced as of 2001 because of depressed commodity prices and declining reserves. Mining has become Cuba's third largest sector for foreign investment, after tourism and tobacco, but its ultimate capacity to contribute to the Cuban economy has yet to be fully established.[61] The latest official figures are rather modest. In 2000 (at the rate of 22 pesos per dollar), nickel and cobalt exports amounted to slightly less than $261 million; copper, a bit more than $58 million; and chrome, just under $12 million.[62]

Biomedical Products. Perhaps no innovation of the revolutionary government has received so much praise from the foreign media as its dedication to developing a world-class biotech industry. Of the regime's commitment to that goal there can be no doubt; during the 1980s vast sums were poured into creating a Center for Genetic Engineering and Biotechnology on a large campus near Havana; Cuban students were sent to Eastern and Western Europe for advanced training; Cuban scientists even established links to U.S. hospitals and research institutions, including the Centers for Disease Control in Atlanta.

"In spite of years of economic isolation and relative impoverishment," writes one British journalist, "the country has built one of the most advanced yet least known biotech industries in the world." The accomplishment is not merely scientific, he continues, but holds out the prospect of a line of exports capable of earning serious money. In particular he notes a Cuban vaccine for meningitis B that is being adapted by GlaxoSmithKline laboratories for use in Western countries, and an anti-cancer vaccine being tested in British hospitals.[63] Another journalist has singled out a Cuban-developed TheraCIM drug that reportedly "has regressed tumors in patients with head and neck cancers," which is being commercialized by YM BioSciences, a Canadian firm.[64] U.S. academic Julie Feinsilver, who has probably studied the industry more extensively than any foreigner, points out some 160 medical-pharmaceutical biotechnology products and a number of agricultural and industrial products produced by Cuban scientists. "Cuba's biotechnology investment," she writes, "may provide large dividends if the extensive scientific infrastructure and human resources are leased to a transnational pharmaceutical company."[65]

At the same time, Feinsilver cautions that the Cubans "have not yet solved all of their problems relating to marketing, sales and distribution networks; competition; patents (others and theirs); credibility in the marketplace; the U.S. embargo; their overall economic situation and economic practices (including the lack of strategic planning: scarcity of resources) . . . and a stressful environment overall in which young scientists must come up with solutions to extraordinarily difficult economic problems."[66] She seems troubled as well by the fact that because of "the ongoing economic crisis," Cubans have rushed to commercialize products "often before they have been extensively tested."[67]

An even less sanguine view comes from José de la Fuente, a former biotechnology researcher, now at Oklahoma State University, who worked in the Cuban industry until the late 1990s. He reaffirms Feinsilver's observation about the precipitous marketing of inadequately tested products, adding that the Cuban industry has often abruptly shifted its priorities to strictly short-term applied research, or alternatively, to "grandiose projects like the creation of a vaccine for AIDS."

De la Fuente also claims that since 1994, the regime has turned its attention to tourism as the solution to attracting foreign capital, which in turn has meant a shortchanging of resources for biotechnology. As a result, no capital improvements have been made on the country's formerly state-of-the-art research facility for nearly a decade. Moreover, the regime's policy of restricting access to computers—one of many measures of totalitarian political control—means that "ordinary scientists and graduate students throughout Latin America and the Caribbean now have more computing power and modern biotechnology tools at their fingertips than heads of some divisions at Cuba's most prestigious biotechnology institutions."[68]

For its part, the Cuban government, through its official daily, claims that thanks to locally created biotech products, including a serum against Hepatitis B, the biotech sector increased its exports by 42 percent in 2001.[69] Unfortunately, not enough data are available on the industry to know how much—if anything—foreign biotech sales currently contribute to the Cuban

CLONED COWS BUT NO MILK

Though the Western media often praises Cuba's achievements in the area of biotechnology, only rarely does it single out cases where vast resources were squandered on projects with no real possibility of success. One such project was the production of Ubre Blanca (White Udder), a cow that holds the world record for milk production (241 pounds—more than four times that of a typical cow—on a single day in 1982). Unfortunately, none of her seven offspring—Ubre Blanca is since deceased—turned out to have her outsized mammary glands. Nonetheless, José Morales, leader of Cuba's cow-cloning team, boasts that the country is "very, very close" to producing its first cloned cow, though he admits that he and his fellow scientists are still unable to replicate Ubre Blanca from tissue that has been in the freezer for seventeen years. "But we do not discard the possibility that we'll be able to do this some day. . . . This project is very important to Comandante Castro." Meanwhile, according to World Bank estimates, Cuba's milk production has fallen by about 60 percent since 1989. [Peter Fritsch and José de Cordoba, "Udderly Fantastic: Cuba Hopes to Clone Its Famous Milk Cow," *Wall Street Journal,* May 21, 2002.]

economy. The announcement cited did not give dollar figures, and in fact those figures do not seem to be readily available. Without them, it is impossible to say to what degree this industry will be able to replace the sugar industry as a major exporter.

Concluding Remarks

As a "normal" Latin American country in the future, Cuba will subsist—like Guatemala, El Salvador, or the Dominican Republic—on a mixture of extractive industries, services, specialty exports, and remittances. With the exception of the last, however, the degree to which the country will prosper will depend less on natural resources or even human capital than on extra-economic considerations, such as Cuba's capacity to attract foreign investment, its access to foreign sources of credit at preferential rates, and its political relationship with its nearest major market in the United States. No doubt the texture and mood of its political life will play a crucial role as well. The inverse is also true: the political synthesis reached among Cubans—and between the state and foreign powers—will play a major role in determining to what degree the country can capitalize on the comparative advantages it may possess.

One thing is clear: there can be no return to sugar. The dream of Cuban nationalists of all stripes—to liberate the island from dependence on a single product—has finally been realized, although not in ways they foresaw or even desired. The challenge that remains, however, is as great as, indeed arguably greater than, any posed by monoculture, particularly a monoculture of the very special and favorable kind that once made Cuba the envy of its neighbors.

3

Property

The Most Socialist of States

As in France, Russia, and modern China, the distinguishing hallmark of social revolution in Cuba has been a drastic reordering of property relations. At first, this meant nationalizing foreign companies long active in agriculture, communications, mining, petroleum refining, manufacturing, and hostelry. Subsequent actions led to the wholesale expropriation of Cuba's locally owned private sector and nearly all urban real estate. Indeed, in one area, Cuba has gone far beyond the countries after which it sought to model itself. By 1988, fully *92 percent* of its agricultural land—historically the country's principal economic resource—was in the hands of the state, compared for the same year with 6 percent in socialist Bulgaria, 8 percent in socialist Poland, 14 percent in the USSR, and 17 percent in the German Democratic Republic.[1] In 1995 dollars, the value of all Cuban takings "far exceed[ed] the value of the property expropriated by the nations of Eastern Europe after World War II and by the Soviet Union after the Bolshevik Revolution."[2]

Given the preponderant role of American business on the island before 1959, such actions were bound to cause enormous losses for U.S. investors. After a lengthy canvassing process between 1966 and 1972, the U.S. Foreign Claims Settlement Commission (FCSC) certified 5,911 claims with an aggregate value of $1.85 billion. Ten corporate giants account for more than half of the total: the Cuban Electric Company ($267.6 million); International Telephone and Telegraph Company ($130.7 million); North American Sugar Industries ($100.9 million); Moa Bay Mining Company ($88.3 million); United Fruit ($85.1 million); West Indies Sugar ($81 million); American

Sugar ($78 million); Standard Oil ($71.6 million); Bangor Punta Corporation ($53.4 million); and Francisco Sugar ($52.6 million). The top fifteen claims account for two-thirds of the total, with claims eleven through fifteen represented by Texaco ($50.1 million); Manati Sugar ($48.6 million); Nícaro Nickel Company ($33 million); Coca Cola ($27.5 million); and Lone Star Cement ($24.9 million). At a simple 6 percent rate of interest imposed by the FCSC, U.S. certified claims against Cuba amounted to $6.44 billion in 2002.

This is a large sum for a small country, particularly one whose economic capacity has been greatly diminished since 1989. Yet Cuba is far from the first Latin American republic to nationalize foreign enterprises. Quite the contrary. While such property transfers have typically taken place under self-styled revolutionary regimes, such as in Mexico (1910), Guatemala (1944–1954), Bolivia (1952), and Peru (1968), they have also occurred under somewhat more conventional ("bourgeois") dispensations. In 1977, Paul Sigmund of Princeton University counted more than fifty cases of expropriation since 1900, ranging from timberlands in Nicaragua to electric power companies in Argentina, from telephone services in Brazil to steel plants in Venezuela.[3]

Nor—if historical precedent is any guide—should Cuba necessarily fear the future costs of compensation. For although the United States has historically insisted on "prompt, adequate and effective" payment for properties taken from its nationals, Sigmund's survey shows that in only a tiny minority of cases have U.S. claims been anywhere near fully satisfied. More typical is the example of American oil companies in Mexico expropriated during the government of President Lázaro Cárdenas in 1938. The original claim for $262 million was eventually settled for slightly less than $37 million (14 percent of the original claim). Another example involves properties taken from the International Petroleum Company in Peru in 1968. The original owners claimed damages in the amount of $120 million, but they received only $27.5 million (23 percent of the original claim). An even more striking case involves three American copper companies taken over by the socialist regime of Salvador Allende in 1970–1973. In 1974, Allende's successor, a military junta allegedly oversolicitous of foreign interests, settled the outstanding claims of $665.5 million for $362 million—slightly more than half what was asked.[4]

The tendency for capital-exporting countries to accept something like ten to twenty-five cents on the dollar for property taken from their nationals is reaffirmed by Cuba's own experience since 1959. After the United States, the second largest source of revolutionary claims ($350 million) was Spain. But by 1988, after two years of negotiation, Cuba agreed to pay a mere $40 million in semi-annual installments over a fifteen-year period in a combination of cash and goods, with a mixed commission determining the type and quality of articles to be accepted in payment.[5] A settlement even more disadvantageous to claimants was concluded in 1966 by Switzerland, which sought compensation for property allegedly worth 18 million Swiss francs (U.S. $4.14 million at 1967 rates of exchange). After what the Swiss later described as "bitter discussions" with their counterparts in Havana, they agreed to buy 40,000 tons of Cuban sugar at the world price, with Cuba earmarking roughly a third of the hard currency it received from the sale for indemnities due Swiss nationals. What made the agreement unique was the capacity of Swiss companies to use sugar in food processing (mostly chocolates). Had the manufacture of confections not figured as an important item on the schedule of Swiss exports, one observer has noted, "it is quite possible that no agreement would have been reached . . . , since the Cubans possess few commodities currently needed by the Swiss economy."[6]

An accord reached with France several weeks after the settlement with Switzerland obliged Cuba to pay 11 million francs (U.S. $2.17 million at 1967 rates of exchange) in twelve nearly equal installments over approximately five years. The National Bank of Cuba was obliged to transfer sums to a special account opened for this purpose in the Bank of France. As relatively favorable as these settlements have been to Cuba, it is perhaps worth noting that a full seven years passed before Havana was even willing to discuss a settlement with these European nations. The eventual conclusion of agreements with Spain and France seems to have been motivated largely by the Cuban government's desire to increase trade with those countries. One might therefore regard such settlements less as an exercise in compensation than "as a quid pro quo for the acquisition of needed commodities or foreign exchange."[7]

This last observation is particularly relevant to the case of the United States. Cuba's official position since at least 1960 has been that it has always intended to pay compensation for U.S. properties; it is the *United States* that refuses to come to the negotiating table for political reasons.[8] This is at best a half-truth; actually the 1960 Cuban law that expropriated U.S. property limited indemnification to a fund created by 25 percent of U.S. sugar purchases in excess of three million tons at the (pre-1959) subsidized price. This was an extremely disingenuous offer, since Cuban sales of sugar to the United States had exceeded the designated amount (and then just barely so) a mere three times between 1929 and 1959.[9] More recent offers by Cuba to discuss property claims have been accompanied by counterclaims for compensation for the longstanding U.S. trade embargo and other offenses, real or imagined.[10] In 1995, Ricardo Alarcón, president of Cuba's legislative assembly, suggested that these could amount to $100 billion, a figure that represents roughly *fifty* times Cuba's annual exports for the previous two years. Four years later Havana almost doubled its demand; a Cuban court found the United States liable for deaths and damages over a forty-year period, making the island apparently eligible for some $181 *billion* in "reparations."[11]

Property Issues and Diplomatic Normalization

However one feels about the rights and wrongs of the issue, property remains at the very heart of the U.S.-Cuban diplomatic impasse. Indeed, powerful legislative barriers have been erected to ensure that no normalization will ever take place until the certified expropriation claims have been settled, or at least until the settlement process has begun.

The Foreign Assistance Act of 1961 (*U.S. Code,* volume 22, section 2515) denies foreign aid to Cuba "until the President determines that such government has taken appropriate steps according to international law standards to return to United States citizens, and to entities not less than fifty per centum beneficially owned by United States citizens, or to provide equitable compensation to such citizens and entities, for property taken from such citizens and entities on or after January 1, 1959, by the government of Cuba." Legislation of a more general type further mandates that the United States vote against loans solicited from multilateral lending institutions by any country that has confiscated the property of U.S. citizens without equitable compensation.

Title II of the Cuban Liberty and Solidarity Act of 1996, U.S. Public Law 104-114—more commonly known as the Helms-Burton Law—lists the conditions for lifting the longstanding trade embargo (which it codifies in Title I) and providing aid to a new Cuban government. Section 205 of Title II defines the characteristics that such a government must possess, including some factors that, though not strictly required, the President is mandated to take into account. They include the consideration that such a government is "taking appropriate steps to return to United States citizens . . . property taken by the Cuban Government . . . or to provide equitable compensation to such citizens for such property." Section 206 goes somewhat further; it requires that in order for the President to find such a government democratically elected, it must be shown to have made "demonstrable progress in returning to United States citizens . . . property taken from such citizens . . . on or after January 1, 1959, or providing full compensation for such property in accordance with international law standards and practice."

Section 207 mandates the Secretary of State to submit to Congress, within 180 days of enactment of the law, a written report containing an assessment of the property dispute question in Cuba, including an estimate of the number and amount of claims "held by U.S. nationals in addition to those claims certified under section 507 of the International Claims Settlement Act of 1949." Section 207 concludes, "It is the sense of the Congress that the satisfactory resolution of property claims by a Cuban Government recognized by the United States remains an essential condition for the full resumption of economic and diplomatic relations between the United States and Cuba."

To be sure, renewal of diplomatic relations is not wholly mortgaged to the resolution of property issues; as a matter of fact, other provisions of Helms-Burton raise the bar still higher—possibly, as some critics have observed, well beyond the conceivable abilities of any transitional regime.[12] Paradoxically, within this context, certified claims of U.S. nationals might well turn out to be the most tractable item on the bilateral agenda, particularly if the United States opts for what is called the "lump-sum" approach. This involves a settlement reached between the State Department and a given foreign government that results in a fixed amount that is then distributed on a pro rata basis among the claimants. Historically these settlements have provided considerable relief for the expropriating government; in the case of the People's

Republic of China, for example, $197 million worth of U.S. claims were eventually settled for $80.5 million. Moreover, under what is called the "doctrine of espousal," these negotiations are binding and not subject to appeal. Further, once claimants have agreed to allow their government to pursue compensation on their behalf, they may not "opt out" of what they may subsequently find an unsatisfactory settlement. Nor, under the same arrangement, may they pursue their unsatisfied claims before either U.S. courts or the courts of the settling country.

Unfortunately, even this fairly forgiving method may lie beyond the bounds of immediate possibility for Cuba, which under present circumstances would be unable to pay any significant portion of the principal ($1.85 billion), leave aside the interest. Any government in Cuba comes to the negotiating table not only with a large bill for expropriations of U.S. property, but a huge hard currency debt with Western Europe and Japan ($11 billion as of 2000), and more than $20 billion in loans owed to the Russian Federation, successor to the Soviet Union.[13]

One alternative is for the U.S. claimants to waive their rights to receive a share of a lump-sum settlement and instead negotiate directly with the government of Cuba for payment in other ways—"restitution of the expropriated assets, investment concessions, payment in commodities other than cash, or compensation by means of Cuban government obligations."[14] Under such circumstances, the U.S. government would have to take measures to assure that those claimants who waive the right to be represented by it would receive "fair and reasonable treatment" by Cuba once they entered into negotiations.[15] (Just what such measures might be, other than normal diplomatic representation, is not clear.)

Such an alternative would not necessarily fully eliminate the need for a lump-sum settlement; those who prefer the latter might share in a small sum—say, $150 million—which, somewhat surprisingly, would provide roughly half the principal (but no interest) to the 5,013 certified claimants who are individuals, largely former owners of small farms or urban real estate. Recent experience in the former East Germany suggests that this might be a viable option for many.

Corporate claimants might prefer direct restitution of land and/or physical plant. Implementation would, however, present some practical difficulties.

Much urban real estate in Cuba owned by U.S. nationals in 1960 has been destroyed or has substantially deteriorated. Land has been subject to multiple transformations, mergers, subdivisions, improvements, and other substantial changes. Some property has been converted to new uses that cannot easily be reversed, or has come to possess substantial public utility. To complicate matters further, since 1994 the Cuban government has been engaged in joint ventures with third parties (often foreign nationals) involving property expropriated from U.S. and Cuban (or former Cuban) nationals.

Even where direct restitution is both appropriate and possible, there are still outstanding issues. Cuba may wish to impose restrictions or requirements on the use of the property by the claimants, or on the claimant's ability to transfer it for a certain period of time. In a few cases, the property may have been improved significantly since expropriation, requiring a complex process of revaluation. Or, in the Cuban case, given the extensive environmental damage that has occurred on the island since 1959,[16] the former owners might be required to commit themselves in advance to a complex process of reclamation. The government of Cuba also might well impose a transfer tax, partly to finance other parts of the program and partly to make sure that restitution does not leave the claimant in a better position than those who have accepted different forms of recovery, such as partial compensation.

Evidently physical restitution will not be appropriate or practicable in all cases, such as in the instance of farmland divided into cooperatives or passed on to small farmers. In such cases, the Cuban government might identify a substitute property that lent itself more readily to transfer. This process, however, would involve complex problems of equivalent valuation. In Eastern Europe this procedure has led to extensive litigation; in Romania alone, some 300,000 court cases contesting valuation have jammed the dockets.

Another way out would be payment through state-issued instruments such as vouchers. These would not be redeemable for cash, but could be used as collateral for loans to pay fully (or in part) for property sold by the state, including shares in privatized enterprises; to purchase real estate put up for sale by the state; to be exchanged for annuities; or to be used as investment instruments. This method has been used in some of the former socialist states of Eastern Europe with some success to resolve the claims of owners of small and medium-sized enterprises who may not be interested in recovering property because of technological obsolescence or deterioration. It has the advantage of bypassing the cash-poor situation of successor states and also avoids the disputes associated with direct restitution. It obviously has the merit of greater flexibility.

Other state-issued instruments include annuities, bonds, promissory notes, stock certificates in privatized enterprises, and other debt or equity instruments. These papers will evidently fluctuate in value, and may depreciate dramatically if Cuba's economy falters. (This has already been the case in the Czech Republic.) As for annuities, their rate of return has been historically rather low. Several methods yet to be tried—but suggested by a leading lobbyist representing offshore interests—include credits on taxes and duties to the extent of part or all of the claim amount; the ability to exchange the claim for other investment opportunities, including management contracts, beneficial interests in state-owned enterprises, or preferences in government contracting. Each of these options would have to be resolved on an ad hoc basis.[17]

Third-Party Contracts and Property Controversies

Unfortunately, property controversies in Cuba cannot be confined to two parties alone. As noted, during the last decade the Castro government began to enter into a large number of joint ventures with foreign (European and Latin American) concerns. In general, these agreements involved the use rather than the sale or transfer of expropriated property; they are, in effect, service contracts that permit the exploitation of land, mines, or enterprises that are still subject to claim by their former owners. Title III of the Helms-Burton law specifically seeks to remedy this situation by empowering claimants of uncompensated commercial property in Cuba to seek redress against present users ("traffickers") in U.S. courts, and Title IV allows for the exclusion from the United States of individuals who do so traffic, or the relevant corporate officers of enterprises, as well as their spouses or children.

Because many of Cuba's new business partners have come from Spain, France, Great Britain, and the Netherlands, Helms-Burton immediately unleashed a furious controversy between the United States and the European Union, with the latter threatening to haul the former before the newly created World Trade Organization. After two years of intensive negotiations, the White

House announced an agreement by which the United States and the EU would establish "disciplines for strengthening investment protection worldwide"[18] in return for administration efforts to seek legislative relief from Title IV. Where countries such as Cuba deny legitimate compensation to expropriated property owners, the signatories oblige themselves to deny to the expropriating state a range of advantages, including loans, grants, subsidies, and political risk insurance. The two sides also agreed to publish a register of expropriated properties, make joint public statements, and coordinate diplomatic representations to the offending state. In exchange, the United States agreed to permanently waive the provisions of Title IV (the authority to do so is within the discretion of the President as the legislation is now written, and has in fact been exercised ever since Helms-Burton was signed into law).

These "disciplines" sound impressive on paper, but, as critics frequently point out, they represent at best a very weak sanction. For one thing, goods and services produced on expropriated properties are exempt from what it classifies as "covered transactions." For another, the agreement applies only to *new* investments made after promulgation of the U.S.-EU understanding. Under the agreement, one critic notes, the United States is in effect "required not only to recognize investments made prior to May 18, 1998, but also must accept that these investors remain eligible to receive governmental commercial insurance." Moreover, the United States "must agree, in effect, that an investor in wrongly taken property remains immune from sanctions in perpetuity."[19]

The U.S.-EU accord also creates additional problems for the future. As David Wallace, general counsel of the Lone Star Corporation, explained, "If current foreign investments in expropriated properties are essentially held harmless by this understanding, restitutionary remedies that ultimately prove critical in resolving many of these claims may be effectively precluded."[20] Yet another problem is that the Cubans may find ways of helping third parties evade the effect of Helms-Burton by disguising their national identity. (As one functionary of the Ministry of Foreign Investment told a business group in Mexico, "We follow a policy of discretion for those who invest in Cuba.")[21] Finally, two of the most important foreign investors in Cuba—Mexico and Canada—are not a party to the U.S.-EU understanding, so that even in the best of cases the effect of the agreement is limited.

To date only one European investor has explicitly recognized the need to take full cognizance of outstanding U.S. claims on Cuban property—Telecom/Italy, or as it is known by its formal acronym, STET. By agreeing to pay the International Telephone and Telegraph Company (original owner of the Cuban Telephone Company) between $25 million and $40 million for a ten-year license to operate its former properties on the island, STET circumvents sanctions under Helms-Burton and is able to sell 1.73 billion shares of stock in U.S. financial markets with a view to expanding Cuba's domestic telecommunications network.[22] More typical, however, has been the acquisition of the rum label of Havana Club by Pernot-Ricard of France over the protest of Bacardi USA, the successor to the original owners. As of mid-2001, Bacardi had won a suit before the World Trade Organization to prevent Pernot-Richard's use of the label, though the European Union has promised to appeal the finding.[23] Similar claims pertain to the use of land belonging to U.S. citizens that has been leased to the Spanish hotel chain Sol Meliá. In the light of such circumstances, one can anticipate that even in the most favorable political environment, with so many other parties involved, negotiations between the United States and Cuba over property issues are bound to be complex, lengthy—and fractious, with some ending up in U.S. courts.[24]

Claims of Former Cuban Nationals

As if 5,911 certified claimants were not enough to keep U.S. diplomats busy, there are also more than 1 million Cuban-Americans (or their heirs) who have lost property in Cuba since 1959. As present-day citizens of the United States (in some cases, native-born), they naturally desire diplomatic support for their own claims in any omnibus settlement between the two governments, and would certainly deploy whatever political influence they could toward that end. Helms-Burton takes cognizance of their claims in a very indirect way in its section 207, which requires the Secretary of State to produce "an estimate of the number and amount of claims to property confiscated by the Cuban government that are held by U.S. nationals *in addition to those claims certified* under section 507 of the International Claims Settlement Act of 1949."[25] The same proviso calls for an assessment of the types of support that the U.S. government could conceivably afford "to help

HELMS-BURTON: CLARIFYING A CONTROVERSY

One of the most persistent misconceptions surrounding the Helms-Burton Law is the notion that its Title III somehow establishes procedures whereby Cubans who subsequently became American citizens may use the U.S. judicial system to recover their expropriated assets.

What Helms-Burton did, however, was to create the civil wrong of "trafficking," which occurs when a party "knowingly and intentionally" engages in the use of or receives a benefit or profit from property taken from a U.S. national without the authorization of said national who holds a claim to the property.

"Trafficking" does not apply in all instances, however. For example, it does not apply to activities involving the delivery of international telecommunications signals to Cuba; the trading or holding of public securities (unless the holder of such securities is a "specially designated national"); transactions incidental to lawful travel to Cuba (for example, a legal visitor who stays in a hotel upon which a claim is pending); or the use of property by an individual who is both a citizen of Cuba and a resident thereof and not an official of the Cuban government or the country's ruling party.

This last point is extremely important. Cubans living in homes abandoned by exiles are not "trafficking" in illegally expropriated property. Thus, the vast majority of claims on which Cuban-Americans might reasonably hope to receive compensation— private homes—have in fact been exempted from Helms-Burton *ab initio*. The only exceptions are residential properties subject to a certified claim or where the property in question "is occupied by an official of the Cuban government or the ruling political party of Cuba."

Having created this civil wrong, the law goes on to provide a remedy—namely, the right of a private party to sue the "trafficker" in U.S. federal courts. It is true that Title III does not require that the claimant must have been a citizen of the United States at the time of taking, but it does require that, in order to sue, the property holder must have had the claim before the enactment of the law (March 12, 1996). This proviso was inserted to prevent the transfer of claims.

Suits before U.S. federal courts must negotiate some very high hurdles. Helms-Burton requires that anyone who wants to use this remedy must meet "an amount in controversy": in this case, no less than $50,000 worth of property. This amount could be determined either by a finding of the Foreign Claims Settlement Commission (FCSC) in the case of certified claimants or by presentation of proof of the fair market value of the property (either the current value or the value when confiscated). Except in the cases of certified claims, which the courts have been instructed to accept, anyone being sued possesses the full right of rebuttal.

In such cases, the rules of evidence would apply to any claims of ownership, and assertions by the plaintiff would likewise be open to rebuttal. While in theory Cuban-Americans could use this reme-dy, the overwhelming majority did not leave Cuba with documen-tary evidence of what they owned and would therefore be hard-pressed to meet the evidentiary requirements of their case.

The definition of "trafficking" further circumscribes the universe of potential defendants. It is possible for a U.S. citizen to sue a Cuban government agency involved in commercial activities (say, Gaviota, S.A., which manages many of Cuba's tourist enterprises). But it is not possible to sue "the Cuban government." Helms-Burton also expressly exempts properties that belong to accredited diplo-matic missions or facilities; thus no one could sue for attachment to the properties of the Cuban Mission to the United Nations in New York or the Cuban Interests Section in Washington, the only Cuban assets physically located in the United States. Further, to be sued, a Cuban government agency would have to have a sufficient nexus with the United States. Because no such agency is present in the United States, it is difficult to see how any such concern could be sued in the federal courts at this time.

resolve claims to property confiscated by the Cuban government that are held by United States nationals *who did not receive or qualify* for certification under section 507 of the International Claims Settlement Act of 1949."[26]

This is far from actually "grandfathering" the properties of Cubans who later became U.S. citizens into the menu of certified claims, as the Cuban official media and also some critics of U.S. policy often assert, but it raises troubling questions nonetheless. On the face of it, Cuban-Americans possess no legal grounds for U.S. diplomatic support for the reacquisition of their former properties. As the Foreign Claims Settlement Commission itself has held, "the principle of international law that eligibility for compensation requires American nationality at the time of loss is so widely understood and universally accepted that citation of authority is scarcely necessary." A United States federal court has likewise held in the *Palacio* case that "confiscations by the state of the property of its own nationals, no matter how flagrant and regardless of whether compensation has been provided, do not constitute violations of international law."[27]

None of this has prevented former Cubans (now U.S. citizens) from organizing to assert their claims. In their view, all existing Cuban state assets should be physically returned to their former owners, with compensation reserved only for cases of dismantled or materially altered property. (Such groups envision enlargement of the compensation fund through the auctioning of property created by the Communist regime, such as the national fishing fleet, and certain defense, intelligence, and energy production facilities.)

To this end, in 1990 a Miami firm established a registry where Cuban exiles and U.S. citizens of Cuban origin could document and enumerate properties seized by the Castro government. The National Association of Landowners (*Hacendados*) posts a warning on its web site that it will vigorously pursue remedies in U.S. courts against third parties who traffic in the former properties of its members.[28] The National Association of Sugar Mill Owners of Cuba has announced an agreement with the Federation of Sugar Cane Workers of Cuba and the National Association of Sugar Cane Farmers (*colonos*)—all three, obviously, exile organizations—to restore pre-1959 work rules in their (presumably recovered) properties. Ironically, these rules include a living wage and maternity leave, as well as two rights denied by the current regime, namely, the right to strike and the right to bargain collectively.[29]

Some sense of what a future Cuban government may face in this regard is dramatically illustrated by the case of Nicaragua. Between 1979 and 1990, the country was ruled by a Marxist regime broadly inspired by the Cuban example; one of its most salient characteristics was—not surprisingly—the expropriation of large tracts of privately owned land and urban real estate. In the decade since that regime was voted out of power, two successive administrations have gradually resolved some 3,300 claims involving former Nicaraguan citizens who have become U.S. nationals. Even so, as of mid-2000, 800 cases were still pending. The delayed resolution of these claims has periodically led some members of the U.S. Congress to withhold economic aid to that country; one bill listed fifty specific cases against which future assistance was mortgaged. Such conditions, Nicaraguan Ambassador Francisco Aguirre Sacasa complained, "involve the United States in the 'micromanagement' of the subject of property [in Nicaragua], and constitute an intolerable intromission in our internal affairs."[30] For his part, Nicaraguan President Arnaldo Alemán—certainly no man of the left—was even more pointed. "Every year," he told the foreign press, "it seems as if more 'nicagringoes' are hatched."[31]

In its required report to Congress, the Department of State estimated in 1996—based on approximately 1.5 million Cuban-Americans resident in the United States, and extrapolations from experience with claims resolution—that "there may be from 75,000 to 200,000 such claims. It is more difficult . . . to estimate the value of such claims, but it could run easily into the tens of billions of dollars."[32] While sidestepping the question of what the U.S. government might owe to former nationals of an expropriating country, the State Department held out "soft" support of various kinds: "ensuring that interested persons obtain the necessary papers to file their claims; encouraging a democratic government to resolve such claims promptly and effectively; monitoring the progress of claims settlement; and where necessary, offering creative solutions to difficult problems." Finally, the State Department suggested that it might provide "informal assistance to claimants seeking to understand the process and present a claim."[33] In effect, the State Department was asserting indirectly that former Cuban nationals are obliged to seek redress for expropriations in Cuban courts. Whether some future Congress will withhold economic and other assistance pending settlement of outstanding property issues involving former citizens of the island remains to be seen, but unfortunately, as the case of Nicaragua illustrates, it takes only one or two determined members to do so.

Possible Redress in Cuban Courts

Even assuming that former Cuban nationals are willing and able to argue their cases before Cuban courts, a series of complicated legal and political issues loom ahead. The first and most important is whether the expropriations were at least legally effective. If so, then the problem is reduced to "determining what remedy should the former property owners be given for the taking of their assets." But if the expropriations were unlawful and legally ineffective, the Cuban government may be said "to have unjustly enriched itself at the expense of the owners and may be holding the properties in the equivalent of a 'constructive trust' for the benefit of the owners."[34] In that case, the Cuban government would be obliged to return the properties or to compensate the former owners or their heirs.

At the time of the revolution, the operative charter in Cuba was the Constitution of 1940.[35] Its article 87 specifically recognizes the existence and legitimacy of private property "in its broadest sense as a social function and without other limitations than those which, for reasons of public necessity or social interest, may be established by law." Its article 24 establishes the circumstances under which expropriations dictated by "public necessity or social interest" can take place. They must be judicially determined; they must serve a public purpose; and they must be indemnified in cash. If these requirements are not met, restitution is required. Moreover, these provisions are not easily pushed aside; articles 285 and 286 impose comprehensive and elaborate procedures for amending the charter, including a two-thirds vote of the legislature and a constitutional convention.

The Fundamental Law of 1959—the first major piece of revolutionary legislation promulgated by Castro's Council of Ministers—replaced (or better stated, superseded) the Constitution of 1940, though it reincorporated many of its provisions. Significantly, the version of article 24 in the 1959 legislation authorized government agencies other than the judiciary to expropriate private property, but it still required the government to pay compensation in bonds or in cash. The same article was also amended to permit expropriation without compensation of the property of collaborators of the fallen Batista regime.

The validity of the Fundamental Law is of crucial importance, because it is the juridical foundation of both the Agrarian Reform Law (1959), which eliminated large private property holdings in agriculture, and the Urban Reform Law (1960), which essentially abolished the private ownership of apartment buildings and other large forms of privately owned urban real estate. Leading figures in the exile community have long questioned whether the Fundamental Law's changes to the 1940 constitution can be valid, inasmuch as the charter's provisions for amendment were bypassed altogether. Regardless of whether the Fundamental Law of 1959 is valid or the original 1940 constitution is still the law of the land, the fact remains that "compensation was required and has not been paid."[36] By either construction, the Cuban government has violated its own nationalization laws.

Much of the property currently in the hands of the Cuban state, or passed on to Cuban citizens by the state, or sold by the Cuban state on foreign markets was acquired not through direct expropriation but through the departure of hundreds of thousands of citizens into exile. This includes not merely apartments, houses, and automobiles, but works of art, jewelry, pianos, and so forth. According to Cuban authorities, this property was "abandoned," which is technically true, but the circumstances of "abandonment"—political persecution, real, imminent, or imagined—violate article 33 of the 1940 charter, which specifically protects the right of free expression. Significantly, the same article was reinserted into the Fundamental Law of 1960, so there can be no question of its relevance here.

The socialist constitution of 1976, which superseded the Fundamental Law, abolished article 87 of the 1940 constitution and also eliminated most of the government's obligations under previous Cuban legislation to compensate property owners. By that time, however, virtually all property expropriations had been completed, and this new charter could hardly be granted the right to operate retroactively. Significantly, a major innovation in property rights was introduced in the 1992 constitution, which authorized the creation of joint ventures (*empresas mixtas*) with foreign investors in tourism, mining, communications, real estate, petroleum, manufacturing, sugar, and construction. As noted, the transfer of any such assets claimed by U.S. citizens lays the ground-work for complicated legal battles in the future.

Insofar as former Cuban citizens are concerned, the largest single area of loss sustained was urban real estate. Castro's 1960 Urban Reform Law not only abolished privately collected rents and nullified real estate contracts, but also allowed residents to "earn" title through rent paid to a government agency over a five- to twenty-year period. Under the doctrine of adverse pos-session (*usucapio*), which figures in the 1988 socialist civil code and also in the 1889 civil code inherited from the Spanish, by the mere act of long-term occupation, current residents have acquired fixed and permanent title (to the buildings, or parts of buildings, but not to the land beneath, which appar-ently belongs to the state).[37] It is therefore extremely unlikely that any future Cuban court would vote to dislodge thousands, possibly hundreds of thou-sands, of current occupants, even if it were foolhardy enough to ignore the potential political consequences.

Some future Cuban government may, of course, seek to defend in its own courts all or part of the expropriations carried out by its predecessor. On what might it base its arguments? United Nations General Assembly Resolution 1803 on the Permanent Sovereignty over Natural Resources (December 14, 1962) empowers any state to take over property for reasons of "public utility, security, or national interest," with "appropriate compensa-tion [paid] in accordance with the rules in force in the State . . . in the exer-cise of its sovereignty and in accordance with international law." In any controversy, national jurisdictions should be exhausted before claims are moved to the state-to-state level. Unfortunately for Cuba, two attempts by the USSR to amend the document to read that any compensation would be deemed "appropriate" if it was in harmony with the expropriating state's domestic laws failed to pass. In the intervening period, interpretations of Resolution 1803 have been so conflicting as to render it almost useless.

The UN Conference on Trade and Development's Resolution 88 (XII) (1972) provides a slightly stronger reed on which to lean; it leaves it to each state to fix the amount of compensation and procedures for adjudication, and mandates that any dispute falls clearly within the sole jurisdiction of national courts without prejudice to what is set forth in Resolution 1803. The same notion is stated even more categorically in United Nations

Resolution 3281 (1974), better known as the Charter of Economic Rights and Duties of States. Unfortunately, such resolutions are not considered binding on UN member nations, and insofar as international *practice* is concerned, it is perhaps worth noting that as of 1994, nearly one hundred countries had completed more than two hundred investment treaties with compensation formulas generally based on benchmarks such as "just," "full," "equivalent," or "adequate." In the case of former Soviet bloc countries, it is likewise significant that they have not only rushed to adopt traditional standards, but have moved toward restitution of properties or compensation of former owners.

A future Cuban attorney general might be better advised to dwell upon the ambiguities of Cuba's own constitutional history. To argue that the 1940 charter is still in effect (since its own amendment procedures have never been followed) would run up against the fact that Cuban history is replete with abrupt, even revolutionary changes—the Spanish conquest, the war of independence, Batista's laws and regulations, and so forth. As Emilio Cueto points out, the validity of each one of these events "would have to be questioned if one wishes to argue consistently that all acts of de facto governments are invalid."[38]

Moreover, Castro's legislation was cleverly crafted to introduce at least the appearance of legality: both the 1959 agrarian reform and the 1960 urban reform—while failing to comply with article 24 of the 1940 constitution and the 1959 Fundamental Law—were essentially folded into the latter, which became a kind of revolutionary super-constitution; hence, the two reforms could hardly be regarded as "unconstitutional." Cueto suggests that claimants might be better off arguing not "unconstitutionality" but "illegality" (no bonds were ever issued, so that no compensation was effectively paid). Even so, he adds, "they may have to accept the constitutionality of these laws, together with the conclusion that property title would indeed change thereunder, and that the compensation provisions thereof (as opposed to their subsequent application) were valid."[39]

Some Problems of Implementation

Even in the unlikely event that a future Cuban government favors the nullification or reversal of revolutionary confiscations, it is by no means clear that it will find restitution a straightforward remedy. First of all, quite apart from identifying property that may have been transformed beyond all recognition, it will be necessary for claimants to produce evidence of prior ownership. Since 1959 many owners have died, and probably, in their haste to leave the island, failed to take appropriate legal documentation into exile with them. Those many heirs whose parents died intestate will have to establish claims to local courts—in Florida, California, Venezuela, Mexico, Spain, or elsewhere. Where the Cuban owners were corporations, these have now been long since dissolved, and there is no juridical person to claim title. Even the tracing of shareholders (or, more likely, their heirs), is bound to be a long, costly, and laborious process. In Cuba itself the chain of title may be difficult or even impossible to trace because the present government has made no effort to preserve old property records, and may even have destroyed many or most of them.[40]

Second, even if restitution is denied as impracticable (and politically unrealistic), compensation does not present a simple, straightforward remedy either. Quite apart from the question of Cuba's extremely limited national resources, determining the appropriate amount to be paid is complicated, even though "adequate compensation" is normally defined as fair market value at the time of taking. Most Western states and some international arbitral tribunals define adequate compensation as net book value, profitability, and—however difficult to quantify—"good will." Some tribunals and publicists, particularly from capital-exporting states, prefer to factor in lost future profits; others (including, significantly, the Iran-U.S. claims tribunal) hold that full value compensation (that is, including future lost profits) is appropriate only in cases of an unlawful government taking.

Cuba might well receive some indirect relief from section 165 of the U.S. Internal Revenue Code, inasmuch as a number of certified claimants who are U.S. taxpayers have already deducted the loss of their property from their 1960 or 1961 income tax returns. (This category includes not only U.S. corporations but also Cuban expatriates who were U.S. taxpayers at the time.) In so doing, such parties effectively transferred their claims to the U.S. government and must abide by the terms of any eventual government-to-government settlement. Moreover, any compensation they might receive from a future Cuban government would be fully taxable, and—significantly—at the rate in force at the time of confiscation. In the 1960s, the corporate tax rate was in excess of 50 percent (as opposed to 35 percent at present); the tax consequences to claimants might well act as a disincentive. Cuba would likewise benefit from the number of American corporations that have already collected insurance on their losses. Such considerations would not, however, apply to former Cuban nationals seeking compensation, who were not eligible for tax write-offs for lost property, or were unlikely to have insured their properties with U.S. or other foreign carriers.[41]

Who Should Pay What?

Some commentators feel that claims against the Cuban state should not be limited to property claims, but include a wider variety of torts—to compensate individuals (particularly Cubans who have remained on the island throughout the Castro period) for involuntary or uncompensated work, unjust imprisonment, loss of life or limb, or even physical or psychological abuse. As two publicists put it, "We see no legal, moral or ethical basis for assigning priority to settling claims against physical property over those claiming civil damages."[42] The inclusion of such claims, however, would open a Pandora's box of possibilities and make litigation—not sugar, tobacco, or rum—the principal Cuban national product for decades to come.

Others believe quite the opposite—namely, that the quest for compensation—whether in property or other areas—goes well beyond what is reasonable to demand of a fundamentally helpless people. The latter, the argument goes, should not be burdened by confiscatory decisions in which they had no part. This argument gains considerable force in light of the fact that fully half the island's current population was not alive at the time the expropriations were decreed. Furthermore, many Cubans who never directly benefited from the confiscations would have to share the burden equally with those who did.[43]

There is an unreal quality to these discussions inasmuch as they ignore the fact that Cuba is essentially a bankrupt country whose infrastructure and habits of work have declined so precipitously since 1959 that the majority of its people survive just above the level of bare subsistence. Any future economic revival will require massive infusions of resources. And any government that seems excessively concerned with sorting out claims—whether those of foreigners or Cuban citizens past or present—rather than addressing the country's immediate needs is likely to lack (or quickly lose) fundamental legitimacy. Paradoxically, this is a view shared by the largest, most militant, and arguably most representative exile organization, the Cuban American National Foundation, which opposed the original creation of the Miami property registry on the grounds that its probable consequence—by raising the specter of imminent wholesale confiscations—would merely shore up support for the current government. "If the goal is to help Cubans, it is negative," one of the foundation's directors told the press. "The exiles' interest is not to recover properties, but for the regime to fall."[44]

Unfortunately, however, the issue of property cannot be waved aside altogether. Without some sort of resolution, it is unlikely that Cuba will be able to attract the capital and credits it requires for national reconstruction. Once again the case of Nicaragua illustrates the perils of ignoring or attempting to finesse the issue. After the defeat of the Sandinista regime in the 1990 elections, its successor was flooded with some 200,000 petitions relating to the violation of property rights, including 1.7 million of Nicaragua's 5.7 million hectares of cultivated land, as well as many houses and urban lots. Ambiguity about titles encouraged land invasions and violent confrontations that initially met with a weak response from law enforcement authorities. During the ninety days between legal award and actual eviction, many intruders caused severe damage to properties. At times, former factory and farm owners were prevented from entering their properties by armed Sandinista union members supported by the National Police.[45] The ensuing violence "arguably constitut[ed] the single most important obstacle to increased private investment and productivity in agriculture, and in turn negatively affect[ed] the rest of the economy."[46]

These dramatic events eventually forced the Nicaraguan government to devise a compensation scheme based on the assessed value of properties for tax purposes. Parties whose property was expropriated under the agrarian reform laws, which in the Nicaraguan case is generally considered to have been legal, are now eligible for compensation in the form of twenty-year bonds at an annual interest rate of 3 percent (indexed to the U.S. dollar exchange rate). Such bonds can either be kept to maturity or used to buy public assets. This program does not, in fact, contemplate anything like full compensation to expropriated parties, since the assessed value is generally less than market value, sometimes substantially so.

In effect, Nicaraguan citizens who do not have a claim on U.S. support have been forced to content themselves with what amounts to a good faith gesture on the part of their government—that, and the hope that the country's future economic growth will make the bonds they have received worth at least their face value at time of redemption. Although the Cuban situation is different in many regards—above all in the number of claimants who can leverage political support in the United States—the Nicaraguan example establishes firmly that the state must make some formal acknowledgment of its obligation, however minimal, to former property owners.

Is There a Way Out?

While the size and shape of an ultimate property settlement between the Cuban state and various claimants—both domestic and foreign—is difficult to imagine at this point, a number of procedural solutions have already been suggested. One is the creation of a binational claims tribunal, composed of distinguished jurists from neutral third countries drawn from a list provided by both the Cuban and U.S. governments. If the two affected parties could not agree on all of the members, jurists could be recruited from the Permanent Court of Arbitration (PCA) or the International Court of Justice in The Hague.

Such a tribunal has already had considerable success in sorting out property disputes between the United States and Iran. Like Cuba, Iran is a country with whom the United States does not maintain diplomatic relations, a nation that is formally classified as a "terrorist state," labors under a strict U.S. trade embargo, and is ineligible for a wide range of U.S. benefits. The latter include tariff concessions under the Generalized System of Preferences (GSP), insurance premiums from the Overseas Private Investment Corporation (OPIC), and support for loans from the international financial institutions (IFIs). Also, like the present government of Cuba, the regime in Tehran regards opposition to the United States and all its works as the organizing principle of its foreign policy, and even, to some extent, the raison d'être of its national and cultural identity.

None of this has prevented the Iran-U.S. Claims Tribunal from holding more than 600 hearings and resolving 4,000 cases by award since 1981. Most observers agree that the tribunal "has resolved disputes over complex issues that m[ight] not otherwise have been resolved" at all.[47]

Because of the broad authority of the President of the United States to conduct foreign relations, he could delegate to a Cuban-U.S. claims tribunal the power to issue rulings that would supersede the adjudications of the Foreign Claims Settlement Commission. While some U.S. claimants might object to this procedure, they might well reach a final settlement more expeditiously by this method than by a government-to-government negotiation. Furthermore, unlike the FCSC, such a tribunal could take full legal cognizance of all property claims of citizens or nationals of the United States regardless of when they acquired their current citizenship, *and* it could also hear claims from Cubans who have been continuously resident on the island. If it were to follow the precedent of the Iran-U.S. tribunal, it could be authorized to hear only those claims that exceed a given amount. (Claims falling below that threshold could be heard by the FCSC or perhaps some newly established Cuban privatization agency.) Finally—for what it may be worth—such a tribunal would be empowered to hear claims by Cubans against the United States for damages inflicted by the U.S. trade embargo or other actions. Moving U.S.-Cuban claims to a presumptively neutral venue would not altogether eliminate politics from the settlement process but would conceivably reduce politics to a level far below what could be expected in a purely bilateral forum.

Another alternative is to borrow from the traditional parameters of bankruptcy law, which, given the present state of the Cuban economy, is perhaps the most appropriate metaphor. In cases of bankruptcy, we are reminded, creditors are forced to refrain from pressing their claims; the debtor is allowed to borrow fresh funds on a privileged basis; and new creditors are given a higher priority than old ones. Old creditors are usually compelled to reach an arrangement with the debtor by which they cancel or restructure part of the debt or convert it into equity. This allows the debtor to emerge from bankruptcy with an opportunity for continued operation.

As in all metaphors, this one is imperfect in actual application because a policy of virtually universal noncompensation of old creditors is likely to undermine the credibility of any Cuban state seeking to reestablish property rights. Moreover, in the Cuban case, outdated technology and a lack of spare parts from former Soviet bloc factories dictate a wholesale modernization—not simply reactivation—of the island's industrial plant. One possible alternative suggested by two expatriate Cuban lawyers[48] would be to convert certain large military bases into free trade zones, with the labor force recruited from demobilized members of Cuba's military establishment. These bases would be converted into poles of industrial development, and claimants could be compensated with shares in these corporations. A particularly appropriate choice would be Guantánamo, one of Cuba's three best ports, which has been a U.S. base since 1901 but would presumably be returned to the island's government in any diplomatic settlement.[49]

Still another alternative would be to separate residential from nonresidential properties, with the Cuban government declaring that the former have in fact passed to their current occupants through the doctrine of adverse possession, while establishing a government agency to sort out claims involving the latter. This would have the advantage of facilitating the rapid privatization of small and medium-sized state enterprises and, at the same time, would presumably make good use of the entrepreneurial skills Cubans have developed over the years negotiating their way through the island's vigorous black market. To make the work of this agency more politically palatable, it might well give priority in the awarding of enterprises to Cubans who have been continuously resident on the island.

Looking Ahead

As noted at the outset of this chapter, most of the settlements for expropriated properties in Latin America have greatly downsized the amounts demanded by claimants. There is no reason to expect the outcome in Cuba to be much different. Quite the contrary: in the Cuban case the profundity and duration of the revolutionary process have led to a more thoroughgoing upheaval of property relations than anywhere else in the region. This renders massive restitution impossible, for practical as well as political reasons. The state of Cuba's economy also imposes sharp limits to compensation. Moreover, the sheer longevity of the regime has led to a situation where many, perhaps most Cubans on the island—whether they like their government or not—have come to have a vested interest in the status quo insofar as property is concerned. In any future negotiations with U.S. claimants, certified or not, the Castro regime (or its neo-*Fidelista* successor) might well find itself operating from a uniquely advantageous position insofar as its own people are concerned. Indeed, on this one issue it could conceivably find a depth of popular support greater than it has been able to summon for many decades.

Paradoxically, however, claimants might not find a successor regime significantly more tractable, even a new regime that, in theory at least, was committed to a wide range of political and economic liberalization. On this subject the last word has hardly been said. Dissident leaders on the island themselves disagree on the shape and extent of the future Cuban state, and we have yet to hear from the Cuban people themselves. Oswaldo Payá Sardiñas of the Christian Liberation Movement has suggested that "those who respect self-determination must support the Cuban people's right to be consulted via referendum on the fundamental issues. . . . It's time to consult the Cuban people at the polls, so they legally can decide what laws should rule their lives."[50] The settlement of outstanding property claims may therefore have to wait upon the resolution of other questions.

4

Security

The Cuban Threat Revisited

Between about 1960 and the collapse of the Soviet Empire in 1989, the nature of the U.S.-Cuban relationship was overwhelmingly shaped and determined by security concerns. Though U.S. business interests were dismayed almost from the very beginning by the radical economic policies of the new regime—particularly its confiscatory practices with respect to agricultural property—and vigorously lobbied the U.S. government on behalf of their interests, expropriations alone would not have been sufficient to disrupt the pattern of normal diplomatic intercourse. Rather, it was Castro's determination to join forces with the principal military enemy of the United States and its allies which overruled conciliatory voices in the State Department and the U.S. Embassy, and led Washington to explore ways of undermining, and even overthrowing, the Castro regime.[1] Having failed that, U.S. policymakers concentrated on limiting and neutralizing Cuban activities overseas, particularly in the Latin American region.

At the height of the Cold War tensions in the 1960s, few in the United States (and for much of the time, in Latin America as well) questioned the fundamental nature of the Cuban threat. This strategic consensus reached something of a dramatic peak during the missile crisis of 1962, but rested upon a longer chain of events going back to the very beginning of the Castro regime.

The revolutionary government was hardly installed in Havana's presidential palace in early 1959 before it was sponsoring expeditions to overthrow governments in the Dominican Republic, Nicaragua, Haiti, and Panama. By its second or third year, it was actively recruiting and training young men to engage in guerrilla warfare against mainland Latin American governments, including Venezuela, Colombia, Peru, even Argentina. In 1967 Castro's revolutionary confederate Ernesto "Che" Guevara appeared in Bolivia at the head of a small insurgent force in an attempt to establish a revolutionary state in the heart of the South American continent. Guevara's capture and death represent the high point of Castro's revolutionary push in the Western Hemisphere. During the 1970s, the Latin American armies gradually liquidated the remnants of Havana-based or Havana-trained guerrilla movements.

From the late sixties to the mid-seventies, Cuba shifted its emphasis to cultivating and influencing leftist (but not openly revolutionary) governments in Latin America, including "radical" military regimes in Peru and (briefly) Bolivia, Salvador Allende's hybrid Socialist-Communist government in Chile, and General Omar Torrijos's comic-opera "leftist" government in Panama. There was a brief reprise of Cuban revolutionary activity in the Central American area in the 1980s, following the unexpected collapse of the Somoza dynasty in Nicaragua and a military regime in neighboring El Salvador, both in 1979; for slightly more than ten years, Havana provided strategic advice, intelligence operatives, economic resources, military training, and weaponry for the Sandinista government in Managua, as well as the FMLN guerrillas in El Salvador. The Nicaraguan adventure collapsed in 1990 with elections in which the Sandinistas were ousted from power and a peace agreement in El Salvador that effectively derailed the revolutionary forces into day-to-day politics.

When not directly involved in the Americas, Cuban troops and intelligence operatives were active elsewhere around the globe, most notably in Africa (Angola, Ethiopia, Somalia, and the Congo), as well as many Middle Eastern countries. In many ways, Cuba acted as a kind of foreign legion for the Soviet Empire, no doubt motivated by a common strategic and ideological vision,[2] but also by the need to provide Soviet rulers with a ready-made rationale to justify—to themselves, to their colleagues, and even to their own people—the huge transfer of resources each year to keep the Cuban government afloat.[3]

Cuba also provided the Soviet Union with an important staging post in the Caribbean. In the final moments of the "special relationship," 12,700 Soviet soldiers were quartered on the island, including a motorized infantry brigade. Soviet submarines periodically called at Cienfuegos on Cuba's south-central coast, and a base at San Antonio de los Baños occasionally serviced Soviet strategic aircraft operating in the North Atlantic area. Not surprisingly, then, Cuba unfailingly figured on the agenda of all major U.S.-Soviet strategic discussions.

Since the demise of the Soviet Empire, a curious debate has ensued over the nature of the residual threat represented by the Castro regime. Some aspects inevitably reflect bureaucratic interests of particular agencies of the defense or intelligence establishments. But much of the discussion has been driven by implicit ideological and political agendas. Stated somewhat telegraphically, those in the U.S. policy community who favor either the status quo or a policy of engagement with the Castro regime tend to minimize or even deny the possibility that the island can or does represent a serious security threat. Conversely, those who favor a more aggressive policy of containment or confrontation argue precisely the opposite.[4]

The debate is further complicated by what might best be characterized as methodological problems. Much of the information we possess about Cuba comes from émigré sources. Debriefing recent arrivals can shed considerable light on many crucial details, particularly if the individual in question has been a government technician or scientist. Unfortunately, the longer some defectors remain in the United States (and specifically, in the overheated exile environment of Miami), the more lurid some of their recollections tend to become. Evaluating their testimony and integrating it within our larger intelligence about the island also present special problems. Within the U.S. intelligence community—whether the subject is Cuba, Iran, or China—one can never damage one's future career prospects by subscribing to worst-case scenarios because in so doing one is "covered" against all eventualities. It is also true, however, that there appears to be a strong bias in U.S. Cuban policy toward leaving well enough alone, which pulls this "worst-case" tendency back in the direction of prudence, reticence, and restraint—excessively so, in the opinion of some. These considerations, when combined with a highly politicized approach to Cuban issues generally, make it particularly difficult to arrive at a broad consensus.

In an attempt to resolve the controversy once and for all, in 1998 the United States Congress mandated an interagency study on the Cuban threat.

It was coordinated by the National Intelligence Council, drawing on inputs from the Central Intelligence Agency; the State Department's Bureau of Intelligence and Research; the National Security Agency; and the Joint Intelligence Center of the U.S. Southern Command (SOUTHCOM). The unclassified version was released to the press in mid-1998.

The report found, first, that Cuba's armed forces had been significantly weakened after the collapse of the Eastern bloc, converting Cuba from one of the "most active militaries" in the Third World to a "stay-at-home force" that has "minimal conventional fighting ability." Among other things, the report pointed to a reduction in budget and force size of more than 50 percent since 1989; severe resource shortages which forced a drastic reduction in training hours; the placing of a substantial amount of its heavy equipment in storage; a critical shortage of spare parts; and the transfer of "significant" numbers of officers to essential civilian tasks—farming, construction, transportation, or other endeavors that undermined basic combat readiness.

The Cuban army, it reported, was generally not able to mount effective operations above the battalion level, while the tiny Cuban navy had no capability to sustain operations beyond the island's immediate territorial waters. As for the Cuban air force, the report maintained that it was incapable of defending Cuban air space against large numbers of high-performance military aircraft, though it conceded that slower, less sophisticated aircraft would be vulnerable to Cuban air defense systems. Special Operations Forces were described as smaller and less proficient than formerly, but still capable of performing selected military and internal security missions.

The Cuban armed forces (FAR) retained some residual strengths, the report found, but these were "essentially defensive in nature." Even so, it noted that intelligence and counterintelligence systems directed at the United States had suffered "little degradation," and that there was a high disposition to share intelligence with U.S. adversaries. It took cognizance of the continued existence of an agreement with the Russian Federation which allowed Moscow to maintain SIGINTEL facilities at Torrens (also known as Lourdes), the largest such facility outside the Commonwealth of Independent States. Its early-warning radar systems were aging but "generally intact," and its military leadership was "combat experienced and disciplined." Balancing all of these factors, the report concluded that Cuba did not represent "a significant military threat to the U.S. or to other countries in the region." This was followed, however, by the caveat that "Cuba has a limited capability to engage in some military and intelligence activities which could pose a danger to U.S. citizens under some circumstances."[5] These circumstances were not specified, at least in the report's unclassified version.

In transmitting the document to Senator Strom Thurmond (R-S.C.) in his capacity as chairman of the Senate Armed Services Committee, Defense Secretary William Cohen hedged further:

> While the assessment notes that the direct conventional threat by the Cuban military has decreased, I remain concerned about the use of Cuba as a base for intelligence activities directed against the United States, the potential threat that Cuba may pose to neighboring islands, Castro's continued dictatorship that represses the Cuban people's desire for political and economic freedom, and the potential instability that could accompany the end of the regime depending on the circumstances under which Castro departs. . . .
>
> Finally, I remain concerned about Cuba's potential to develop and produce biological agents, given its biotechnology infrastructure, as well as the environmental health risks posed to the United States by potential accidents at the Jaraguá nuclear power facility.

Given the rather equivocal nature of the two documents—one, the report; the other, the cover letter—it is not surprising that the secretary failed to close debate on the subject. Oddly enough, both friends and enemies of U.S. Cuban policy glossed over the cover letter and to some extent even the ambiguous nature of the findings themselves, accepting or rejecting its principal conclusion according to their own particular agendas. "Politicized Pentagon Study Misses Abiding Nature of the Threat from Cuba, Promotes Wrong Response," read the title of one press release by a Washington-based security think tank. "The Pentagon's analysis," the body read, "will be shamelessly exploited, like Pope John Paul II's recent visit to the island, to provide political cover for the campaign to add Fidel Castro's regime to the growing list of communist dictatorships with which the United States is 'engaging' at the expense of its traditional commitment to freedom—and quite possibly at peril to its national security."[6] For his part, Congressman Lincoln Díaz-Balart (R-Fla.), a major spokesman for the exile community in Miami and a longtime advocate of the U.S. economic embargo of the island, likewise took strong objection to the report. "Despite the end of the Cold War," he declared on the floor of the House of Representatives, "Castro continues to espouse a hard line, using apocalyptic rhetoric, proclaiming socialism or death, ranting about a final reckoning with the United States, and punishing any Cuban who advocates genuine political or economic reform."[7]

By way of contrast, "Cuba's Fictional Threat to the United States" was the title of an editorial appearing in the *Chicago Tribune* on May 14, 1998. Referring to the Defense Department report, it argued that "you don't need to be Karl Von Clausewitz to figure out that after the gusher of Soviet subsidies dried up in 1989, Cuba has barely been able to keep food on the table and the lights on in Havana, much less maintain an attack force that could threaten anyone." Indeed, the editorial added—and here, the heart of the message—"if the Castro regime poses any threat to the U.S. at all, it could be far more effectively handled through direct contacts and negotiations rather than recriminations and isolation." Professor Raymond C. Duncan, formerly of the U.S. Naval War College and a longtime advocate of normalization of relations, drew a similar lesson. "If the Pentagon makes a national security assessment and says that Cuba is no longer a national security threat, then why have an economic embargo law?"[8]

The controversy over the Pentagon report was rekindled four years later by the discovery that the principal specialist on Cuba at the Defense Intelligence Agency who apparently drafted the report—one Ana Belén Montes—had been acting at the time as an agent in the service of Cuban intelligence.[9] Meanwhile, debate continues on such pregnant topics as Cuba's links to international terrorism or its capacity and willingness to engage in (or be an accessory to) biological warfare. While Cuba is hardly a major concern of the American public generally, opinion surveys reveal that when specifically asked to address the subject, most people continue to harbor a vague sense that the island represents some sort of threat, albeit perhaps a low-level one.[10] It cannot be surprising, then, that the U.S. government reflects that sentiment, however ambiguously or imprecisely. The question remains, however, to *what* extent Cuba constitutes a challenge to U.S. national security. In his letter to Senator Thurmond, Secretary Cohen pointed to several sensitive areas; this chapter will explore each of them and also take up some that he did not mention.

The Cuban Military and Its Strategic Doctrine

Any strategic evaluation of Cuba must begin with a curious fact that renders it an anomaly among Communist states. It is fundamentally a military dictatorship whose ultimate authority rests principally upon the loyalty and commitment of an officer class. "The sources of Castroism are military," writes Irving Louis Horowitz, professor emeritus at Rutgers University. "The personnel which made up the regime at the outset and continues to rule, has been military." Though the Communist Party has grown greatly in size since the mid-1960s, this "does not necessarily signify an expansion of civilism; only that it is a paramilitary party in charge of managing a dependent state machinery."[11] Although this finding is a quarter-century old, it is hardly out of date. Indeed, since the Ochoa affair in 1989,[12] the power of the armed forces (under the dictator's brother and designated successor, General Raúl Castro) has expanded to comprehend the all-powerful Interior Ministry, the agency that controls the forces of domestic repression. Likewise, as noted in chapter 2, the vitally important Sugar Ministry has in recent times been taken over by a flag officer serving in the Revolutionary Armed Forces.

Until 1989, Cuba had the longest term of conscription of any Latin American country, and individuals were required to participate in annual military training until age fifty. After that, they were (and to some extent, still are) liable for call-up in times of emergency. Although many of these requirements still exist on paper, in practice Cuba no longer possesses the resources to maintain such large standing forces, and many young people now find it possible to do alternative service. Nevertheless, Cuba is resisting a broad Latin American trend toward the abolition of conscription altogether. Although all armies provide a certain measure of political and strategic indoctrination to their conscripts and officers, both commissioned and noncommissioned, no other country in Latin America does so as thoroughly and rigorously as Cuba.[13]

While Cuban military capabilities have obviously suffered since the loss of Soviet aid, Phyllis Greene Walker, an expert on the subject, insists that they nonetheless remain impressive "when considered solely in terms of human resources. In having at its disposal the troops of the FAR [Revolutionary Armed Forces], the MININT [Ministry of Interior], and the MTT

[Territorial Militia], the Cuban government would conceivably be able to assemble a force of over a million in the event of a national security crisis. In addition, the entire population is organized into defense zones, whose command would be taken over by the armed forces in time of war. . . . As a whole, the institution still maintains a credible defense posture despite problems."[14] As General Raúl Castro puts it, Cuba still has "armed forces very large for the size of our country and for our economy."[15]

In the past, the Cuban military had an important "internationalist" mission that took it to countries near and far. Indeed, from 1969 to 1988, approximately 300,000 Cuban soldiers saw service overseas. Since 1989, however, its resources have been overwhelmingly directed toward protection against an invasion from the United States, which continues to be regarded as the country's principal enemy. At first glance, this objective would seem to be based on a rather remote eventuality, but apparently that is not how the Cuban military sees it. Its basic outlook, reported Major General Edward Atkeson, U.S. Army (retired) of the U.S. Army Land Warfare Institute after a visit to the island, "closely resembles our own [perception of the threat] posed by the Warsaw Pact at the height of the Cold War. We did not consider it likely, but the risks on the downside were so great that we had to devote substantial resources and effort to deterring it and preparing a viable defense."[16]

The fundamental strategic doctrine of the Cuban military at present can be subsumed under the heading "War of All the People," which is to say, an understanding that the island can never be defended from foreign invasion by conventional set-piece battles, but only by mobilizing the population as a whole, assigning particular importance to the territorial militias. The experience of the Gulf War, in which the Western allies virtually eliminated Saddam Hussein's tank and airborne capacities by carpet-bombing at the very beginning of hostilities, also convinced Cuban service chiefs of the need both to disperse and bury their equipment. Thus during the last decade, a considerable network of underground tunnels has been constructed for the pre-positioning of arms and provisions. At the same time, greater emphasis has been placed on training for guerrilla operations, sniper activities, special forces operations, and even— if necessary—a retreat to mountainous and rural areas.[17] As military historian Richard Millett has acutely observed, this kind of strategic planning takes little or no cognizance of the only context in which an American invasion is even remotely conceivable, namely, "after and related to an already raging civil conflict within Cuba"—which is to say, under far less advantageous circumstances than the War of All People doctrine contemplates in the abstract.[18]

The exclusive focus on the United States, and the presumed imminence of an invasion, however remote, has unquestionably provided a useful doctrinal glue for the Cuban military. After all, there is no way—short of announcing its active support of the existing Cuban regime—that the United States can disprove the "hypothesis of conflict" taught in Cuban service schools. On the other hand, by stressing this mission to the exclusion of all others, the Cuban military exposes the population to what might be called "mobilizational exhaustion," which leads to massive diversion of valuable time and resources. Moreover, to the extent that the Cuban government achieves one of its major foreign policy objectives—to improve relations with the United States—it "risks undermining credibility of the threat and contradicting official statements of the intractability of the major potential foe."[19]

The Cuban military also possesses two secondary domestic missions, neither of which is directly relevant to its threat posture to the United States. One is a domestic security mission, which is to say, to provide an ultimate guarantee to the regime's survival in the event of serious political disorder. So far the armed forces have been able to remain aloof from such eventualities, and they prefer to continue to do so, since a direct confrontation with the populace would undermine the military's carefully cultivated image as a legitimate expression of the people rather than as a watchdog of higher authority, its role elsewhere in Latin America. Fortunately for the Cuban military, the Interior Ministry has troops of its own which so far have proven equal to the task.

The other is an economic mission that calls upon senior officers to take charge of the new mixed enterprises that are being formed in conjunction with foreign capital. Outstanding among these is Gaviota, S.A., a kind of holding company that works closely with investors in the tourist sector, the fastest growing (indeed, practically the only growing) sector of the Cuban economy.[20] The limited economic reforms that have made this role possible have also consolidated the regime's hold on the officer class, which now has access—unlike most Cubans—to abundant amounts of foreign currency. This new role presumably assures its continued political loyalty. On the other hand, it is not necessarily compatible with the traditional role and responsibilities of the professional military and could eventually contribute to an institutional identity crisis. "Serious problems could develop," writes one specialist, "should the FAR be seen (as) willing to sacrifice professionalism for the sake of economic gains."[21] The same is even more true if the economic well-being of the military class becomes so conspicuously superior to that of the population at large as to introduce waves of popular resentment to which so far, at least, the Cuban military has been largely immune.

Those who believe the Cuban threat is greatly exaggerated often point to the fundamentally defensive posture of the Cuban military. But at the end of the day, it is difficult to see what else it could be. Cuba is not in a position to invade the United States and never has been. The Cuban security challenge to the United States and to the region as a whole has always been more diffuse. Whether *that* has changed, and to what extent it has changed, remains a matter of opinion. So, also, is the question of whether or not the threat, even if it continues to exist, remains sufficiently serious to merit a more energetic U.S. response.

Guantánamo

For nearly a century, the United States has maintained a naval base at Guantánamo Bay, about fifty miles east of Santiago in Cuba's Oriente province. Guantánamo is a deep-water port capable of accommodating the largest ships in the world and for many years was one of the principal U.S. naval installations overseas. The basis of the U.S. presence there is a treaty concluded with the first independent Cuban government in 1903, an agreement which Fidel Castro himself ceremoniously tore up at the rostrum of the United Nations in New York in 1960. Although the United States continues to send the Cuban government a peppercorn rent for the facility, Havana habitually refuses to cash the checks by way of denying the legitimacy of the foreign presence. It also denies the Americans access to Cuba's water supply, so that since the early 1960s the Navy has been forced to establish its own desalinization plants.

A curious truce nonetheless prevails between the United States and Cuba on the subject of Guantánamo. On one hand, the base is separated from the rest of the island by barbed wire and land mines.[22] On the other, a shrinking handful of Cuban civilians are employed there, passing checkpoints regularly each morning and afternoon. Although Cuba's official media often speaks of it as a probable point of entry for a U.S. invasion force, it more nearly resembles a military base somewhere in the continental United States being run by a skeleton crew prior to being definitively closed.

How important is Guantánamo to U.S. security? The base was originally established to provision coaling ships. Technological changes have rendered this original mission obsolete. Nonetheless, naval authorities are loath to concede as much. In fact, a recent base commander, Captain Larry E. Larson, denied emphatically that it had lost military value. Rather, he told an American newspaper, "It is the perfect location to support naval operations in the Caribbean." In support of his view he noted that the closest naval bases to the region were in Norfolk, Virginia (1,100 miles away); Jacksonville, Florida (888 miles away); and Roosevelt Roads in Puerto Rico (600 miles away). In time of war, he explained, without Guantánamo, American ships in the Caribbean in need of repair would require at least a two-day turn-around in the journey to Norfolk.[23] This is a curious statement in light of the fact that there are no ship repair facilities at the base.

General John Sheehan, commander-in-chief of the U.S. Atlantic Command in Norfolk, concedes that Guantánamo will never again be "a fully functional military facility as has been traditionally characterized." The fleet training center there, he explained, is being moved out because such things can be done less expensively from points in the continental United States. But, he added, "I think you'll see GITMO [Guantánamo] being put in a caretaker status because it's essential for strategic reach reasons." When asked to elaborate, he said that the base "offers a place that you can go to from some place like the Dominican Republic or Haiti by helicopter . . . you should never miss the opportunity to keep that kind of capability in a place should you need it for some other part of the Caribbean."[24]

For a time Defense Department officials talked about turning Guantánamo into a multilateral antinarcotics center or a headquarters for joint exercises. The former project was of momentary interest to some Washington bureaucracies since the failure in 1998–1999 of negotiations with Panama over a residual presence in that country following the withdrawal of American troops under the Carter-Torrijos treaties.[25] Since then, the department has lost interest in the idea, establishing instead forward operating locations (FOLs) in Ecuador, Curaçao, and Costa Rica.

For their part, civilian authorities in Washington have tended to dismiss Guantánamo as an expensive relic of the past (closing it would save $100 million a year), of no real use in today's high-tech world. One Clinton administration official even confided to the press that "we are prepared to enter into negotiations with a democratically elected government in Cuba to return the base or renegotiate the rental arrangement."[26] Given the resentment toward U.S. presence across the political spectrum in Cuba prior to 1959, it is at least arguable that surrendering the base to a post-Communist regime would grant that government an instant dose of nationalist credibility, which over the longer term would far better serve broader U.S. strategic interests than a largely symbolic physical presence.

The terrorist attacks on the World Trade Center and the Pentagon on September 11, 2001, and the decision of the Bush administration to respond to them with military operations in Afghanistan have abruptly transformed Guantánamo into a more valuable strategic asset, the ideal venue to confine and interrogate captured Taliban militants. Unlike Guam or other locations that were considered for this purpose, Guantánamo's status as a foreign naval base offers some compelling legal advantages, "inasmuch as it has no federal civilian court to which the detainees might petition for release, appeal a conviction or conjure up other legal arguments."[27] At the same time, government officials revealed somewhat offhandedly that complementary contingency plans envision use of the base as a temporary refuge for up to 10,000 Caribbean boat people in case of a huge humanitarian crisis—either in Haiti or elsewhere, including, presumably, Cuba itself.[28]

Few would argue that Guantánamo is essential to the national security of the United States, but in the changed circumstances of post–September 11, it is no longer possible to treat it as merely a relic of earlier times, or even a convenient boondoggle for empire-building military planners. Instead, it is likely to figure in the agenda of normalization talks when they occur, possibly providing the Cuban government with valuable negotiating leverage or even the potential for significantly more sizable compensation for continued use of the facility.

Lourdes

During the 1970s, the Soviet Union erected a major electronic listening post at Lourdes, in the outer Havana suburbs. Manned by 2,000 officers of the GRU (Soviet military intelligence), during the Cold War it was the largest Soviet SIGINTEL site abroad. Lourdes was built to monitor U.S. commercial satellites and sensitive communications dealing with the U.S. military, merchant shipping, and Florida-based NASA programs. Since then, according to Russian sources, the Russian Foreign Intelligence Service (SVR) has established a communications network center at the facility for its agent network in North and South America. In recent years Russian interest in the site has been increasingly driven by economic considerations—namely, as a way of acquiring unprotected commercial information.

Since its establishment, U.S. commentators, politicians, and security experts have long expressed considerable concern about this base, which received some $90 million in new equipment and facilities from the Russian Federation between 1996 and 1998. Perhaps not surprisingly, throughout the 1980s and 1990s, Congress revisited the issue repeatedly in various legislative projects—most notably, section 106(d) of the Helms-Burton Law, which specifically requires the President to withhold from any state belonging to the former Soviet Union "an amount equal to the sum of assistance and credits, if any, provided on or after such date by such state in support of intelligence facilities in Cuba, including the intelligence facility at Lourdes."

Whatever legitimate security concerns the base might once have justified, however, they have been superseded by two considerations. The first is the decision in late 2001 by Russian President Vladimir Putin to dismantle the Lourdes facility in its entirety and ship its equipment home. This would save the Russian Federation roughly $200 million that was formerly paid to Cuba each year. Not incidentally, it would also dramatically improve Putin's (and Russia's) relations with the United States.[29]

The second is that Lourdes has been rendered largely obsolete by Western technological advances in telecommunications. Starting in the 1980s the United States long-distance telephone system (including computer storage and transmission) moved from one based on microwave transmission to one employing fiber optics, which have a much higher carrying capacity and greater resistance to data error. Microwave links, which typically use satellite relays, are now used primarily as a backup for fiber routes and often carry no traffic at all.[30] Meanwhile, the United States has made enormous strides in improving its encrypting facilities. It would appear, in fact, that Russia's continued interest in the base during the Yeltsin years was dictated purely by domestic political considerations (as a sop to the Russian military, allowing it to claim that in spite of everything it still possessed a global reach[31]—even though in fact geography is irrelevant when it comes to monitoring international satellite communications). This point about technological obsolescence is crucial in light of Fidel Castro's subsequent offer to lease the base to the Chinese. The latter are reported (in the Russian media) to have accepted.[32] How much they are willing to pay for access to a fundamentally useless facility—if in fact they ever do so—remains to be seen.

Germ Warfare

One of the few areas where the Castro regime has significantly advanced Cuba's economic development during the past four decades has been the development of an extensive biomedical industry. Indeed, by Caribbean and even Latin American standards, Cuba is now something of a pharmaceutical superpower, producing vaccines that are sold in much of the world. In recent years, however, serious concerns have been raised by the potential use of this new scientific capability to produce biological weaponry.

The question of whether Cuba does or does not have a biological weapons program (as opposed to a biological weapons *capability*) periodically surfaces as a major scientific and foreign policy controversy in the United States. On this score many prominent figures in the U.S. policy, military, and academic communities believe the threat to be nonexistent. General John Sheehan, who visited the island in March 1998 after his retirement from the Marine Corps, reported that he saw no evidence—either on the ground or from intelligence reports—that the country was working on biological weapons. Professor Jonathan Benjamín Alvardo of the University of Nebraska, a specialist on Cuban scientific policy, is reassured by the fact that Cuba became a signatory to the Biological Weapons Convention as long ago as 1972. As he puts it, "Accession to, and compliance with, this agreement virtually assures that Cuba will not engage in any activities that will lead to the development or production, transfer or deployment of a biological weapons capability." To do so would be a "serious breach of international law. . . . At this time such an undertaking is very unlikely."[33]

Professor Harlyn Halvorson of the University of Massachusetts, who has visited Cuba on numerous occasions and praised the accomplishments of its biotech industry, denies the possibility of a germ warfare program. So does a Cuban physician specializing in microbiology who now lives in the United States; he points out that it would be illogical to develop medicines and drugs in the same place as biological weapons "because the systems of filtration and separation could be contaminated."[34]

The most newsworthy American personality to endorse this point of view is former President Jimmy Carter who, during his visit to the island in May 2002, asserted that he had been told prior to his trip by U.S. intelligence experts "on more than one occasion" that Cuba was not sharing any scientific information that could be used for terrorist purposes. He also seemed completely satisfied by assurances from Cuban scientific officials that the country had no plans for agreements with Libya or Iraq. (He specifically put the question to them.)

Almost immediately, both the White House and the State Department contradicted the former president's remarks. John Bolton, undersecretary of state for arms control and international security, told the press that the United States believed that Cuba "has at least a limited offensive biological warfare research and development effort." Another (unidentified) State Department official even went so far as to advise the press that the particular official who briefed Carter "was not an expert on biological weapons." In subsequent days, the White House backed Undersecretary Bolton, leading President Carter to complain that the statement was made deliberately to sabotage his trip to Cuba.

Then, suddenly, the Bush administration started to backtrack. When asked about the Bolton remarks, Defense Secretary Donald Rumsfeld claimed "not to [have] seen the intelligence that apparently led" Bolton to assert the claim. "We didn't say [Cuba] actually had some weapons," asserted Secretary of State Colin Powell somewhat defensively. "But it has the capacity to conduct such research," a point surely not in dispute. Oddly enough, the forty-seven lines devoted to Cuba in the State Department's annual report on terrorism (which appeared somewhat opportunely at roughly the same time) made no mention whatever of bioterrorism.[35] Several weeks later, moreover, in testimony before the Senate Western Hemisphere Subcommittee, Carl Ford, assistant secretary of state for intelligence and research, opined that Cuba's biological weapons research program remained at the "developmental" stage and had not expanded into a full weapons program.[36]

In some respects, this controversy merely casts into sharp relief the highly ideological purposes for which intelligence findings are often conscripted. On one hand, the formal posture of hostility of the U.S. government toward the government of Cuba (and vice versa)—not to mention domestic political constituencies determined to believe the worst of the Castro regime—periodically inspires remarks such as those enunciated by Undersecretary Bolton. On the other hand, strong countervailing forces are at work as well. The facts themselves may be the least important element in the mixture. On the particular subject of Cuban biological weaponry, one security official told a journalist that "we've known all about this for some time now, but it's considered too delicate a matter to be discussed publicly. On a political level it doesn't square with maintaining stable relations with Cuba, which are potentially volatile." The same news report went on to say that "very much in spite of the Pentagon's concern on the subject, the primary military and political objective of the U.S. is not to create tensions or perceived or imagined threats to Castro and the Cuban military." One officer remarked that Castro is "a dangerous character capable of just about anything if he feels himself cornered. Don't forget he's the same guy who insisted that Khrushchev fire missiles at us during the October [1962] crisis."[37]

Without speculating on what kinds of classified intelligence inspired such remarks, it may be useful to review here the kinds of information or allegations that lie in the public domain. The major sources here are inevitably defectors, both Russian and Cuban.

There is, in the first place, a Soviet defector who now lives in the United States and writes under the pseudonym of Ken Alibeck. A military doctor and ex-colonel in the Red Army, Alibeck spent seventeen years working on germ warfare, developing military uses for viruses, anthrax, and the bubonic plague. At the time of his defection in 1992, he was the subdirector of the Russian germ warfare program. In his book[38] and in interviews with the *New York Times*, Alibeck relates that in 1990 he visited Cuba with Major General

Yuri T. Kalinin, vice-minister of the medical and microbiological industries of the USSR. (General Kalinin's duties included supervising the production of biological weapons.) Although the publicly stated purpose of the visit was to discuss creation of a new plant dedicated to simple cell proteins, Alibeck returned from the visit with an entirely different impression.

"Since 1988 the Cubans were after us to help them construct a new microbiology plant," Alibeck told a U.S.-based journalist. "The processing of the single cell would use the protein obtained from sugar, something the Cubans possess in abundance." Almost immediately the two Soviet officials surmised that what the Cubans were really after was something quite different. "They wanted us to build a huge reactor appropriate to a large-scale plant. We suspected that this had nothing to do with anything industrial or pharmacological. . . . We knew that the Cubans had a new biological complex outside of Havana, a very expensive and sophisticated one that was totally beyond the normal scale appropriate to a poor country."

Kalinin had been to Cuba before, and in private conversation with Alibeck confided to him that he was convinced the Cubans were producing biological weapons. "Their installations of microtechnology are full of secret, closed areas, exactly like ours," he recalls his superior saying. For his part, Alibeck could not help recognizing in Cuba certain technical facilities of a type normally required to produce biological arms—an observation that does not, to be sure, establish that the facilities were dedicated to that purpose. Returning to the Soviet Union, Alibeck had occasion to discuss his visit with other members of the Biopreparat, the agency responsible for producing both medicines and germ weaponry. He asked his colleagues where the Cubans had obtained so much sophistication and capacity. The response was, "From us, of course."[39] The Cuban government has denounced Alibeck's declarations as "ridiculous and full of fantasy."

Another even more sensational account comes from ex-Major Florentino Azpillaga, a former Cuban intelligence official described as one of the deserters "of highest rank and greatest credibility." He came forward with additional information upon reading Alibeck's declarations to the Spanish-language edition of the *Miami Herald*. He claims to have heard Fidel Castro sometime between 1979 and 1981 reveal the existence of a germ warfare program in a tape that was played for army or intelligence agencies. The information was so highly classified that all those who heard it were required to sign a document acknowledging that they were privy to a "state secret."

Azpillaga also recalls having been ordered to deliver a package obtained by a Cuban operative in Japan to a doctor working in a laboratory known as the Polo Científico del Oeste at Cubanacán, a suburb east of Havana. Azpillaga's superior, Major Armando Hernández Hernández, specifically told him that the package contained "a key element used in germ warfare that had to be delivered to a house . . . where this sort of work is being carried out."[40]

Another Cuban defector—this one directly from the scientific community who left the island in 1992 and now lives in Switzerland—claims that Cuba is experimenting with migratory birds for use in biological warfare. Dr. Carlos Wotzkow recalls working at the Instituto de Zoología on a project whose supervisor reported directly to Fidel Castro himself. Among other things, the staff attempted to "inoculate the leptospiras virus into mites and migratory birds." Wotzkow's statement came a year after chickens in New York state were infected with a strange virus that causes encephalitis, a malady of a type common in Asia and Africa but previously unknown in the United States.

Wotzkow's account was supported by another émigré scientist from Cuba, Professor Luis Roberto Hernández, professor of entomology at the University of Puerto Rico in Mayaguez. He told journalists that when he worked at the same institute, he knew of a project organized to identify and produce viruses as "passengers" on migratory birds. This work, he added, took place in a secret laboratory on a farm outside Havana, formerly the property of ex-President Carlos Prío. Ironically, he adds, its research on the habits of migratory birds received assistance from the U.S. scientific community.[41] Hernández also stated that over the last few years Cuba had developed studies on the Culex mosquito, the principal vector of the encephalitis virus. Of particular interest to Cuban scientists was its resistance to certain insecticides. This is the same mosquito that has caused serious health problems in the northeastern United States during the last several summers.[42]

More recently Alvaro Prendes, a former Cuban air force colonel now living in Miami in exile, claims that in the basement of the Luis Díaz Soto Naval Hospital, experiments are being conducted on cadavers and live animals with anthrax, brucellosis, equine encephalitis, dengue fever, hepatitis, tetanus, and a variety of other bacteriological agents. Documents smuggled out of Cuba in 1998 by Prendes and other defecting military officers purport to establish that five chemical and biological weapons plants operate throughout the island.[43] They also suggest that experiments are underway in the use of insects, rats, even household pets as contaminants, and that Cuban scientists have developed tetanus-carrying antipersonnel mines with infected needles, supposedly used for perimeter security around forced labor camps. According to one news analysis, it was these apparent revelations that caused Defense Secretary William Cohen to qualify the tone of his evaluation of the Cuban threat in his report to Congress.

Given the highly technical nature of the subject, the laity can hardly be expected to form an authoritative opinion on the Cuban germ warfare threat. Nor is it in a position to evaluate information from defectors. At first blush, however, it is difficult to see why Cuba would wish to deploy biological agents against the United States, particularly given its own geographical proximity; presumably it would be impossible to fully insulate itself from the side effects. An even greater mystery is why, in the absence of a direct confrontation or a credible U.S. military threat, Cuba would seek to spread viruses in the United States. Such an act, if its origins were firmly established, would obviously be sufficiently provocative to trigger the very reaction the regime apparently wishes to avoid—namely, a U.S. military invasion. On the other hand, a germ warfare capability might simply be the ultimate deterrent to assure that—come what may—the United States will never introduce troops on the island.[44] It is even possible that some of the defectors are double agents, spreading false tales intended to stay the hand of a (supposedly) aggressive U.S. military. Or maybe the defectors' stories are made up out of whole cloth, a collage of fantasies intended to curry favor with the U.S. government and Cuban-American community.

Certainly if Cuba is producing biological arms, a more probable motivation is the need for hard currency, with the market being other rogue states.[45] It is also possible that Cuba is transferring legitimate processes that nonetheless can be easily adapted to lethal uses. In this connection some importance might be ascribed to the visit of Cuban Vice President Carlos Lage to Tehran in October 2000. Lage began his visit with a tour of a plant under construction by a joint Iran-Cuban society to produce vaccines and biomedical products. The entry of Cuba into the Iranian pharmaceutical market seems odd, however, given that

Tehran has long boasted that in spite of the U.S.-led embargo, it is capable of producing 97 percent of the medicine it needs.[46] José de la Fuente, formerly a researcher at Cuba's Center for Genetic Engineering and Biotechnology (CIBG), is disturbed by the sale to Iran of recombinant protein production technologies in yeast and Escherichia coli, as well as "large scale purification protocols for both soluble and insoluble proteins synthesized in or excreted by them." He writes, "There is no one who truly believes that Iran is interested in these technologies for the purpose of protecting all the children in the Middle East from hepatitis, or treating their peoples with cheap streptokinase when they suffer sudden cardiac arrest."[47]

One cannot help noting a similar, apparently embryonic, relationship with Syria, whose vice-president, Mohammed Zouheir Macharka, headed a large delegation to Cuba in June 2002. While the stated purpose of the visit was to "strengthen the friendly relations and cooperation between Cuba and Syria and exchang[e] viewpoints on issues of mutual interest," the Syrians were also scheduled to tour Havana's Center for Genetic Engineering and Biotechnology.[48] There have also been reports in the press concerning a possible financial connection between Cuba's biotech industry and Saddam Hussein's Iraq.[49] To what degree these exchanges represent a problem for U.S. security depends, of course, on its own sense of the Iranian, Syrian, or Iraqi threat as much as or more than the Cuban.

The Juraguá Nuclear Plant

In 1976, the Soviet Union and Cuba concluded an agreement to construct two 440-megawatt nuclear power reactors at Juraguá near Cienfuegos, about 180 miles south of Key West, Florida. Actual construction began in 1983. When brought on line, the two plants were expected to provide 15 percent of the island's electrical supply. The first reactors should have started up around the end of 1993, but the breakup of the Soviet Union and the switch to market relations between Moscow and Havana delayed completion.

U.S. security advocates have long viewed this nuclear project with alarm, often referring to it as a potential "Cuban Chernobyl."[50] As in the case of Lourdes, Juraguá has inspired a torrent of legislation, most notably section 111 of the Helms-Burton Law which specifically requires the President to "withhold from assistance . . . any country an amount equal to the sum of assistance and credits, if any . . . by that country or any entity in that country" to the Cubans to complete this nuclear project. For their part, arms control activists, some academics, and Cuba policy activists have insisted that "there is no possible [nuclear] threat for the United States in Cuba today."[51] Or if there is, then the United States should step in and help complete the project, thus assuring that it would pose no health hazard.[52]

To resolve the controversy, in 1992, Senator Bob Graham (D-Fla.) asked the U.S. Government Accounting Office (GAO) to produce a full-scale study of the Juraguá project.[53] Much of the information in the GAO study was of a technical nature, well beyond the ken of the nonscientific reader, encompassing such arcane questions as the quality of construction of the (uncompleted) first reactor, its welds, its monitoring facilities, even the value of simulators used to train future nuclear personnel. (There was also some discussion of the potential seismic dangers of the Cuban site.) In the end, however, both the GAO and the Nuclear Regulatory Commission confessed that they were unable to address congressional and public concerns in a definitive way, largely because of incomplete information. Even so, Congress appropriated $3 million in the 1998 Defense authorization bill to construct a nuclear radiation detection facility in Florida specifically to monitor leakage from Cuba.

The debate over the significance of the Juraguá facility suddenly became moot, however, in late 2000 when Russian President Vladimir Putin announced on a visit to Cuba that the project was being abandoned, supposedly at the request of Cuban President Fidel Castro himself.[54] It is highly unlikely that any other country or combination of countries will step into Russia's place, since a consortium of Western financial and engineering concerns (from Britain, Italy, and Brazil) has concluded that it would cost $750 million just to finish the first reactor.[55] A study undertaken separately by Electricité de France reached roughly the same conclusion.[56] These are astronomic sums for Cuba, given the size and state of its economy, much less its perilous credit standing. Far from being a security threat to the United States, the rotting hulk near Cienfuegos is rather a grotesque monument to Fidel Castro's outsized ambitions, his poor choice of strategic partners, and the waste of millions of dollars' worth of resources.

Narcotics

Like many Caribbean islands, Cuba sits astride the major routes for the shipment of illegal narcotics to the United States. The U.S. government, however, has tended to minimize or even deny any possible Cuban involvement in the traffic, and even, during the Clinton administration, to emphasize Cuban "cooperation" with U.S. drug interdiction efforts.[57] For example, the entry for "illicit drugs" in the Central Intelligence Agency's 1995 *Fact Book* mentioned virtually every nation in the hemisphere except Cuba. When this apparent omission was pointed out to agency director George Tenet by Congressman Lincoln Díaz-Balart (R-Fla.), the former did not defend the text but rather claimed that it was merely "an oversight." The oversight, however, was not corrected in the 1996, 1997, or 1998 editions. Cuba finally appeared under this entry in the 1999 *Fact Book* but only to the extent of being characterized (page 127) as a country whose territory "serves as a transshipment zone for cocaine bound for the U.S. and Europe." It gives far more attention and space to Costa Rica, Belize, and Antigua-Barbuda (pages 19, 51, and 120, respectively), presumably because more illicit traffic is routed through those three nations than through Cuba.

Other U.S. government agencies specifically charged with drug enforcement likewise regard Cuba as a very minor offender, if indeed an offender at all. No less an authority than former drug czar General Barry McCaffrey, U.S. Army (retired), has roundly insisted as recently as March 2002 during a visit to the island that he saw "no evidence at all that the Cubans are in any way facilitating drug trafficking. Indeed," he added for emphasis, "I see good evidence of the opposite. I strongly believe that Cuba is an island of resistance to drug traffic."[58] John C. Varrone of the U.S. Customs Service, testifying to a congressional committee in January 2000, phrased his findings rather more cautiously. "Our enforcement experience in the Caribbean," he explained, "has led us to believe that the role Cuba plays in non-commercial smuggling can best be characterized as that of a method that smugglers use to thwart end-game interdiction efforts." To which he added, "By this I mean that Cuban authorities typically do not respond to their presence in Cuban waters and air space and that there are limitations on law enforcement exchange and operational coordination between the U.S. and Cuban governments." He avowed, however, that "we do not have any evidence or intelligence that this use of Cuban waters to thwart our interdiction efforts is promoted, supported or coordinated in any way by Cuban government forces."[59] In other words, rather than serving as an active participant in the traffic, Cuba is an innocent victim of its geography and of inadequate resources to police its borders.

A slightly more pointed account was given at the same hearing by William E. Ledwith, chief of international operations for the Drug Enforcement Agency. He described the Cuban government's performance in interdicting narcotics "mixed," but professed to derive some comfort in the fact that Havana had concluded agreements with several governments—including the United Kingdom, Italy, the Bahamas, and France—as well as the United Nations Office for Drug Control and Crime Prevention (UNODCCP).

"Cuban authorities," he continued, "on occasion have arrested individual drug traffickers; but historically, the Cuban government did not respond aggressively to incursions by these traffickers into Cuban territorial waters and airspace." In part, he added, echoing his Customs Service colleague, this may be due to lack of resources. "In addressing the role of Cuba in the international drug trade," he said,

> DEA must rely on international media sources, as well as other foreign law enforcement agencies for much of our information regarding drug arrests and seizures by Cuban authorities. The DEA does not have a presence in Cuba. Therefore, we have no formal contacts with Cuban authorities, and we cannot independently corroborate much of the alleged Cuban involvement in drug trafficking.[60]

General Edward Atkeson, cited earlier in the context of his visit to Cuba and a long session with President Castro himself, describes the Cuban chief of state as somewhat perplexed by the situation. He [Castro] "painted a picture of frequent flights by small private aircraft violating Cuban sovereign territory, depositing their packages in the water to be picked up by high-speed boats operating from 'mother' ships traversing the Straits of Florida." At any moment, the general was told, "there may be as many as a hundred ships in the narrows, which at night or in fog are difficult to identify." The problem, Castro is cited as saying, "is partly lack of fuel, but even more, the lack of U.S.-Cuban governmental coordination because of 'irrational' U.S. law and policy."[61]

This view of Cuba's role in the universe of narcotics trafficking is sharply questioned by Rep. Ileana Ros-Lehtinen (R-Fla.), Rep. Benjamin Gilman (R-N.Y.), chairman of the House International Relations Committee, and Rep. Dan Burton (R-Ind.), among others.[62] At the January 2000 hearing cited above, Ros-Lehtinen insisted that in spite of the official position of the DEA, many of its officials—under condition of anonymity—have told a very different story to members of her staff. They say, she claims, that "documentation exists detailing the activities of drug runners who go from the Bahamas and other neighboring Caribbean nations to Cuba for loading and unloading of drug shipments. They also refer to sightings and logs of air traffic into Cuba suspected to be related to the drug trade." She went on to say that "statements of former spies and high-level Castro officials indicate that drug trafficking activities are a directive from the Castro brothers executed by their senior leadership."[63]

For its part, the Cuban government heatedly denies these allegations. José Luis Ponce of the Cuban Interests Section in Washington calls the allegations "an outrageous lie. The Cuban government," he insists, "is not involved in any drug trafficking. Many people in the United States would like to build a campaign against the Cuban government in order to use it as a pretext for foreign intervention in Cuba that could even be a military intervention."[64] Undoubtedly Ponce is at least partially correct: while not necessarily advocating an invasion of the island, Cuba's most vocal accusers are among the firmest anti-Castro figures in American political life. Their motives may be suspect; so, however, may his own.

It may indeed be, of course, that the findings of the CIA, the DEA, and the Customs Service (as well as the U.S. Coast Guard) are based on the best evidence available. This means not only that the members of Congress cited above are misinformed, but also that virtually all of the testimony of defectors, as well as a string of reports in the daily press (much of it, admittedly, based in Miami), are false. Many allegations have in fact proven to be just that. Others have not been substantiated sufficiently to justify judicial action. The matter is further complicated by the fact that U.S. intelligence sources profess to find a significant difference between the evidence of Cuba's involvement in drug trafficking before and after 1989, when General Arnaldo Ochoa and several high-ranking Cuban intelligence agents were tried for a multitude of sins,

CUBA AND DRUGS: AN END TO EXCEPTIONALISM?

Although Cuba has for many years heatedly denied involvement in drug trafficking, a recent report by the United Nations Office for Drug Control and Crime Prevention strongly suggests otherwise. According to its *Global Illicit Drug Trends 2002,* from 1995 through 2000, Cuba led the entire Caribbean in cocaine and marijuana traffic—23.8 tons of the former and 21.5 tons of the latter—ahead of the Bahamas, the Cayman Islands, and Haiti.

The report was based on government reports, research by Interpol, and findings of specialized international organizations. Precisely how the UN Office for Drug Control and Crime Prevention arrived at these figures is not clear; for its part, Cuba failed to submit reports to the agency for the years 1998 and 2000. Also, in contrast to other reporting countries, Cuba refuses to submit information on domestic drug use.

Articles appearing in the Cuban official press concede that there is a growing drug problem on the island. Cuba's penal code already provides stiff sentences for drug trafficking, including the death penalty. A decree-law issued in January 2003 additionally provides that persons who traffic in drugs or cultivate drugs, or who knowingly allow their property to be used for those purposes, will lose their homes and farms. As one veteran observer of Cuba has noted, "It is not surprising that drug consumption would come to a country that, ten years ago, had little trade or contact with international tourism and now welcomes nearly two million tourists per year." Nonetheless, he added, given the island's impoverished economic state, it is remarkable that "there is enough purchasing power to support even an 'incipient' market for illegal drugs." [Philip Peters, "Cuba Responds to 'Growing' Drug Problem," *Lexington Institute Cuba Report,* March 2003.]

including drug trafficking. The notion that Cuba is a drug-free zone—unique to its region—invites both admiration and wonderment, but also a modicum of skepticism, even by those not normally obsessed by the Cuban "threat." It is also true, however, that alone among Caribbean states, Cuba possesses a government with sufficient authority and intelligence resources to render the island a drug-free zone—if that is indeed what it wished to do.

An alternative hypothesis is that, rather than a transshipment point for drugs themselves, Cuba has become a major center for the laundering of drug money from the Caribbean. This prospect first suggested itself following the publication of a full-dress survey of the Cuba economy by the United Nations Economic Commission for Latin America (CEPAL) in 1997.[65] According to the Commission's team of economists, the island was receiving somewhere between $800 million and $1 billion in remittances *each year* from Cubans overseas.[66] The figure was so unusually large that Ernesto Betancourt, a Cuban émigré scholar and former director of Radio Martí, was encouraged to work through the numbers in the report.

Among other things, Betancourt found that in order for the figure to reach $800 million, about 200,000 émigrés would have to remit $4,000 annually to their relatives on the island (or 400,000 émigrés, $2,000 each; or 800,000 émigrés, $1,000 each). This seemed highly unlikely in view of the fact that a recent poll of Cuban residents revealed that fully two-thirds received no money from abroad, and of those who did, the overwhelming majority received less than a thousand dollars a year. He juxtaposed this against the fact that 70 percent of U.S. residents of Cuban origin (408,000 of 580,000) earn less than $25,000 a year, "which does not leave too much disposable income for remittances."

He also questioned whether the Cuban government was capable of absorbing $800 million in remittances from a political and sociological point of view. At the 1997 official rate of exchange (one dollar equals twenty pesos), $800 million would amount to 16 billion pesos, representing more than 133 percent of the *total* Cuban government revenues for 1996. "This level of remittances, Betancourt observed, would reflect not only "a very high concentration of wealth in the hands of enemies of the revolution, or at least disaffected elements," but also give the relatives of bitterly antigovernment overseas Cubans a "buying power far in excess of that of the state."

Were those figures to be true, Betancourt concludes, "there would be a very perverse relation within Cuban society between political power and economic power." By way of comparison, a Cuban army colonel currently makes around 8,400 pesos a year, and a hospital director around 7,200 pesos. Such massive disparities between recipients of remittances and party loyalists would be intolerably destabilizing to the political system. The most plausible explanation for the numbers is that they mask income generated by money laundering and drug trafficking.[67]

To be sure, the fact that CEPAL cannot satisfactorily account for so huge a number under the rubric of "remittances"—many eyebrows were raised at this aspect of its report—does not automatically substantiate Betancourt's hypothesis. Nonetheless, the money must be coming from *somewhere*. As if to respond to these troubling questions, that agency's subsequent report on the Cuban economy downgraded its estimates of remittances to (a still hardly credible) $700 million.[68]

Espionage

During the heyday of its association with the Soviet bloc, the Cuban state developed one of the most professional intelligence services anywhere in the Third World, trained mainly in the former German Democratic Republic. The Directorate-General of Cuban Intelligence (DGI) operated around the world, but its proudest achievements were no doubt associated with protection of leading Cuban authorities. Indeed, in July 1987 Cuban television aired a series on CIA operations in Cuba, which supposedly revealed among other things the degree to which almost every Cuban agent recruited by Washington was in fact a double agent working for the DGI.[69] Certainly Cuban intelligence has demonstrated its capacities in one important regard—its effective neutralization of several plans by the Kennedy administration in the United States to assassinate President Fidel Castro.[70]

Since the end of the Cold War, there has been some controversy over the degree to which Cuban espionage remains in a position to threaten the United States. The issue emerged in the media and the political community in 1998, when eight individuals were arrested by the FBI regional office in Miami, charged with attempts to infiltrate and spy on U.S. government agencies and on the Cuban-American community. By the time the accused were brought to trial in late 2000, the indictment was supported by considerable evidence, including applications for employment in defense-related agencies, as well as the death certificate of a five-year-old child who died in California in 1969 which, the FBI explained, was to be used as a cover of identity.

The FBI also found dozens of computer diskettes with addresses of DGI contacts, copies of others from the "principal center," receipts, and copies of orders and instructions. Some diskettes recovered in the apartment of the ringleader contained codified documents contemplating "the possibility of sabotaging or damaging planes and hangers in an unspecified Florida locale," later identified as Boca Chica Naval Base in the Florida Keys and McDill Air Force Base in Tampa.

By mid-1999, the U.S. attorney had widened the indictment to include two more spies and accused all of them of belonging to the so-called Wasp Web. The purported leader of the group, Gerardo Hernández, whose *nom de guerre* was Manuel Viramontes, was also charged with involvement in the 1996 shoot-down of planes belonging to Brothers to the Rescue.[71] Born in the United States, Viramontes was taken to Cuba by his parents in the late 1950s, and eventually became a pilot in the Cuban military, with which he saw combat service in Angola. His American citizenship became of considerable value to him when he apparently defected in a crop duster plane in 1988, since he was able to produce a Chicago birth certificate. He later became a pilot for Brothers to the Rescue, and also became involved in a fringe exile group, Partido Unidad Nacional Democrática, that was subsequently discredited by involvement in drug trafficking.[72]

While the Wasp Web case was being prepared for trial, two of the accused—a married couple—concluded a plea bargain with the U.S. authorities. Charged with trying to penetrate the headquarters of the U.S. Southern Command, they were given a reduced 42-month sentence in exchange for information that led to the expulsion of three Cuban diplomats at the United Nations in New York.[73] At roughly the same time, a federal court in Miami sentenced another Cuban couple to seven years' imprisonment for having reported to Cuba on the movement of planes at Homestead Air Force Base and the movement of cargo on the Miami River, and for attempting to infiltrate Miami's Latin American Chamber of Commerce. The couple had also parked outside of Fort Bragg, North Carolina, to report the movement of troops. By way of mitigation, the accused claimed that they had been forced into espionage work by the Cuban government, which held their families as hostage, but in fact only the woman's mother was resident on the island.[74]

Some security experts regard these cases as examples not of any Cuban espionage threat but rather proof of the relative impotence and amateurishness into which Cuban intelligence has fallen since the end of the Cold War. One such expert was quoted in the Miami press as saying that the Wasp Web "is not a first-class operation." Among other things, Viramontes/ Hernández neglected the first rule of espionage, which is compartmentalization. Moreover, on one occasion he lost a computer full of codes. Havana reduced his budget so that he was frequently late in paying his rent on a modest apartment.[75]

The U.S. military authorities were likewise scornful of the efforts of Viramontes's group. "It never reached the point of threat because we were very well aware of it," affirmed General Charles Wilhelm, commander-in-chief of the U.S. Southern Command based at Homestead Air Force Base in the Miami area. "We took extraordinary measures to assure our protection first, and above all to secure the information that left headquarters."[76] The real objective of the group was in all likelihood the Miami exile community, epicenter of anti-Castro sentiment in the United States and circum-Caribbean. "They [the Cuban authorities] are obsessed with Miami," according to Francisco Avila, an ex-DGI agent who for twelve years following his defection worked for the FBI. "They want to know everything about it— what brand of cigarettes the people are smoking, [even] the kind of automobiles they are driving."[77] For his part, Cuban President Fidel Castro admitted in a television interview that he had spies in the United States, but only to monitor U.S. political groups, particularly those likely to engage in terrorist activities against the island.[78]

Extraordinary efforts by the defense included recruiting active and retired U.S. officers to downplay the vulnerability of military facilities to Cuban infiltration,[79] bringing a counterintelligence specialist from Cuba to present his government's case,[80] and suggesting that Brothers to the Rescue "provoked" the shoot-down.[81] Nevertheless, a jury that included no Cuban-Americans found all five defendants guilty of conspiring to spy on the

United States. The leader of the group was sentenced to life in prison and the others to long periods of incarceration.

An even more curious case, mentioned in the first section of this chapter, was that involving Ana Belén Montes, a Puerto Rican-American employee of the Defense Intelligence Agency, who was regarded as the Pentagon's leading expert on Cuba. During the hearing at which she pleaded guilty of espionage, Ms. Montes acknowledged that "she had received the identities of four American undercover intelligence officers and provided the Cuban authorities with reams of other secret and top-secret military and intelligence information."[82] Under her plea bargain, she was sentenced in October 2002 to twenty-five years' imprisonment. Law enforcement officials have declined to say, however, whether her case was in any way related to the activities of the Wasp Web.

On the face of it, it is difficult to see exactly what Havana hoped to gain through these espionage activities, particularly those of the Wasp Web. One possible explanation was aired in the authoritative *Jane's Defense Weekly* (March 6, 1996), which reported that Havana was training commandos in Vietnam for operations against U.S. military installations in the event of a U.S. invasion. "Havana's strategy," it explained, "is to attack the staging and supply areas for U.S. forces preparing" for such an operation. "The political objective would be to bring the reality of warfare to the American public and so exert domestic pressure on Washington." The fact that such an invasion is next door to inconceivable—as far as the United States is concerned—would not necessarily reassure the Cuban government, which, like all regimes of its type, lives in a state of permanent paranoia and insecurity. The revelation of two centers of Cuban espionage in the United States underscores the fundamentally hostile relationship that continues to exist between the two countries, as well as the Cuban disposition to expend valuable resources on protecting the island from improbable threats, but possibly little else.

Terrorism

One of the most vociferous arguments on Cuban policy in recent times has been the question of where the island's government fits, if at all, in the pattern of global terror and the club of "terrorist states." In the past, certainly, there could be little doubt about Cuba's involvement in violent efforts to over-throw governments in Latin America, or even to stage sensational bank rob-beries in the United States. Since the end of the Cold War, however, the subject has become so politically and ideologically volatile that no definitive conclusions can be offered here.[83]

During the Clinton administration the very notion of "rogue states" was dismissed as undiplomatic and inept; Secretary of State Madeleine Albright preferred the softer term "states of concern." As State Department spokesman Richard Boucher later explained, "a more general phrase" was needed given "a certain evolution" within each of the countries that formerly figured on the terrorist list.[84] Even so, Cuba was still bracketed with Iran, Iraq, and Libya, in view of the fact that it continued to harbor terrorists (notably from the Spanish ETA) and maintain links to designated foreign terrorist organi-zations (such as the Colombian FARC and the IRA).

Since the Bush administration took office, the old name of the list has been restored, and Cuba is still on it. One critic of the first State Department report issued since the change of administrations (*Patterns of Global Terrorism, 2000*), while conceding that Cuba's official rhetoric is "at times unfounded and offensive," notes that the new document stands out both for its brevity and the fact that it employs a lower standard of evidence for Cuba than for Syria, Libya, Iran, Iraq, and so forth.[85] He might also have added that Castro's visits to such places and his expression of political solidarity with Islamic extremism[86] may be dictated more by a desire to obtain oil at prefer-ential prices or under favorable credit arrangements (efforts that so far have been fruitless) than any operational interest in their subversive activities at home or abroad.

That Fidel Castro himself may harbor sufficient hatred of the United States to wish it "brought to its knees"—as he declared during a tour of Iran, Syria, and Libya in May 2001—cannot be in doubt.[87] At the same time, his country is indirectly but strongly dependent on the economic welfare of the United States, as demonstrated by the ripple effect of the September 11 attacks on the World Trade Center and the Pentagon. (Two important results were an immediate drop in tourism and air travel worldwide, which strongly affected Cuba's most important industry, and a drop in remittances from U.S.-based Cubans as a result of the onset of an economic recession.) Just how far Cuba dares to go—in its own interest—in trying to "bring America to its knees" (as if such a thing were possible for a wretched Caribbean island) is another question. A world in which the United States was hungry and defeated would inevitably be one in which Cuba would be even hungrier still.

Conclusions and Prospect

For the most part, such conventional military threats as Cuba has been able to pose in the past have been neutralized by its precarious economic situation, the loss of a powerful strategic partner, the gradual divergence of its military establishment toward sugar, tourism, and other business enterprises,[88] and technological challenges that are beyond its capacity to meet. Certainly from the perspective of doctrine, the United States remains the enemy for Cuba's military and intelligence establishment, and to the degree that the government is capable of pursuing some of its projects—particularly in the area of germ warfare—its threat potential cannot be written off altogether. If it is, as seems more than possible, a center of money laundering for drug kingpins, it plays an unwholesome international role, but one in no way different from other Caribbean islands that otherwise maintain normal and even cordial relations with the United States.

At this point, however, it may be that the most serious danger Cuba represents to the United States is a massive exodus of people, produced either in response to heightened repression, an abrupt transition to a more open form of political organization, or an unpredictable accident (such as the assassination or sudden disappearance of President Fidel Castro). Under such circumstances the United States would presumably be forced to order a military response to control the influx of refugees and prevent potential clashes between Cuban authorities and Cuban exile groups involved in rescue activities.

A group of U.S. security specialists, convening in 1997 to think through this scenario, was frankly unsure how to meet its challenges.

> Given this discomfiting prospect [the conference report read] the matter of discrete military options, short of deployment of U.S. forces, was

briefly addressed, and an effort made to highlight those that might put the onus of escalation on the Cuban government.

Such options might include increased surveillance, the tightening of economic sanctions, or the imposition of a blockade, presumably carried out with the acquiescence, if not support, of our European allies.

But it was also recognized that at such an uncertain time the Cuban regime could opt to pursue actions to force U.S. retaliation, thus precipitating an outright war.

The report went on to say that no consensus had been reached "on the range of responses that might be appropriate in the event of 'end game' in Cuba." While some conference participants apparently suggested that a more conciliatory response toward the Cuban government by the United States, even to the point of providing it with additional resources, might stem such an outflow, others pointed to the "fundamental contradiction" of such a proposal, namely, "to lend legitimacy to the regime, therefore ultimately delay[ing] a transition."

> The consideration of these options [the report went on to say] nevertheless remains very important given [that] the historical record shows "end games" usually come about quickly, and leave little time for lengthy deliberations before decisive action is required.
>
> [But] given the increasing levels of repression and the deteriorating security situation in Cuba and limited United States options, it was concluded that security issues have become the most important issue in U.S.-Cuban relations.[89]

A retired U.S. intelligence official reminds us that since the 1960s, popular disaffection on the island has led to three seaborne migrations, "confronting U.S. administrations with costly, urgent, and confounding security and humanitarian crises." A fourth such migration could well be imminent, since the regime's current difficulties "seem substantially to exceed the problems that preceded previous mass sealifts." He is particularly troubled by the impact of formal dollarization of the Cuban economy since 1993, a measure that has introduced new and sharp inequalities in Cuban society. While the government apparently understands the gravity of the social problems thus engendered, it has, he writes, "offered no palliatives or explanations about how . . . to narrow gaps in income, consumption, and privilege between Cuba's dollar and peso classes."

To the degree to which Castro refuses further economic reform, he continues to undermine the stability of his own regime. According to the 1997 conference report,

> To continue on the present course inevitably will compromise every cherished article of the revolutionary faith that Castro has upheld for over four decades. The dual economies he tolerates are more difficult to monitor and tax. The proliferation of standards and rules invites transgressions and lawlessness. Crime and corruption, including narcotics trafficking and use, will persist and large numbers of Cubans will engage in criminal activities. Racial and urban-rural tensions will increase as those with access to dollars improve their standards of living while others continue barely to subsist. Violence and theft by one group against the other may become the dominant types of crime. These trends will erode the Revolution's legitimacy as the hypocrisy of Castro's promises becomes more and more blatant. And finally, they generate frustrated expectations for more fundamental economic and even political reforms. . . . Any half-way measures between continued tolerance of current conditions and a sweeping crackdown would solve none of the ideological and social dilemmas while sowing confusion and unrest.

Under these circumstances, Castro may eventually decide that "he has no alternative but to purge Cuba of that large new materialistic segment of the population that has virtually no ties with or allegiance to the revolutionary principles and values he has preached for over 40 years." Thus the regime itself—in its present and evolving form—carries within it the embryo of a major migration crisis with serious security implications for the United States.[90]

Yet even the peaceful disappearance of the Castro government and its instant replacement by something far more appetizing to the United States and to Cuba's neighbors—the best of all best-case scenarios—would not automatically end the threat of mass migration, use of the island as a base for international criminal activities, or drug trafficking and money laundering, as demonstrated by the respective cases of Haiti, Jamaica, and Panama. Indeed, to the degree to which the country fails to reestablish its lost economic viability, it might be inclined to turn to drugs with redoubled dedication. Again, Haiti is a case in point. Having failed to achieve a minimal political consensus after the expulsion of the Duvalier clan and the military caste that supported it, the western half of Hispaniola today is the principal point of entry into the United States of cocaine shipments from Colombia and elsewhere (53.9 *tons* between 1998 and 1999).[91] This sort of threat is far more palatable than the kinds posed by Cuba in the past, but hardly an invitation to complacency; a Cuban "problem" may prove in the end more costly and contentious than the Cuban threat ever did.

5

Tourism and Environment

The Cuban Reentry

Since the onset of the so-called "Special Period," the one sector of the Cuban economy to register significant and continuous growth has been tourism. In and of itself this represents a remarkable ideological, cultural, and definitional turnaround. For many years—indeed, from almost the onset of the revolution—the Castro regime regarded this industry as inextricably linked to the humiliating presence of affluent (and arrogant) Americans, gambling, prostitution, and the mob—in other words, as a breeding ground for every manner of "bourgeois" vice.

The U.S. trade embargo effectively closed off Cuba's principal source of foreign tourism in 1960–1961; for its part, the regime's own sense of revolutionary identity largely put an end to leisure travel from other Western sources. Between 1960 and 1989, tourism in Cuba remained extremely modest in scope and largely restricted to visitors from the Eastern bloc—vanguard workers, Communist Party officials, or ordinary citizens of Soviet bloc countries whose currency was worthless elsewhere, and to whom travel to other warm-weather areas in the West was largely closed. These visitors had to cope with outdated and poorly maintained hotels, surly and inattentive service, and second- or third-rate cuisine. Indeed, during the first twenty years of the revolution, sixteen hotels were closed, and hotel capacity was reduced by 50 percent.[1]

Politics aside, Cuba's sudden embrace of foreign tourism after the loss of its principal financial patron cannot be wholly surprising. Tourism was a major industry and primary source of hard currency and employment in pre-revolutionary Cuba. Indeed, in 1957, which is to say the penultimate year before Castro's assumption of power, tourism was the country's second largest generator of foreign exchange, producing more revenue than tobacco and surpassed only by sugar. As one student of the subject has noted, throughout the 1950s, "Cuba's share of the Caribbean tourist market ranged between 18 and 21 percent . . . , and most visitors to the island were from the United States."[2]

Castro's economic team could not fail to note the impact of tourism on the economies of Cuba's Latin American neighbors during the thirty years that the island had virtually withdrawn from the industry. By century's end the figures were nothing short of spectacular. According to the World Tourist Organization, Rio de Janeiro in Brazil took in $3.6 billion in the summer of 1999 alone, making it that city's principal economic activity, representing fully 8 percent of the city's Gross Domestic Product. During the same year, Quintana Roo, the Mexican state geographically closest to Cuba, welcomed roughly 4 million tourists and earned $3 billion, or 37 percent of Mexico's entire receipts from the industry. Another region near Cuba, Punta Cana in the Dominican Republic, received 2.6 million visitors in 1999, leaving $2.6 billion in foreign exchange and generating employment for 200,000 persons— astounding numbers for so small and so poor a country.[3]

Compared with Quintana Roo, where the only real attractions are the beaches of Cancún and the nearby Mayan ruins at Palenque, or the Dominican Republic, where beaches are virtually the only draw, Cuba would seem to be far better positioned in the Caribbean market. Unlike its neighbors, the island enjoys a "substantial land mass, . . . geographical diversity, [an] enormous range of existing and potential attractions, cultural and architectural history, and a combination of an educated work force and low incidence of crime."[4] A Cuban-American travel professional who visited the island in October 1998 affirmed these advantages but also took note of widespread prostitution in Havana, "museum quality" hotels, a crumbling infrastructure in the old districts of the capital, and food that was "monotonous and lack[ing in] variety."[5]

A report on the industry in early 1996 noted that 80 to 95 percent of visitors to Cuba bought relatively low-cost packages, and they differed significantly from visitors to other Caribbean destinations. They tended to be "younger, slightly more adventurous individuals, generally without children and with less money to spend."[6] Part of the island's appeal was precisely the fact that it was an inexpensive destination. By the end of the decade, however, visitors were beginning to spend more per capita and stay somewhat longer.

Moreover, the island's tourist authorities have lately set out to attract affluent visitors. In July 2000, Belgian entrepreneur Thierry Nicolas announced the imminent opening of the Cuban & Caribbean Express, a joint venture between the Cuban state and the Chemin de Fer Belge (SNCB). Some $28 million, it was announced, will be invested to rehabilitate rolling stock into luxury fittings, including Jacuzzis, smoking rooms, bars, even business centers. ("Not only the only luxury train in the Caribbean," affirmed Nicolas, "but without doubt the most beautiful hotel in Cuba.") The train was scheduled to be put into service in December 2001, but the promoters claimed that they were "inundated" with reservations or inquiries, particularly from Japan, more than a full year in advance.[7]

Meanwhile, Cuba has attracted considerable numbers of Latin American visitors by widely advertising medical services at cut-rate prices. In 1997, for example, it was reportedly earning $25 million a year from low-cost face-lifts and liposuction, as well as innovative treatments for night blindness, vertigo, and neurological disorders. Plans were reported underway to build new alcohol and drug addiction centers, as well as to refurbish pre-revolutionary medical spas. Some of these cutting-edge treatments may be less effective than claimed, particularly the treatment for night blindness, which U.S. physicians claim is incurable. Others have expressed concern that Cuba is "charging exorbitant prices [for what is actually being offered] and violating accepted procedures in its rush for dollars."[8] While that may be, the government agency responsible for this activity, SERVIMED, has aggressively marketed these services, and with considerable success.[9]

Cuba in the Caribbean: Some Comparative Facts and Figures

Since the early 1990s, Cuba's tourist industry has experienced extraordinary growth—an average of 20 percent *a year* for the 1994–2000 period—the highest in the region.[10] A decade after reentering the market, Cuba stood as the Caribbean's fifth most popular destination.[11] This achievement is largely due to a crash program of hotel construction and refurbishment—much of it the result of joint ventures with foreign investors—and the opening of seven new international airports. According to official Cuban figures, 1.7 million people visited the island in 2000, spending $2 billion.[12] The same source claimed 1.9 million visitors in 2001, a figure that was lower than expected but still represented a modest increase.[13] This compares dramatically with 132,900 visitors for 1980 or even 340,000 for 1990.[14] The island's late start in the tourist sector is reflected in its share of the Caribbean market. In 1999, Cuba accounted for only 8 percent of the Caribbean market, while Cancún accounted for 14.3 percent, and the Dominican Republic fully 13 percent. Though rapidly increasing, Cuba's supply of international quality hotel rooms stood at 32,000 in 1999, compared with 50,000 for the Dominican Republic.

Though Cancún has only 25,000 rooms, they tend to be of higher quality, and occupancy rates have continually run higher than Cuba's (79 percent versus 63 percent in 1999). Cancún also derives considerably more financial benefit from fewer visitors by attracting a far more upscale clientele, and by having developed an extensive infrastructure nearby of restaurants, shops, and bars. For its part, the Dominican Republic has captured an important segment of the middle market from both Western Europe and the United States, a share that is bound to increase if the U.S. ban on travel to Cuba remains in place.[15]

The Cuban government has announced plans to develop 172,500 rooms by 2010, which is to say, an average of 14,000 rooms a year. This "very aggressive rate of expansion" seems to be based on the assumption that all U.S. travel and trade restrictions will be lifted by that date, and that $22 billion will be available for investment in hotels alone, much of it coming from U.S. and foreign corporations. Two travel specialists from the United States thought that the government's plans fell short of its goals by roughly 6,000 rooms a year. Apart from an increase in physical plant, the same authorities suggested that the quality of food and services would have to improve to continue present growth rates. There would also have to be an expansion of offerings, moving beyond all-inclusive packages to time-share and resort villages.[16]

One area where Cuba continues to operate at a disadvantage, not only vis-à-vis Cancún and the Dominican Republic, but many of the smaller Caribbean islands, is that it receives relatively few cruise ships, most of which depart from or call at U.S. ports. (The Cuban Democracy Act of 1992 forbids any ship calling at a Cuban port from making a similar call at a U.S. destination for a full six months.) These restrictions prevent Cuba from tapping into a fast-growing industry, one that has the additional advantage of requiring relatively little infrastructure investment by the host country. In 1995 Cuba opened its first cruise ship terminal in Havana; a second was scheduled to open in 2001, with two more under construction in Santiago and Mariel as part of a $12 million joint venture with the Italian enterprise Costa Crociere. The London-based P&L and the Norwegian Kloster Cruise were reported exploring similar arrangements.[17] Eventually the Cuban government expects to welcome as many as 100,000 tourists a year in this way.[18]

Background to Growth

Significant changes in Cuban law have been required to bring about Cuba's impressive reentry into the tourist industry. Decree-Law 50 established more favorable provisions for foreign investment in that sector than for other industries as long ago as 1982. It exempted investors from certain taxes and licenses; freed them from many of Cuba's cumbersome regulations; and allowed them to lease Cuban installations and to contract with the state for Cuban workers. (Shortly thereafter, in 1987, Cubanacán was created to provide a Cuban partner for foreign ventures.)[19]

Apparently recognizing the need to deepen the incentives to foreign investment following the collapse of the Soviet Union, the Cuban government amended its constitution in 1992 to recognize and protect private foreign property. Another measure, obviously related, was the decision the following year to permit the dollar to circulate legally for the first time since 1959. Decree-Law 147 in 1994 created a new Ministry of Tourism, and as if to respond to the burgeoning industry, the Cuban tourist agency (INTUR) and Cubanacán were broken up into a number of separate entities to render the state sector more agile.

As of 1997, Cubanacán was operating four- and five-star hotels, mainly in Varadero, Santa Lucía, and Santiago; Gran Caribe, a new government entity, was doing the same in Havana, Varadero, and Cayo Largo; and Gaviota, S.A. and Horizontes—new creations—were in charge of three- and four-star hotels. It should be noted that the Cuban system of designations (five-star, four-star, and so on) are far more generous than the standard used by most hoteliers in the Caribbean, Western Europe, and elsewhere. For example, the author stayed at the Golden Tulip Parque Central in Havana in early 2001; though deemed worthy of five stars—Cuba's highest designation for an urban establishment—it was basically a first-class rather than a luxury facility.

Precise and up-to-date figures on foreign investment in Cuba's tourist sector are hard to come by. As of 1998, the Cuban government announced the existence of twenty-one joint ventures representing $600 million in capital investments. The provisions of the contracts are unknown but were initially reported to be quite favorable, including a free lease on the land, exemption from tariffs or other inputs, tax-free repatriation of profits, even guaranteed ownership rights for twenty-five years, renegotiable for fifty years.[20] (As time has passed, however, the Cuban state has introduced new taxes and overhead charges.) Typically the Cuban government turns over existing hotel facilities to foreigners, who supervise the upgrades, train most of the personnel, and share roughly 50 percent of the profits.[21]

Lately the Cuban government has been constructing new hotels in conjunction with foreign investor-operators. Cuba's principal partners have been the Spanish chain Sol Meliá, the Dutch Golden Tulip chain (a subsidiary of KLM airlines), and various Mexican, Canadian, and Italian companies. Although a far-flung international enterprise, Sol Meliá reports that Cuba has consistently been its most profitable market in recent years.[22] Indeed, so much is this the case that the company has chosen to forgo a presence in southern Florida, a Hobson's choice dictated by the restrictions of the Helms-Burton Law.[23]

Most tourists are brought to Cuba by foreign investors operating under marketing and managing contracts. They make their money by bringing in planeloads of tourists who have purchased prepaid packages in their countries of origin. They tend to sell their tours through wholesalers, who demand higher commissions to promote and sell less popular destinations.[24] While Helms-Burton has affected some hotel concerns, its effect on tour operators, travel agencies, consolidators, wholesalers, and suppliers is minimal, even if they operate within the United States. This is so because the law only forbids trafficking in confiscated property, not doing business in Cuba itself.[25]

By 2010, Cuban officials expect to receive some 10 million tourists, who will spend $5 billion, roughly half the hard currency generated by the entire

Cuban economy in 1997. This projection is based on all kinds of optimistic notions—not merely the lifting of the U.S. travel ban, but an unprecedented flood of foreign investment. It also assumes that overseas participants in joint ventures will continue to feel comfortable with the welter of curious regulations and restrictions that currently shape (or misshape) the Cuban economy. For example, hotel operators are not allowed to go out and hire people on the open market; rather, they are obliged to hire their workers from a pool administered by a government agency, to which they also remit their salaries. As has been widely reported—and which the Cuban government freely admits—roughly 95 percent of this amount is confiscated, ostensibly at least, to redistribute to the rest of the population in the form of social services (the so-called *prestaciones sociales*). The tourist worker receives 5 percent of his or her salary, though in nearly worthless Cuban pesos. The appeal of tourist work lies in the fact that those employed in the industry have access to dollars in the form of tips.[26]

In addition, all foreign enterprises are subject to Cuban taxation, which includes a 30 percent income tax, an 11 percent tax on labor force utilization, a 14 percent social security tax, personal property taxes on cars, and documentary fees.[27] Some economists believe that this is making Cuban labor disproportionately expensive, particularly relative to other Caribbean countries.[28]

The backward linkages into the Cuban economy, such as they are, suffer from all of the inefficiencies associated with nonmarket systems. One unidentified Spanish businessman was quoted in the Madrid daily *El País* as saying "as long as the [economic] system doesn't change, and private enterprise is forced to operate with so many controls, the Cubans will not really prosper."[29] There may well be a systemic ceiling to tourist growth. On the other hand, the constant possibility that the U.S. travel ban will be lifted at any moment acts as a tantalizing stimulus to non-U.S. investors, encouraging them to soldier on regardless of present obstacles.

Impact of Tourism on the Cuban Economy

To say that tourism has become the engine of growth in Cuba is not to say that it has reached anything close to its full potential. In 1997 Cuban authorities claimed that the industry guaranteed jobs for 130,000 Cubans,[30] while the leader of the tourist workers union claimed 63,000 members.[31] Even if the numbers have doubled since then, this is a tiny percentage of the Cuban labor force of roughly 4.5 million. A more interesting question is how deeply tourist revenues penetrate beyond the immediate circle of those who work directly in the industry.

Minister of Tourism Ibrahim Ferradaz claims that Cuba retains 22 cents of every tourist dollar.[32] This is somewhat in excess of the Bahamas, whose prime minister has remarked that his island chain keeps 19 cents of every tourist dollar,[33] a comparison that raises serious questions about Minister Ferradaz's credibility, given that—unlike Cuba—the Bahamas possesses an active and vigorous small business sector and is not forced to import as many of its inputs.

Economists specializing in the tourist industry paint a far more modest picture. María Dolores Espino finds that in 1998, only 81,000 Cubans were employed in the industry (about 2 percent of the labor force). More to the point, she insists that the figure has held constant since 1996, the first year for which data were available. Commenting on the total impact of tourist spending on the local economy, she writes that it

> is a combination of direct and indirect (induced) effects. It is calculated by multiplying tourist expenditures by a tourist income and/or employment multiplier. The value of the multiplier depends on the portion of income that leaks out of the local economy at each round of circulation. These leakages include payments for import or raw materials, rent and profits paid to nonresidents, and savings by residents. The larger and more diversified the economy in question, the lower the leakages and the larger the value of the multiplier.[34]

In other words, the more economic activity in a given country, the more dollars (or other external currencies) can be retained at each round of exchange. Where there is no small business sector, no productive agricultural sector, no light industry to speak of, a vast number of inputs, from food to light bulbs, have to be imported. Or, as another team of economists puts it, from an input-output point of view, tourist sectors should be heavily related to other domestic economic sectors. "If government policies inhibit the flow of tourist dollars, or reroute them to other sectors of the economy, the multiplier impact is clearly altered."[35]

The expansionary effect of the multiplier is also affected by supply constraints. That is to say, it rests on the notion that demand stimulates supply, but in the Cuban case—in spite of the modest market reforms of the economy beginning in the 1990s—the economy does not facilitate this process. The multiplier effect is further curtailed, Espino explains, by "continuing government policies designed to keep the tourism sector separate from the Cuban economy. The total impact of tourism on the Cuban economy is probably not much larger than the direct income and employment that these expenditures create."

By way of comparison, she finds the tourist income multiplier for small island economies in the Caribbean to range from 1.58 for Jamaica to 0.65 for the Cayman Islands, with others situated somewhere in between (Bahamas, 0.78; Antigua, 0.88; Bermuda, 1.03; Dominica, 1.20). At somewhere between 0.74 and 0.84, Cuba's is "one of the lowest values in the literature. Though a small reduction has been reported in the import component of the economy at large and of the tourism sector, these are more than counterbalanced by leakages due to taxes."[36]

One area where the tourist dollar has spread beyond the ken of the government or the joint ventures lies in the area of *paladares, casas particulares,* and private taxis. Paladares are home restaurants where the seating is limited to twelve persons at a time and where all the "employees" must be members of the immediate family. Casas particulares are private homes that rent out rooms to foreign tourists for dollars. Private or "gypsy" taxis are self-explanatory. It is extremely difficult to measure this part of the tourist economy because in spite of licensing and fees, much self-employed economic activity remains outside government control. Many Cuban entrepreneurs opt not to seek licenses, fearful of becoming targets for purges if government policy should abruptly change—something that has happened in the past. Or they refuse to apply for licenses because of artificially high taxation—so high, indeed, that at times it is difficult to see whether the purpose is revenue collection or the extinction of individual enterprise. Moreover, some enterprises are engaged in activities not covered by the licenses—underreporting income, renting out more rooms than permitted by licensing, serving food without declaring it part of one's business, or bringing in friends to work in paladares.[37]

Another area of self-employment related to tourism has to do with artisans, artists, and others who are permitted to sell their works in open-air markets, particularly the important one near the cathedral in Old Havana. It is difficult to estimate how many people are engaged in this sort of work, but it is obviously extremely negligible in terms of the overall workforce and even more in terms of its share of tourist revenues. Current estimates of the entire self-employed population in Cuba run at 150,000 persons, slightly more than 3 percent of the workforce. Even so, the vast majority of the self-employed are not engaged in enterprises related to tourism—for example, plumbers, electricians, tailors, and bicycle and automobile mechanics.[38]

If we accept the Cuban official figure of 22 cents on the dollar, this means that for 2000 the island netted a paltry $440 million from tourism. If we go on to assume that the island reaches its most ambitious target of grossing $5 billion in the year 2010—again, using Minister Ferradaz's calculations—the country will net only $1.1 billion, which is not an impressive figure when contrasted with the roughly $6 billion a year which Cuba formerly "earned" from its membership in the Soviet family of nations. To be sure, fundamental changes in the way Cuba's domestic economy is organized would conceivably increase significantly the production, employment, and income multipliers. Within the existing model, however, tourism remains an island of productivity with relatively minor relevance to the rest of the Cuban economy.

This is not to say that it has no important extra-economic consequences. The opening of Cuba to foreign tourism, like the legalization of the dollar, has generated both new opportunities and new social tensions. The presence of (relatively) affluent foreign visitors, many from neighboring Latin American countries, has opened a window onto the world for ordinary Cubans and provided them with a means to test some of the notions retailed by the official media. It has also undermined and to some extent discredited the notion that selfless devotion to the revolutionary ideal of equality ultimately brings greater satisfaction. (A popular joke in Havana during 1993 was that a public opinion survey found that the ambition of many Cuban children when they grew up was to be either a foreigner or a tourist!)[39] The evident disproportion between the income of workers in the tourist sector—hotel clerks, bellboys, waiters, taxi drivers, and so forth—and that of highly educated technicians, doctors, and teachers, has raised serious questions among younger Cubans as to whether a university education is even worth pursuing.

Finally, the drastic contrast between hotels and resorts, where food and drink are abundant, and the perennial shortages in the ration stores cannot but provoke anger and resentment. As one dissident put it, the handful of Cubans making dollars in the tourist sector contrasts painfully with the "low net income to [sic] the Cuban economy, the critical situation being faced in basic services, and the [meager?] supply of goods and medicines to the population, with no change in sight."[40] Tourism is thus a double-edged sword: it provides enough new resources for the regime to secure its core constituency in the armed forces and the party, but not enough to restore long-term economic growth. At the same time, it may well be generating dangerous political fallout, or put another way, it represents a lethal time bomb.

To be sure, Cuba is not the only Caribbean country for which tourism is but a partial solution to its economic ills and socially a mixed blessing. The difference, however, is that for thirty years, thanks to the Soviet subsidy, Cubans had become accustomed to a higher standard of living than they currently enjoy, and before that, thanks to a protected place in the U.S. domestic sugar market and a vigorous private sector, Cubans enjoyed a significantly higher standard of living than other countries in the region. While tourism has provided immediate relief to a country suddenly deprived of much of its external resources, alone it can never deliver the goods and services Cubans have historically come to expect, especially when the economic system itself is purposely designed to limit the diffusion of its benefits.

The Tourism-Environment Nexus

Much of Cuba's future as a major tourist destination depends upon its stewardship of its natural and man-made environment. Whether it has done so in the most environmentally responsible way is, like so many other subjects involving the island and its government, a matter of controversy. In some environmental circles, Cuba is seen as something of a model for developing countries, or even—in at least one case—for developed countries like the United States. One American who visited Cuba in 1992 fulsomely praised it as "an environmental and egalitarian utopia. There are few cars and no smog.

There is no graffiti, no commercial billboards and signs. The streets are cleaned, trash is picked up. Everything is recycled, nothing wasted."[41]

This view stands in stark contrast to the affirmation of Dr. José Oro, former director-general of the Department of Natural Resources in Cuba's Ministry of Basic Industry, now living in exile. "The environmental degradation [in Cuba] is rapid. We have the industrial production of Honduras and the pollution of East Germany."[42]

The one environmental achievement of the regime beyond dispute is, not surprisingly, intimately involved with the pursuit of the tourist dollar, namely, the restoration of Old Havana. An almost completely intact model of an eighteenth-century Spanish port city, it has been saved—paradoxically, by Communism—from the kind of tasteless urban redevelopment that has disfigured the central parts of Mexico City, Montevideo, and Buenos Aires, though by the late 1980s, it was crumbling under the weight of neglect and the harsh sea air. It is now being sensitively redeveloped by a new agency under the direction of the official historian of the city, a man of immense culture and great organizational abilities.[43]

The rush to create new facilities for foreign visitors has not always produced such happy outcomes. A crash program in the early 1990s to build hotels, with roads and auxiliary structures to service them, mainly on sand dunes, produced new episodes of soil erosion. To render the keys on the northern and southern sides of the island accessible to tourists, a program was established to join the archipelago by a continuous ribbon of stone roads (called *pedraplenes,* which are stone and earth embankments). The effect has been to close off substantial portions of seawater from the area between the coastline and the keys, producing severe damage to native flora and fauna. "Sea life has been drastically reduced in all these areas, with an accompanying decrease in fishing resources," writes one specialist. "Entire marine areas have been reduced to salty lagoons, with low oxygen levels and little life."[44] In recent years the Cuban government has been at pains to reassure the international environmental community that such practices have come to an end, though it has not said what, if anything, has been done to repair the damage already inflicted.

Another specialist looked at two particular cases, one where ecotourism policies were being pursued successfully; the other less so. The first was the Sierra del Rosario, which was formally designated a biosphere reserve by UNESCO in 1985, and which was receiving assistance from the United Nations Development Program. The region, he found, was subject to international regulations requiring protection, study, and preservation of its forest. Permission to live in the area was restricted. The residents themselves were self-sufficient and responsible for the protection of the area. The local hotel has only 25 rooms, which necessarily limited the number of tourists. Nature trails had been designed, and residents were being trained as guides.

The second was the National Park at Ciénaga de Zapata, which had been divided into 182 protected areas of varying management specifications. This region is one of the world's major neotropical wetlands, home to 15 varieties of mammalian species, 160 species of birds, 27 of reptiles, and 3 of amphibians. The Zapata peninsula is one of the island's richest areas of bird species. Of Cuba's 20 native species, fully 17 have been sighted here. Unlike the Sierra del Rosario, he reported, this region has poor roads and is severely understaffed, forcing scientists to double as park rangers. Lack of fuel for vehicles, combined with the absence of hand radios, made it impossible to manage so large a park. As a result, it was necessary to allow many fires to burn out naturally. The park director also expressed concern that nonnative vegetation was killing indigenous species. Since his report was written in the early days of the "Special Period," during which Cuba was under severe economic constraints, it leaves open the question of whether the problem was one of resources rather than political will.[45]

Dr. Carlos Wotzkow, a Cuban environmental scientist who left the island in 1992 and is now living in Switzerland, offers a rather different view. In the case of the Ciénaga de Zapata, his criticism is unsparing. He reports that the New Integrated Forest Enterprises are engaged in unselective logging there for charcoal production, though in fact many trees are left to rot on the roadsides because of a lack of transportation. There is also a program—the so-called Turquoise Plan—to engage in clear-cutting to open land for subsistence farming. This procedure, he writes, "has not produced, nor will it ever, the anticipated results in the areas deforested for that purpose." Entire palm groves have completely vanished from this park, as the Youth Army knocks them down looking for baby parrots, which can be exported for hard currency.[46]

Attempting to split the difference, one of the authors cited above puts it this way: "Cuba is neither an ecological disaster nor a paradise. Environmentally destructive decisions have been taken in some instances, while preservation concerns have won in others." He goes on to say that "Cuban experts in the field are aware that the most critical profit versus environmental protection decisions have yet to be made. Growing environmental awareness at the grass roots, the population's relatively high level of scientific education, the lowest cost of some environmentally sound methods, and the acknowledged importance of environmental protection to long term tourist revenues, all provide limited grounds for hope." But, he adds, "the economic and political forces militating against environmental protection remain formidable and should not be underestimated."[47]

The Formal Structures of Environmental Protection

On paper, at least, Cuba seems to be at least as responsible as any of the major developed countries where a high degree of environmental awareness is the norm. It is, for example, a signatory to at least twenty-five environmental treaties, including the Convention on Nature Protection and Wildlife Preservation in the Western Hemisphere; the International Convention for the Conservation of Atlantic Tunas; the International Plant Protection Convention; the Convention on the Prevention of Marine Pollution by Dumping of Wastes and Other Matter; the Protocol Concerning Cooperation in Combating Oil Spills in the Wider Caribbean Region; the Protocol on Substances that Deplete the Ozone Layer; and the Convention on Biological Diversity.

Cuba also possesses a full range of environmental laws. These include Law 33 of 1981, which requires environmental assessment of all investment projects, and establishes a coordinating agency (COMARNA) to oversee the environmental impact of new projects, composed of representatives from state agencies, provincial environmental commissions, and mass organizations; Article 27 of the 1992 constitution, which commits the country to environmental protection and links it to sustainable development; and Law 81 of 1997, which replaces Law 33, and designates the Ministry of Science, Technology, and the Environment (CITMA) as the principal agency in charge of advancing environmental policy and directing its enforcement.

Law 81 sets forth a three-tiered system of environmental standards and establishes the requirement of environmental impact assessments (EIAs) on new projects. Still, its enforcement provisions are weak and ill defined; it establishes no basis for the imposition of fines; and CITMA's independence of other agencies and superior bodies (like the Council of Ministers) is not established by law. Nor does it establish a procedure for remediation in the event of a negative finding.

Particularly remarkable is the lack of any independent sources of environmental investigation and civic action; as if to underscore this point, the major Cuban environmental "NGO," Pro-Natura, is physically housed in the Ministry itself. Even at a conference of U.S. and Cuban scientists in 1997 sponsored by the Inter-American Dialogue, where "consensus [was achieved] on all key issues," participants from the U.S. side could not suppress the "general impression" that "NGOs in Cuba are not independent of the Cuban government and do not play the same role in independent advocacy as NGOs in the United States." It is doubtful that they were fully reassured by the insistence of Pro-Natura's vice-president that Cuban NGOs are "independent from the government and play an extremely important role," much less that the organization "receives no funding from the government and is supported completely by contributions from individuals."[48]

Systemic and Ideological Constraints on Environmental Protection

In the 1960s and 1970s, many Western scholars were aware of serious environmental problems in Eastern Europe and the Soviet Union, but until the late 1980s, their full extent was unknown. When these problems were revealed after the Berlin Wall fell, they surpassed the scholars' worst assumptions, particularly as they related to air and water pollution and the loss of topsoil and other agricultural resources. Under Marxism's labor theory of value, natural resources were either regarded as free goods or assigned a very low valuation in economic planning, thereby creating an incentive for their wasteful exploitation. In centrally planned economies, managers tend to be rewarded by output rather than by prudent stewardship of resources, and the most serious sanctions are saved for those who have failed to fulfill assigned production quotas.

In the socialist countries of Eastern Europe, as in the Soviet Union, the ministries responsible for environmental protection were folded into the same ministries that were responsible for economic growth, and investment planning tended to favor building new production capacities rather than retrofitting older ones. Thus older plants were kept in production if they met output goals, regardless of the pollution they generated. In agriculture, the tendency was toward large-scale organization of resources, combined with the heavy use of mechanized equipment and the excessive use of pesticides. In addition, water was frequently diverted toward irrigation. Indeed, two students of Cuba have written, "Agriculture was the heaviest polluter of water and soils in the former Soviet Union." Finally, lacking any permanent interest in the land, agricultural workers had little incentive to conserve resources.[49]

Given the immense influence that Soviet economics had on Cuba's agricultural and industrial policies for nearly thirty years, it surpasses all credibility that the island's environmental regime has escaped wholly unscathed, and in fact it has not. Apart from the restoration of Old Havana, there are only three positive notes in the Cuban environmental record—the most outstanding is the government's program of reforestation, although, as we shall see, even this is not without problems. The other two are not the consequence of concrete decisions but "accomplishments" forced upon the island by circumstances beyond its control: the abandonment of plans to pursue a program of heavy industrialization, vetoed by the Soviet Union; and the collapse of the Soviet Union itself, which, by plunging the country into the austerities of the Special Period, put an end to many economic activities associated with environmentally destructive practices.

Forestry Policies

Because so much praise has been heaped upon the revolutionary government for its forestry policies, they deserve careful examination. Like most Caribbean and circum-Caribbean countries, the depletion of forestlands in Cuba has been underway since the Spanish conquest. Between 1491, the year before Columbus' arrival, and 1959, the year of Castro's assumption of power, the total amount of forest cover in Cuba declined from roughly 72 percent to 14 percent. From 1959 until 1992, according to official figures, 14,000 hectares were reforested annually, so that by the final year the cover had increased to 18 percent of national territory. This would make Cuba virtually the only country in the region that has reversed deforestation trends.

In addition, by the early 1990s, Cuba had developed a cadre of more than 1,000 forestry engineers and biologists, as well as close to 2,000 forestry technicians. It was virtually the only country in the region for whom forest management was a serious career, requiring specialized training, and (with the possible exception of Costa Rica) the only one deploying qualified personnel across virtually the entire forested land surface.

Of the resources devoted to this program there can be no doubt: between 1960 and 1990, 1.5 *billion* trees were planted in Cuba. By the late 1980s, COMARNA was claiming that for every hectare of trees logged, 16.9 hectares of new trees were being planted. Unfortunately, many errors were committed along the way. The initial emphasis was on eucalyptus, chosen because of its rapid growth pattern and because it was believed—erroneously, as it turned out—that it would help arrest soil erosion. Other species selection was likewise ill informed. For example, the casuarinas planted in the 1960s in beach areas such as Varadero, Santa María del Mar, and Guanaba for shade and esthetic reasons were responsible for "extensive erosion as their shallow and dense roots—not naturally found in these areas—interfered with normal sand shifts."[50] As a result, the trees had to be massively uprooted in the 1980s. Poor species selection resulted as well in extremely low survivability for hardwood trees planted in areas normally associated with coffee growing.

The researcher quoted above calculates that tree mortality rates in Cuba were in the range of 47 to 73 percent, depending on the density of plantings. (The Cuban government's official figure is 40 percent.) He attributes his own higher estimate to the failure to follow proper seedling care procedures, including extensive weeding, during the initial years of reforestation. Despite massive planting of fruit trees, the island has suffered persistent fruit shortages, presumably because of poor plant maintenance.

Moreover, some of Cuba's agricultural policies purposely inflicted a high mortality rate on existing tree stocks. Castro's decision to plant a green belt of coffee farms around Havana led to the extinction of many fruit orchards (as well as market gardens), though it turned out that the soil and locale of the area were inappropriate for coffee cultivation.[51] Anxious to imitate Soviet-style farming, the Cubans also uprooted numerous species to allow heavy tractors and combines to operate unobstructed over huge state farms. Land clearing tasks were assigned to mechanized military brigades, which typically "drag[ged] a chain between two tractors or army tanks, pulling along the way any vegetation they encountered."[52] One astonishing result was to nearly obliterate the island's stock of palm trees. Following clearing procedures, the land itself was subject to a heavy infusion of chemicals and fertilizers imported from the Soviet Union. Once these had done their destructive worst, the reclaimed lands were simply abandoned.

In a 1995 conservation assessment of the major ecoregions of Latin America and the Caribbean, the World Bank and World Wildlife Fund found that two of Cuba's five ecoregions—the tropical broadleaf dry forests (formerly extending across much of the island) and the flooded wetlands (the Zapata swamps)—were endangered. Of the remaining three, most broadleaf forests (found in the country's highest altitudes), coniferous pine forests (in the province of Pinar del Río and the Isla de la Juventud), and the cactus scrub (in the southeast) are considered vulnerable. The survey summarized its findings on Cuba as follows:

> In relative conservation terms, Cuba is not doing significantly better or worse than other neighboring nations. Nevertheless, the Cuban forests continue to be threatened by human activities, in particular by excessive logging, the expansion of agroforestry activities, and by slash and burn agriculture. The latter is surprising since slash and burn agriculture is usually associated with landless peasants seeking farmland, a problem not expected in a country where most land is government owned.[53]

In effect, then, Cuba's forestry accomplishments have been achieved "at a very high economic cost";[54] in proportion to investment in resources, time, skills, raw materials, and labor, the result has been at best unremarkable. Indeed, according to one specialist, "Under current conditions, . . . Cuba has limited potential in the forestry industry" and is compelled to import fully 55 percent of its wood product needs.[55] The exigencies of the Special Period may indeed have also brought an end to reforestation; in 1992, for example, only 500,000 seedlings were planted, although the target was 4 million.[56] Law 77 (1995) opened the industry for the first time to foreign investment, and Cuba was reported to be seeking foreign investors for a seedlings project. Joint ventures with European or other partners may finally provide the incentive for more responsible stewardship and produce results more proportionate to investment.

Agriculture

One of the leitmotifs of the Cuban revolution has been the expansion of the land area brought under cultivation, particularly for sugar. At the same time, the size of holdings has increased considerably, thanks to a land reform that virtually abolished large private property in agriculture. Both of these trends have had environmental implications. The rush to increase the size of land under cultivation forced the government to choose between constructing adequate drainage facilities or massive importation of chemical inputs (herbicides, pesticides, and fertilizers). It chose the latter, since chemicals and fertilizers were readily available from its Soviet partner and therefore far less expensive.

Other Soviet-inspired innovations were the introduction of heavy equipment in agriculture and the massive introduction of irrigation. Prior to the revolution, machines were used only to prepare the soil for sugar cane planting; these were light tractors that inflicted minimal damage to the land surface. By 1990, Cuba had 77,800 tractors, a total surpassed only by much larger countries such as Argentina, Brazil, and Mexico, and even COMARNA's official data conceded that 24.2 percent of the country's agricultural land was affected by compaction. (Other estimates place the number somewhat higher.)

The deterioration of Cuban soil was doubtless underway at the time of the revolution; however, subsequent economic policies have in all probability accelerated it. These include central planning practices which disregard differences in physical, hydrological, and environmental characteristics of the soils in different parts of the country; a tendency to reward political loyalty and administrative docility over technical competence; and a tendency to follow blindly the Soviet and Bulgarian models of vertical integration of crops, which precludes the introduction of alternative crops between large tracts of sugar cane because these would impede mechanized harvesting.[57] In the later years of the Cuban-Soviet alliance, an elaborate system of irrigation was created, but inadequate drainage aggravated, and in some instances produced, soil salinization.

The precise amount of soil erosion in Cuba is unknown, but in some agricultural areas it may be as high as 90 percent. Two specialists argue that the extent varies considerably, but regardless of crop, it is pervasive, affecting at least half of all cropland. It is particularly widespread but perhaps not as severe in lands planted with perennials such as coffee, cocoa, and citrus—with over 90 percent of those lands affected—but it is also highly prevalent in pastures and in lands planted with sugar cane. It is also very prevalent in tobacco plantations.[58]

Heavy reliance on chemical inputs has contributed to changes in the chemical composition of the soil and caused the "acidification of many Cuban soils,"[59] but it has also introduced highly toxic chemicals (organochlorine, for example) that are banned in the United States and other countries because they constitute a threat to human health. While this problem exists in other Central American and Caribbean countries, it is more serious in Cuba because it has relied much more heavily on chemical inputs. By 1989, approximately 34,000 tons of pesticides and herbicides were being produced or imported. Dr. José Oro, a Soviet-trained geologist who defected to the United States in 1990, claims that chemical pollution affects about a million acres of Cuban soil; of this total, some 20 percent, he claims, is severely polluted.[60]

Water

Since the revolution, the Cuban government has been actively involved in the construction of dams and reservoirs; indeed, this program is often touted as one of the most important achievements of the revolution. On paper, certainly, the statistics are impressive: between 1959 and 1987, the country's stored water capacity increased by a factor of nearly 150, from 48 million cubic meters to 7,000 million cubic meters. Even so, by the late 1980s, 1.3 million residents did not have access to running water, and 5 million were not connected to sewage systems. Water shortages are endemic in the countryside but also apparent in the city of Havana, where the piping system, installed by the U.S. Army Corps of Engineers during the second occupation (1906–1909), has deteriorated to such a degree that tourists are advised not to drink the tap water, and tankers delivering water to residents are apparent throughout the city.

To some degree this problem is the consequence of concrete political decisions. Through the early 1980s, water was free in Cuba; consequently, there was no incentive to conserve it. Also, water resources were allocated on the basis of a central plan rather than price (cost). Not until 1989 did the government institute water-pricing policies, which charged enterprises producing rice, sugar, and mixed crops for "excessive" consumption.

Moreover, the gain in reservoir capacity must be balanced against the contamination of a considerable amount of water in aquifers. That is, salinization has come to afflict significant amounts of underground water sources, partly because of overextraction and partly by retention of water in large surface stores. The result is that water flows are not being allowed to reach and recharge coastal aquifers, resulting in the infiltration of seawater.

The construction of massive irrigation systems has also reduced the amount of water flowing to aquifers, and in some places the needs of sugar, citrus, and rice have had to be served from water drawn from aquifers. The obvious result is salinization, followed by the eventual abandonment of formerly productive lands. In addition, many surface waters have been contaminated by industrial wastes and the runoff of chemicals associated with agriculture. Although the dramatic increase in irrigation and storage facilities was apparently driven by a desire to increase agricultural production, it is now lower on a per capita basis than it was in the 1950s and 1960s.[61]

Industrial Pollution

Industrial pollution has been a far less serious problem in Cuba than in Eastern Europe and the Soviet Union, partly because the country's propitious geographical and climatological situation provides a natural system to carry pollution out to sea and partly because, within the socialist international division of labor, Cuba was assigned a primarily agricultural role. Since the collapse of the socialist community of nations, the island has moved to tourism, whose impact on the environment has been relatively (though not entirely) benevolent.

Even so, the country's major industrial activity—sugar production—is a major source of pollution. The rush to expand the amount of land under cultivation led to the elimination of many creeks and wetlands, the leveling of tree fences, soil compaction from heavy equipment, waterlogging caused by improper drainage, and the generation of smoke and soot from burning fields. Mills are particularly notorious for discharging toxic wastes into neighboring bodies of water; for example, in 1985 Fidel Castro was told—much to his surprise—that shrimp no longer lived in Nipe Bay because of high levels of water pollution.

Other agricultural or agriculture-related industries are also polluters. For example, the paper industry is one of the main sources of contamination of surface waters because of the direct discharge of waste into ditches and ponds. The same is true for the production of both fertilizer and torula yeast, a form of animal feed for cattle, poultry, and swine. Waste from the Havana Club rum distillery in La Habana province has been reported to be seriously contaminating the marine shelf near Havana's eastern beaches.

Cuba's small but increasingly active mining, cement, and oil industries are likewise cause for concern. The Moa Bay nickel mining concession— expropriated from the Gulf Freeport Sulphur Company and now leased to Sherritt International Corporation of Canada—is likewise discharging large quantities of pollutants into streams, rivers, bays, and ultimately the ocean. Further environmental damage is being visited on the area by Sherritt's use of calcium carbonate in the form of coral sand in its processing procedures. It is obtained from a large reef nearby, reported to be (for the moment) the second largest in the world. All of Cuba's cement plants are significant sources of air and water pollution, but the newest plants at Mariel and Cienfuegos are reported to be particularly heavy polluters.

Since the collapse of the Soviet Union and particularly since the end of the favorable oil-for-sugar deals, Cuba has been actively searching for domestic sources of petroleum, often with the assistance of foreign investors. The rush to increase production has caused extensive damage to beaches from residues and waste products from wells drilled east of Havana. The country's three refineries, largely fitted with Soviet-era equipment, are considered among the heaviest polluters in the country. Cuba has fewer motor vehicles than the United States, but the ones it does have tend to be more polluting. This includes pre-1959 U.S.-made cars, a surprising number of which are still in operation, and Soviet and Eastern European vehicles not equipped with catalytic converters or other pollution abatement equipment.[62] The government's fleet of cars and the vehicles used by tourist enterprises, are, however, being gradually replenished with more environmentally friendly vehicles.

The Urban Environment

After the triumph of the revolution, the Cuban government made a conscious effort to discourage migration from the countryside to Havana, partly by investing more heavily in the provinces, partly by purposely neglecting to construct new housing in the capital. The result, however, has not been wholly in accordance with the original vision. Returning to Havana after a twenty-year absence in 1993, an American of leftist sympathies who had worked for the government in its early days found that the city "had approximately doubled in population . . . , Castro's socialist planning notwithstanding." Since very little construction had taken place, "congestion and pollution, along with urban neglect" were the order of the day.

Particularly striking to this visitor were the polluting Hungarian and Czech buses, which made it difficult for him to breathe in certain parts of the city. "There were even times," he writes, "when I could smell the exhaust smoke in my room on the eighteenth floor of the Havana Libre." Adding to the poisonous bus emissions were the "thick exhaust gases generated by ubiquitous Soviet Ladas and the dwindling number of old American clunkers of the fifties." Without repair facilities, most automobiles had to operate without tune-ups, adding to exhaust pollution. "In a word, emission controls did not exist in Havana or in the rest of Cuba."[63]

The pell-mell growth of the population of Havana (and indeed, of urban Cuba in general) has introduced enormous stresses on basic services. For example, 50 percent of the capital's sewer system is not functioning adequately or at all. This is particularly serious because in 1959 it was already forty years old, and the useful life of such a system is generally fifty years when properly maintained. Many of the resources that might have been devoted to upgrading the system were expended elsewhere, including wars in Africa that involved not only thousands of soldiers but also teachers, administrators, and construction workers.

A particularly unfortunate victim of Cuba's environmental policies (or lack of them) has been Havana Bay, which is now classified by the United Nations Development Program as one of the ten most polluted bodies of water in the world.[64] As long ago as 1982, two visiting Soviet experts concluded that from a biological point of view the bay itself was "practically dead," largely due to pollution from the discharge of organic matter, 70 percent of which flows through the storm drainage system and the three rivers that flow directly into the bay. Two critics of the Cuban government's environmental policies conclude that "many billions of dollars" will be necessary to modernize Havana's physical infrastructure and begin reversal of its environmental deterioration.[65]

The "Special Period" and the Environment

Ironically, the collapse of the Soviet Union and the end of Cuba's "special relationship" with the socialist community of nations has produced some benevolent (if not always intended) environmental consequences. The gradual refitting of Cuba's industrial plant with Western equipment is reducing pollution, but at a rate far slower than would otherwise be the case if foreign investment were allowed to operate as freely as it does elsewhere in Latin America. The breakup of state farms into UBPCs (Castro's current version of agricultural cooperatives), complete with the introduction of quasi-market incentives, has somewhat reshaped the attitude of farmers toward their land and equipment, which they no longer regard as entirely expendable. A sharp reduction in fuels, fertilizers, and other agricultural inputs have forced changes in agricultural techniques; instead of the heavy use of chemicals, Cubans are discovering, or rather rediscovering, the benefits of organic farming. This has led to a rush of favorable commentary from foreign visitors who seem unaware that the new agricultural model "is essentially pre-revolutionary Cuba's agricultural model."[66] Unfortunately, organic farming can only exist alongside a more productive agricultural model; alone it cannot feed a country. Indeed, the widespread use of draft animals, which draws kudos from environmentalists, is normally the hallmark of low productivity and rural poverty in backward countries.

During the early 1990s, critical fuel shortages caused the government to import hundreds of thousands of bicycles from China, which were used by citizens for their ordinary transport needs. This had the effect of both reducing pollution and improving the cardiovascular health of users. At the same time the composition of the Cuban diet—formerly high in fats and carbohydrates—changed to more fruits and vegetables (sometimes available in the new farmers' markets, sometimes from home gardens). On the other hand, as pointed out in chapter 1, the overall intake of calories declined, sometimes to dangerously low levels.

These modest advances cannot, however, fully compensate for the rush to construct tourist facilities in ecologically fragile zones, or to increase crude oil production in areas formerly considered off-limits, such as coastal areas. Cuban government representatives make much of the lack of resources, particularly since the onset of the Special Period,[67] but arguably a far greater danger to the Cuban environment comes from an excessively authoritarian political system wholly lacking countervailing forces and influences. As Dr. Wotzkow puts it, "As long as Cuba continues to languish under a government like the one it presently possesses, wholly lacking a program of environmental education, and with an army of specialists who are not allowed to freely exercise their skills, any intention to save our national patrimony will remain, as it has up till now, reduced to a modest list of recommendations with no practical import."[68]

The Environment and the Future

Contrary to the assumptions of many, both inside and outside of Cuba, a transition to another form of government in the foreseeable future is by no means inevitable.[69] Assuming that some significant changes do occur, however, a new environmental authority will face enormous tasks. Cuba's entire industrial plant will have to be reevaluated from the point of view of environmental impact, and some of the worst offenders may have to be shut down. Meanwhile, the Cuban government will have to devote large sums— as much as $236 million according to one estimate[70]—to achieve full environmental remediation. The bulk of the resources to render Cuba's industries more environmentally friendly will inevitably have to come from within, but some foreign assistance may be available. One source could well be the World Bank's Global Environmental Facility, a fund created in 1991. Recent grants to the Latin American region have targeted biodiversity, climate change, and water initiatives. The amount of money involved is not negligible; as of 1996, for example, the World Bank's overall environmental portfolio was already $11.5 billion (153 projects in sixty-two countries); moreover, such allocations leveraged an additional $14.5 billion from other sources, including the Inter-American Development Bank. As of now, however, Cuba is not a member of either institution.

Another possible source of funding might well be the United States Agency for International Development (AID). Although competition for AID grants is fierce, particularly among the poorer countries of the Caribbean Basin, Cuba is particularly well-situated geographically to receive some sort of priority, and unlike many circum-Caribbean countries, already possesses a significant eco-scientific establishment. As the conference report cited earlier emphasized, "situated just 90 miles apart and separated only by the Straits of Florida, the two countries are irrevocably connected to each other by their shared natural resources. As a result, what one country does to affect the environment has a significant impact on the other."[71] An oil spill in Cuba, for example, would affect marine life in both countries.[72] Size and proximity alone thus suggest a continuing U.S. concern with the Cuban environment. Finally, to the degree to which environmental degradation detracts from Cuba's capacity to support its population, migratory pressures on the United States, already very heavy, will be further compounded.

The issue of Cuba's environmental future is not merely one of resources, however, but also transforming the rules of the game. A new set of laws will have to prioritize environmental protection, set out procedures for remediation, and establish practicable enforcement mechanisms. Old plants will have to be allowed to operate under less stringent regulation until they can be phased out, while income from privatization (assuming that it occurs) will have to be partially earmarked for remediation projects.[73] However these challenges are addressed in practice, the environment, like so many other aspects of Cuban society, will remain subject to permanent tension between past and present, between a revolutionary history that cannot be unlived and a market-oriented future that ultimately cannot be avoided.

6

Immigration

The Coherence of Differences

Since the United States broke formal diplomatic relations with Cuba in late 1960, the one area where both countries have maintained profound, continuous, and even fruitful contact has been in the exchange of population. Indeed, it is not an exaggeration to say that immigrant issues lie at the heart of the nonrelationship, demonstrating an astonishing degree of complicity on the part of both parties along a narrow but crucial band of issues. For the United States, the benefits have been both practical and political. Initially it gained a complement of well-trained professionals and energetic business people and for many years thereafter, scored valuable propaganda points in the Cold War by pointing to the large number of Cubans who "voted with their feet" and chose to leave Castro's communist utopia. Although geopolitical circumstances have changed, the provisions that make it possible for Cubans to leave the island for the United States remain in force—frozen by laws that no Congress has yet been motivated to repeal, amplified by diplomatic accords, and consolidated by an important domestic political constituency.

For the Cuban government, U.S. openness to immigration from the island has likewise provided concrete benefits. The most important of these has been the voluntary expatriation of the country's most dissatisfied citizens, which initially permitted the rapid and expeditious consolidation of the new regime and subsequently provided a convenient safety valve against political exhaustion and disillusionment with the revolutionary project. Even today the prospect of emigration to the United States defuses pressures for political and economic change. In addition, the émigrés leave behind houses, apartments, automobiles, and other property for redistribution. Moreover, in recent years at least, remittances from the overseas community have proven an important source of hard currency for the Cuban government and have provided a social safety net for many needy families and individuals. Nevertheless, four decades of out-migration, largely to the Miami metropolitan area, have also summoned to life a kind of counter-Cuba—an alternative model of development that acts as a permanent adversary, goad, and reproach to the revolutionary government and, to some degree, to those Cubans who remain on the island.[1]

For this curiously coherent relationship between two adversaries to work, the process of population movement must occur in an orderly and predictable manner—not in occasional spurts that can quickly spin out of control, creating domestic political problems in the United States, as occurred in 1980 with the Mariel boatlift crisis.[2] It was precisely the prospect of "another Mariel" that led U.S. authorities to hammer out a new migration protocol with the Cubans in 1994. Although this accord and another, supplementary agreement reached the following year have not fully resolved the outstanding differences on migration questions, taken together, they have apparently put an end to massive and unregulated outflows of people.[3] To be sure, this happy situation can last only as long as the Cuban government is willing and able to enforce the existing agreements. Any drastic change, loss of control, or political upheaval raises once again the prospect of uncontrolled immigration—forcing the United States to revisit a series of unpleasant issues.

A Brief Policy History

Prior to the revolution, few Cubans emigrated to the United States, not only because the island was among the more prosperous of Latin American countries, but because U.S. immigration policy was based on quotas derived from the 1920 census, which included few Americans of Cuban descent. The quota system was abolished in 1965, but by that time the United States had already made it relatively easy for Cuban nationals to enter the country on a parole basis (that is to say, without visas). Even those who entered the country illegally were immediately given temporary refuge, which eventually turned out to be permanent. The new arrivals from Cuba were even given financial assistance, first under a contingency provision of the Mutual Security Act of 1954, then under the Cuban Refugee Program established by

President Kennedy in 1961, and subsequently by resources earmarked in the Foreign Assistance Act of 1962.

The latter two indulgences were originally based on the assumption that the new Castro regime would not last long and that the Cubans encamped in Florida and elsewhere in the United States would soon return to their homeland. After the failure of the Bay of Pigs expedition and other efforts to rid the island of the revolutionary government, the U.S. government was left with the task of devising a permanent status for recent Cuban arrivals. Although there is normally no way to shift from parole to immigrant status, exceptions can be made by act of Congress.[4] This is precisely what was accomplished by U.S. Public Law 89-732 (1966), better known as the Cuban Adjustment Act, which specifically states that Cuban natives or citizens who have been paroled into the United States since January 1, 1959, and have been physically present in the United States for two years (subsequently shortened to one year in the Immigration Act of 1980) may "adjust" their status and, in so doing, gain eligibility to apply for permanent residence. The benefits of this provision were automatically extended to the spouse and child of the applicant.

Between 1966 and 1994, the Cuban Adjustment Act provided the basic framework for population exchange, and indeed, about 750,000 Cuban nationals entered and settled in the United States between 1959 and 1990 alone. During this time, and particularly in the 1980s, the efforts of other ethnic and national groups to get Congress to repeal the legislation were as unsuccessful as the efforts to extend its benefits to others.[5] What finally led to a change in U.S. policy was the collapse of the Soviet Union, and with it, an end to the financially advantageous "special relationship" between Moscow and Havana. The effect on the Cuban economy was little short of devastating; by some estimates, the country experienced a 40 percent drop in Gross National Product between 1990 and 1993, and reports of hunger and even starvation were widespread.

Faced for the first time with antigovernment demonstrations, on August 6, 1994, President Fidel Castro announced that his government would no longer attempt to prevent people from leaving Cuba by sea. U.S. President Bill Clinton responded less than two weeks later by affirming that henceforth Washington would bar entry of Cuban rafters into the United States. Instead, the U.S. Coast Guard was ordered to detain rafters at sea and take them to the U.S.

naval facility at Guantánamo Bay until they could be repatriated to Cuba. Unfortunately, this bold policy announcement did not significantly stem the tide. That was not accomplished until September 1994, when Cuban and U.S. diplomats met in New York and concluded a new migration agreement. Among other things, the Joint Communiqué announced that the United States government was discontinuing its practice "of granting parole to all Cuban migrants who reach U.S. territory in irregular ways." For its part, the Cuban government pledged to "take effective measures . . . to prevent unsafe departures." To further discourage such departures, the United States committed itself to admit a minimum of 20,000 Cubans each year, based on applications submitted by relatives, classification as authentic political refugees, or successful draws in a lottery.[6]

A subsequent meeting of U.S. and Cuban officials in Toronto, Canada, in May 1995 produced further policy modifications. Cuba agreed not to encourage irregular departures and committed itself to take back those rescued at sea by the U.S. Coast Guard or others, pledging that "no action" would be "taken against those migrants returned to Cuba as a consequence of their attempt to [emigrate] illegally." (Formerly those caught attempting to escape had been prosecuted and jailed.)[7] It also agreed to accept Cuban nationals then detained in Guantánamo or elsewhere who were ineligible for admission to the United States—presumably because they had criminal records or were mentally defective. The U.S. government agreed that all other Cuban rafters would be paroled into the United States on a one-time-only basis but issued stern warnings that in the future those picked up at sea would be promptly returned.

Presumably in response to the opposition of the Cuban-American community to these accords, in subsequent years the U.S. Congress revisited legislation relating to Cuban immigration, reaffirming on each occasion its exceptional features. In April 1996, for example, the Senate voted to retain the Cuban Adjustment Act until a democratic government was in place in Havana (U.S. Public Law 104-208, Title VI, section 606). A year later, Congress went even further in the Nicaraguan Adjustment and Central American Relief Act (NACARA), specifically exempting Cubans from regulations that normally deny adjustment to migrants who enter illegally, work in the United States without authorization, or remain in the United States beyond their authorized stay.

If the Cuban Adjustment Act appears to be cast in stone, so too in a quite different way do the 1994–1995 migration accords. This much seems clear from the recent case of Elián González, a small boy who fled the island on a raft with his mother, her boyfriend, and several other adults in late 1999. One of the few survivors of the trip—his mother was among those who perished—he was plucked out of the water suffering from dehydration and sent to a hospital in nearby Broward County, Florida. Then, through an apparent bureaucratic misstep, he was paroled to relatives in Miami (technically he should have been returned to Cuba as soon as he was able to travel). Once in their custody, however, Elián's Miami kin refused to surrender him to the immigration authorities. At issue—at least to all appearances—was an extremely nasty family quarrel. The boy's father, who had remained in Cuba, demanded his return, while his great-uncle and other members of his Miami family hastily applied for political asylum on little Elián's behalf.

Their resolve found enormous resonance in the Cuban-American community and led to an exhausting process of litigation. The overarching legal question was whether a six-year-old was legally competent to decide whether or not he wished to remain in the United States as a political refugee; following judicial precedent and family law as it is practiced in all fifty states, the federal courts eventually decided that he was not, and that in a contest between a father and a great-uncle, the advantage inevitably lay with the father. In the face of continued resistance by the Miami family, at dawn on April 22, 2000, federal agents converged on the house where Elián was staying, seized him, and promptly returned him to his father, who had flown to Miami from Cuba to claim his son. Eventually the two returned to the island.

The domestic political consequences of this drama were rapidly felt. Although the overwhelming majority of Americans supported the decision of the courts, the Cuban-American community of South Florida—into which the Democratic Party had made significant inroads in the 1992 and 1996 presidential elections—turned with a vengeance upon the Clinton administration and its candidate in the November 2000 presidential election, arguably determining the outcome of an excruciatingly close national race.

Although the Clinton administration must have sensed that sending Elián González back to Cuba could well exact a significant political price in the electoral college,[8] failing to do so would not only have contravened the findings of the federal courts and long-standing INS regulations, but would also have put the Cuban government in a position to claim that the United States had violated the migration accords—a violation that constituted an open invitation to Havana to unleash "another Mariel." Indeed, Fidel Castro himself hinted as much publicly more than once during the weeks of the "Elián crisis." On balance, the risk of returning Elián to Cuba—if it was a risk—was worth taking for the Clinton administration, since the negative political consequences of "another Mariel" would have spread far beyond Florida.[9]

Cuba and Haiti Compared

At first blush it would seem that the Cuban Adjustment Act and the Cuban provisions of NACARA contradict the 1994–1995 migration agreements—the former inviting people in, the latter excluding them. It would be more accurate to say that together, they represent a compromise. The U.S.-Cuban accords continue to hold out a special status for Cubans who manage to physically touch ground in U.S. territory, but they deny it to those who do not. Since 1995 Cubans rescued on the high seas have generally been treated much as boat people from other Caribbean islands; that is to say, they have been forcibly returned to their point of origin.[10]

Ironically, the "wet foot–dry foot" distinction applies not only to Cubans but to Haitians—and for that matter, to other nationalities as well. In fact, it was originally established by an opinion drafted in 1996 by the Office of Legal Counsel at the Department of Justice in a case involving Haitians. There are, of course, some crucial differences. Haitians (or for that matter, Barbadians or Jamaicans or Dominicans) cannot "adjust" out of their parole status, and therefore remain in legal limbo in the United States. But unlike Cubans, Haitians (or Barbadians or Jamaicans or Dominicans) are free to return whenever they wish as far as their own governments are concerned. While the Castro regime now agrees to take back boat people—indeed, it insists that *all* Cubans who have fled to the United States should be promptly returned—it refuses to consider repatriation of those Cuban citizens who have been in the United States for a number of months and are therefore presumably "contaminated" by what the Castro regime is pleased to call "the Miami mafia."

The logic of this position seems somewhat elusive, given that repeal of the Cuban Adjustment Act has long constituted Havana's principal demand in migration talks with the United States. Cuban officials argue that the law constitutes an unwholesome lure that encourages its citizens to needlessly risk their lives crossing the Florida straits, supposedly on rickety vessels, many perishing in the process.[11] (In fact, the overwhelming majority of arrivals have no apparent knowledge of the law and are motivated simply by the knowledge that hundreds of thousands of their countrymen have somehow managed to settle in the United States.) In any case, a simple change in Cuban government policy—a willingness to repatriate all those who succeed in landing on U.S. territory, no matter how long they have managed to stay—would immediately deprive the United States of any justification for separate treatment of Cuban arrivals. As one U.S. immigration official explained to this writer, "Precisely because we can't return Cubans, like other Caribbean nationalities, we can't detain them; if we could return them, we could detain them for illegal entry." A more drastic turn in Cuba's fortunes—a change of political regime—would likewise call into question the necessity of a special procedure to "adjust" Cuban arrivals, and in fact the Illegal Immigration Reform and Immigrant Responsibility Act of 1996 (U.S. Public Law 104-208) even establishes the automatic repeal of the Cuban Adjustment Act once the President of the United States has "certified" that Cuba has a democratically elected government.

During the 1990s, similar arguments were used by critics of U.S. policy toward Haitian and Cuban migrants, though not at the same time or by the same people. During 1990–1991, a strict economic embargo had been imposed on Haiti to punish its military leaders for having overthrown the elected government of Jean-Bertrand Aristide. One devastating side effect was a refugee crisis, as thousands of Haitians fled their country for the United States, typically in balsa wood boats. Those who survived the journey long enough to be picked up by the U.S. Coast Guard were taken to camps in Guantánamo Bay, while members of Congress and the Bush administration quarreled over who was responsible and what to do with the rafters. Rep. Romano Mazzoli (D-Ky.) conceded that the embargo was "clearly contributing to the dimensions of the debacle in Haiti itself, the economic debacle. It obviously doesn't make it easier for people who live in Haiti who want to stay there."[12] To which Rep. Dante Fascell (D-Fla.) added, "The embargo which is now in place to force a [political] change . . . in Haiti may work some day. Meanwhile, [it] is creating a disaster for poor people," encouraging many of them to emigrate.[13]

Critics of U.S. policy toward Cuba likewise have periodically advanced the same notion that denying that country access to U.S. markets and trade has created conditions that induced many Cubans to want to leave, often under irregular circumstances. At the very least, however, Cuba's irrational economic system, which in many ways is organized to create scarcities, contributes as much or more to poverty on the island as the economic embargo.

Both Cuba and Haiti have been the subjects of the same argument concerning the morality of returning refugees to venues where governments deny citizens basic rights. "Can the administration honestly certify," demanded Rep. William Lehman (D-Fla.) in 1991, "that Haiti is now a stable and safe place for these fleeing people? I certainly doubt it."[14]

"We are moving down a very slippery slope," remarked Rep. Bob Menéndez (D-N.J.) four years later, when the subject was Cuban refugees, "when domestic anti-immigrant sentiments determine our foreign policy toward the most brutal regime in the hemisphere."[15]

"Forced repatriation by the United States of Cubans fleeing the tyranny of Castro's Cuba," added Rep. Chris Smith (R-N.J.) "is repugnant, immoral, and it is extremely naïve."[16]

"If it was wrong to return desperate Haitians to the hands of a two-year-old Haitian dictatorship," thundered Rep. Robert Torricelli (D-N.J.), "it certainly cannot be justifiable to do so to the hands of a 35-year-old dictatorship."[17]

Insofar as sanctions are concerned, important differences between Haiti and Cuba exist. The Haitian embargo was adhered to by virtually all of that country's traditional trading partners, rendering its effect far more devastating than the embargo imposed on Cuba, which is respected by the United States alone. Also, the fact that Haiti's economy is relatively open rendered it far more vulnerable to international economic pressures than Cuba's, and therefore suggested a more obvious and direct link between it and the massive flight of people. Even so, the failure of the Haitian embargo to achieve its objective—the resignation of a de facto government and an invitation to

Aristide to return to power—ultimately forced the United States to occupy the country militarily, whereas the failure of the Cuban embargo to achieve *its* objective has led to calls for its unilateral and unconditional suspension. Insofar as the purpose of U.S. policy in Haiti was to find a moral justification for returning boat people, however, the Clinton administration's decision to invade the country and reestablish the Aristide government can be justified on its own terms. On the other hand, it sets a troubling precedent for the resolution of future migration crises in the Caribbean region: if all else fails, it seems to suggest, one can always change the government of the country exporting people, by military force if necessary.

The Four Waves

Roughly 1 million Cubans have emigrated to the United States since 1959, but they do not constitute a homogeneous whole in terms of their political histories; their socioeconomic extraction; or even, increasingly, their education and racial composition. Chronology and social status are closely correlated; there is, as one student of the subject has found, "an inverse relationship between date of departure and social class."[18] The Cuban exiles arrived in four waves. The first conforms to the popular conception of Cuban exiles purveyed by the press and major electronic media in the United States—the island's wealthy, "white" elite. That is to say, it was largely composed of owners and executives of big firms, sugar mill owners, cattlemen, representatives of foreign companies, and well-established professionals. These people arrived in the United States with no intention of remaining; rather, they were convinced that it was only a matter of time before Washington toppled Castro, and many of the members of the expeditionary force that met its end at the Bay of Pigs were recruited from the sons of this group. Its numbers virtually doubled after Fidel Castro declared on December 2, 1961, that he was a "Marxist-Leninist" and quite possibly had always been one. This migration was more middle class but also included a fair number of skilled workers.

The second wave was brought to the United States between 1965 and 1974 through regular air evacuations established by joint agreement between the two governments, assigning priority to those with families already in the

United States. Even so, the process of selection was complicated, with each government producing its own lists. Cuba specifically barred the departure of professionals, technicians, or skilled workers, as well as young men of military age. Most of the people who emigrated in this wave were either working class or lower-middle class; many were encouraged to leave by the decision of the government to shut down some 55,000 small businesses, so that the motivations for departure were probably as much economic as political. Some 250,000 Cubans entered the United States in this fashion.

The third wave is associated with the Mariel affair—about 125,000, approximately 18 percent of the whole as of 1995. This group was strikingly different from its predecessors—71 percent were blue-collar workers (factory machine operators; carpenters; masons, bus, taxi, and truck drivers, for example). It was also the first group in which blacks were present in noticeable numbers. A full 19 percent of Marielitos had been in jail in Cuba, though the vast majority of these (70 percent) were ordinary criminals; the rest qualified as political prisoners. Many of the crimes for which ordinary criminals were convicted in Cuba, however, would not have been regarded as such in the United States. Although the U.S. media made much of the presence of hardened criminals, this group represented a mere 2 percent of the total.

The fourth and final wave comprises those who have trickled into the United States as boat people in the 1980s or have been granted entry permits by the U.S. Interests Section in Havana since the conclusion of the 1994 migration agreements. The latter—never less than 20,000 in any year and normally somewhat in excess of that number—are divided into three categories: (1) applicants who can claim close family relationships in the United States or are sponsored by an employer, usually on the basis of possessing special skills; (2) refugees—that is, people who can provide evidence of a well-founded fear of persecution based on race, religion, nationality, social group, or political opinion; and, the largest single category, (3) winners of a lottery drawn from a pool of people who have registered at the U.S. Interests Section in Havana. Still, the Cuban government has the final say on who is permitted to leave and who is not; mere readiness on the part of the United States to issue an entry permit is not sufficient to assure departure.

As noted, over time the kinds of Cubans moving to the United States have changed, dramatically so since 1990. Because definitions of race are different in the United States than in Cuba (and, for that matter, in the Dominican Republic, Venezuela, Panama, and Colombia), it is difficult to pinpoint the exact change in ethnic composition, except to say that the first wave of Cuban immigration was decisively "white," while subsequent waves became increasingly less so. By one estimate, as many as 22 percent of the latest wave would be regarded as "nonwhite" (e.g., black or mulatto) in the United States.

It is easier to chart the differences in education and social class. Twenty-five percent of the first wave—but only 7 percent of the Marielitos—had graduated from college. The proportion of post-1990 émigrés who are college graduates has increased to 18 percent, though the surprisingly high percentage of those without a high school diploma—28 percent—raises interesting questions about the vaunted universality of education in Cuba. Fully 32 percent of Cubans who have entered the United States since 1990 are recipients of various welfare programs—public housing or rent subsidies, food stamps, Medicaid, Supplementary Security Income (SSI), or Temporary Assistance to Needy Families (TANF). This figure is roughly similar to that of new immigrants from Mexico (32 percent) or Haiti (31 percent), but greater than that of their counterparts from Colombia (26 percent) or even El Salvador (26 percent).[19]

Moreover, the academic performance of the children of these immigrants does not augur well for the future, even when compared to those of other recent arrivals. A survey of 1,200 students of recent foreign extraction conducted in the greater Miami area in 1991–1992 (the Children of Immigrants Longitudinal Study) found that students of Cuban origin who were enrolled in public schools had one of the lowest grade point averages (2.14) in the sample, trailed only by Dominicans and Haitians. Even those students of Cuban origin who attended private schools turned in a mediocre grade point average (2.64). Even more striking is the fact that Cuban students in the Miami-Dade public schools had the highest dropout rate among children of immigrants, "a remarkable outcome," two sociologists observe, "for children of a relatively advantaged group supported by a strong ethnic enclave."[20]

A Different Kind of Immigration?

These indicators suggest what other data confirm—that Cuban immigrants are beginning to resemble arrivals from other Caribbean countries. For example, in one survey completed in 1999, a full 40.4 percent of households headed by the Cuban-born in the United States were living in or near poverty.[21] The comparable figures for arrivals from other Caribbean countries were 57.5 percent of households headed by migrants from Haiti, 63.7 percent of those from the Dominican Republic, and 48.5 percent of those from the Caribbean generally. The 28 percent of Cuban immigrants without a high school diploma (31.3 percent in this particular survey) is roughly comparable to the figure for their counterparts from Haiti (34.9 percent) and only slightly better than the Caribbean average (33.3 percent). What is particularly striking about these numbers is that fully 80 percent of the Cubans in the sample had arrived in the United States before 1990.[22]

The numbers also suggest the possibility that the principal drivers of Cuban emigration to the United States since at least the early 1990s—and quite possibly before—have been economic rather than political. This is obviously a highly controversial subject, and U.S. officials have been understandably reluctant to address it directly. When pointedly asked to comment on the distinction, Undersecretary of State Peter Tarnoff told a congressional committee in 1995, "Cubans flee the island for a variety of reasons." But he boldly added that "many of the migrants interdicted by the U.S. Coast Guard have told U.S. officials that their primary motive for fleeing Cuba was economic."[23] Secretary Tarnoff went on to explain that "Cuban migrants who claim to be fleeing for political reasons are being screened by the INS."[24] He might have added that since 1994, roughly 3,000 persons a year have been entering the United States from Cuba under this category.[25]

Additional evidence supporting Secretary Tarnoff's assessment comes from Gene McNary, Commissioner of the Immigration and Naturalization Service during the 1989–1993 Bush administration. Testifying before a congressional committee in 1991, he noted that even though all legal immigration from Cuba was suspended for a thirty-month period in the mid-1980s, when it was resumed in 1987, "even with the pent-up demand this should have caused, legal Cuban immigration to the U.S. has not exceeded 3,800 per year" since then.[26] All the other Cuban entrants for 1986–1990 (an average of 7,500 a year) were spouses or children of U.S. residents or citizens, not people requesting political asylum.[27] The sudden increase in the number of Cubans wishing to leave the island after 1991 would seem to be directly traceable to the collapse of the Soviet Union and the end of Moscow's generous subsidies to the Castro government, rather than any particular change in the Cuban political system or its treatment of ordinary citizens. Even within the Cuban-American community in Florida, recognition of the fact seems to be growing, inasmuch as a substantial plurality of Cuban-Americans polled in the mid-1990s agreed that the time had come to significantly limit immigration from the island.[28]

To be sure, the line between political and economic motivations for emigration cannot always be neatly drawn. As one authority has written, "Since all societies are simultaneously and inextricably political and economic, . . . political and economic conditions are entangled. . . . When people grow politically disaffected, when they lose faith and trust in their government and its cause, they can no longer be disposed of as simply economic immigrants."[29] Nevertheless, it is difficult to maintain that—with the exception of a few outstanding cases, usually well known to U.S. officials—those Cubans wishing to leave the island since 1994 have been motivated by a fear of explicit political persecution. Admittedly, Cubans applying for exit permits are denied the basic rights of citizens in free countries, but in this way they do not differ from the mass of their fellow citizens. Were the United States to open its doors to all those unhappy with the broad political arrangements in their countries, most of the states of the Third World would empty out.

A Larger Perspective

The willingness of the United States to accept large numbers of Cubans each year is based on a hostile bilateral relationship which sometime in the future will come to an end—either by a change of government in Cuba or the ultimate acceptance of that government by the United States. At that point, Cubans will be subject to the same filters applied to other nationalities, and also exposed to some of the questions already being raised about the desirability of current levels of immigration generally. These questions are not frivolous, nor are they wholly based—as is sometimes claimed—on xenophobia or racism.

In 2002, the immigrant population of the United States was 33.1 million, the largest ever recorded in the country's history, and a 67 percent increase over 1990. According to a study by the Center for Immigration Studies, more than one of ten U.S. residents is now foreign born, compared with less than one of twenty in 1970. Moreover, the foreign-born population is growing at roughly 6.5 times the rate of the native-born population. In and of itself this need pose no problem, but there are differences in the kind of people emigrating now compared with the past, and in the impact of these new cohorts on public services. In effect, the flood of newcomers has dramatically increased the supply of unskilled workers in the labor force (41 percent of high school dropouts in 2001 were immigrants).[30]

Moreover, current immigrant cohorts do not seem to be replicating the patterns of social mobility historically associated with new arrivals. As one demographer explained, "Today's established immigrants (those who have lived in the country eleven to twenty years) are much poorer, less likely to be homeowners, and less likely to have become citizens than established immigrants in the past." The economic position of established immigrants has declined not only in relation to earlier newcomers, but also—even more dramatically—in comparison with natives.

The Center for Immigration Studies analysis produced these startling facts: in 1970, established immigrants were actually *less* likely than natives to have low incomes (25.7 percent of immigrants were living in or near the poverty level compared with 35.1 percent of natives), whereas in 2000, the figures were drastically reversed—41.4 percent of immigrants versus 28.8 percent of natives. In 1970, established immigrants were almost as likely to be homeowners as natives (56.8 percent versus 63.4 percent); in 2000, the numbers were 45.5 percent versus 69.5 percent. In 1970, the overwhelming majority (63.6 percent) of established immigrants became citizens; thirty years later, the number hovered at 38.9 percent. In 1970, only 7 percentage points separated natives from newcomers in the rate of high school completion; by 2000, that difference approached 25 percentage points. Although all immigrants make some economic progress over time, today's newcomers start out far poorer, and declining educational attainment diminishes their long-term prospects in American society.[31]

The declining quality of foreign immigrants poses serious problems for law enforcement, housing, education, and medical services. This is particularly true in Florida, where—to quote one member of its congressional delegation—"the influx of refugees has strained access to . . . numerous vital programs that citizens of my district support with their tax dollars. Until we face the facts regarding the impact of immigration on the United States, Americans who depend on these programs will continue to be short-changed."[32] The situation has become particularly acute in the Miami area, which is fast becoming a center for illegals from all over the world, inasmuch as—in the words of one INS official—"it already has a large immigrant population, making it easy for illegals to readily disappear into existing communities."[33]

Until now, officials of state governments in warm-weather regions have attempted to address these problems by petitioning the federal government for additional funds to cushion the impact of new arrivals. As the problem expands beyond the boundaries of Florida and California to nontraditional areas, however, a national debate on immigration policy will doubtless be heard in Washington, with certain impact on all of the nations and mini-states of the circum-Caribbean, which since 1970 have been providing slightly more than a third of all newcomers to the United States. Cuba will be sheltered from this debate only as long as the current political impasse between Washington and Havana persists.

The Economic Dimension of Immigration

If the current migration agreements remain in force through 2010—which is to say, if there is no qualitative change in the nature of U.S.-Cuban relations by the latter date—the United States will have acquired at least an additional 432,000 Cuban immigrants.[34] If the newcomers continue to resemble demographically those that have entered between 1994 and 2000, they will evidently constitute a considerably poorer community than those of the first or second waves (the "historic" emigration). Still, even poor immigrants can play an important role in the economic life of their parent country, largely through remittances.

This is a subject that has only recently attracted the attention of the U.S. press and Latin American governments. Remittances from the United States, which are growing at the astounding rate of 15 percent annually, now constitute a major source of support for Latin American populations, particularly some of the poorest families and communities. According to a report prepared by the United Nations Economic Commission for Latin America and the Caribbean (ECLAC), in the year 2000, $16.5 billion was transferred to all of the countries of the region, a sum nearly equal to Cuba's Gross National Product. This figure is undoubtedly conservative, since it rests on data gathered from banks and transfer agencies and does not include dollars from family members who return home for visits, which might well double the amount.

The largest recipient is, obviously, Mexico, the country that has by far the largest number of nationals living and working in the United States. It is estimated to receive $8 billion a year from these remittances, a source of revenue second only to oil exports. But even small countries have come to rely upon such transfers. For example, in the Dominican Republic remittances are the second largest source of hard currency after tourism; in Ecuador the second largest after crude oil; in El Salvador the third largest after coffee and foreign assembly plants.[35]

There are no authoritative figures for remittances to Cuba. Some estimates run as high as $800 million or even $1 billion a year, but for reasons indicated in chapter 4, these estimates are scarcely credible. Western Union admits to transferring $49 million a year to the island; the U.S.-Cuba Trade and Economic Council in New York puts the figure at $425 million. The latter figure would presumably include cash carried into the island by visiting Cuban-Americans, currently numbering about 120,000 a year. If the latter figure is correct, remittances may well rival—or even exceed—tourism as the island's principal source of hard currency.

One recent study surveying Mexico, Guatemala, El Salvador, the Dominican Republic, and Colombia found that the governments of the countries, recognizing the value of remittances, have devised specific policies to coax even larger transfers from their expatriate communities in the United States. These include eliminating import duties on capital goods or mandatory earmarking of a portion of remittances for development funds; creating financial instruments based on remittances ("remittance bonds" in Mexico) or exempting dollar accounts from foreign exchange regulations; creating incentives to convince immigrants abroad to spend remittances on job-creating investments; and establishing government outreach to expatriate communities through the creation of hometown organizations. (In 1998 there were 400 such Mexican bodies in the United

States; the governments of El Salvador, Guatemala, and the Dominican Republic are trying to encourage their migrants to follow suit.)[36]

The role of hometown associations was vividly highlighted in one newspaper account dealing with the Mexican state of Guanajuato, which was reported to receive $800 million a year from its migrant population in the United States. "Emigrant remittances feed families," it related. "They build houses and maintain plots of land. Thousands of towns owe their infrastructure—electricity, paved streets, drinking and waste-water systems—almost entirely to the investment of millions of migrants."[37] The state's governor, Vicente Fox (now president of Mexico), launched an imaginative plan to persuade emigrants to form their own partnerships, pool their money, and start businesses in their home villages, with the state government assuming responsibility for training workers and managers. Under this program ("Mi Comunidad"), eight factories had been built by 1999, and ten more were on the drawing boards.

Remittances play a similar role in fueling small business in El Salvador. Indeed, one survey found that fully a third of the microenterprises in its sample had been established through funds from relatives in the United States. While entrepreneurial families typically draw on dollar transfers for consumption as well, the authors of the survey report were surprised to find that in El Salvador they were "much more likely to be invested in small businesses than in Mexico." Between 44 and 48 percent of remittances were invested in Salvadoran small businesses, replacing what would be bank credits, if such were normally available (which in most cases they are not).[38]

These detours through other countries are necessary to emphasize the degree to which the Cuban case diverges from broader regional trends. First, because of deep political differences, Cuban-Americans have a lower propensity to remit dollars to their homeland than do Mexican-Americans, Dominican-Americans, or Salvadoran-Americans. While the latter groups may not particularly admire the political arrangements in their homelands, they tend to look beyond them to family considerations. Second, unlike Cuba, other countries do not foreclose the possibility of a migrant returning to permanently resettle. (Indeed, probably a strong plurality of emigrants to the United States from Latin America hope to return to their homelands eventually.) The absence of a return flow to Cuba is crucial, since studies show that in many parts of the world, migrants send money home for their own use upon anticipated or actual return, including the purchase of land, housing, vehicles, and durable goods. Having foreclosed this possibility, the Cuban government assures that remittances will remain well below the economic potential of the expatriate community. Third and most important, again unlike Cuba, other countries do not typically forbid expatriates from acquiring productive assets. Finally, unlike nationals of nearby countries, Cubans cannot use dollar remittances from relatives abroad to produce sources of income through commerce, for the obvious reason that with very few exceptions (notably, home restaurants) government policy forbids the operation of small businesses.[39]

While dollar recipients in all the countries of the circum-Caribbean use part of their remittances for consumption, in Cuba people have no other choice. Moreover, because items beyond the most basic are unavailable in government stores (and sometimes not even there), Cubans who receive dollars from their relatives have nowhere else to spend them but in the so-called Hard Currency Recovery Stores (*Tiendas de Recuperación de Divisas*). It is therefore not much of an exaggeration to say that most of the remittances end up in the hands of the Cuban government and its overseas suppliers.[40] A significant change in the way that the Cuban economy is organized would, evidently, increase the multiplier effect of remittances manyfold.

Some Demographic and Socioeconomic Predictors

Paradoxically, the actual value of remittances to Cuba is directly linked to survival of the current regime—or what amounts to the same thing—the willingness of the United States to take in a floor of 20,000 émigrés each year, replenishing an expatriate labor force capable of sending money to relatives on the island. All things being equal, a change in U.S. policy—either dictated by a political transformation within Cuba or the recognition and acceptance of its existing government by Washington—would bring an end to the current migration policy. That in turn might well bring about crucial changes over time in the demography of the Cuban-American community, changes fraught with serious economic consequences.

Some sense of just what those consequences might be can be gathered from the situation that existed in 1994, which is to say, just before the current migration accords came into being. At that time, according to U.S. Census

U.S. TREASURY RESTRICTIONS: A DOUBLE-EDGED SWORD

Until early 2003, U.S. Treasury regulations restricted remittances of Cuban-Americans to their families on the island to $1,200 a year. In practice, however, it is highly doubtful that these provisos ever succeeded in limiting transfers to that relatively modest sum. Cuban-Americans can easily send additional funds through third countries. Nor is there any effective control on the amount they take into the country when visiting their families—once a year according to U.S. Treasury regulations, but in some cases probably more often, again by routing themselves through Mexico, the Dominican Republic, or other countries nearby.

Critics of U.S. policy have long argued that these travel restrictions are both unrealistic and inhumane, since they legislate how often Cuban-Americans need to visit their families without reference to concrete situations. And in artificially limiting the amount of remittances, critics have argued, U.S. policy invites Cuban-American citizens or residents to violate the law. Presumably in response to this criticism, in March 2003 the Bush administration raised the cap on remittances to $3,000 a year.

The more established elements of the exile community have traditionally opposed allowing remittances altogether—partly out of conviction that such a restriction would deprive Castro of crucial resources and lead to his early demise and partly because so few of its members (unlike more recent arrivals) still have relatives on the island. To the extent that the exile establishment favors stricter, rather than more lax, U.S. Treasury controls, it overlooks the significant role that remittances play in undermining the morale of the Communist Party's cadres and discrediting Castro's revolutionary project.

figures, the Cuban-American community was growing at a very modest rate; in 1990, its rate of increase was about 10 percent below the national average, and sharply below that of other Hispanic groups. It was also an increasingly older population, ironically mirroring the demographics of the island itself.[41] (In

1990, for example, the average Cuban-American was 37 years of age.) The same census figures reported an increasing age differential between expatriates arriving before 1980 (52.7 years) and those entering between 1980 and 1990 (38.8 years). As with older-than-average populations everywhere, the Cuban-American community was increasingly characterized by high mortality and low fertility. The economic implications of such a demographic shift are obvious—to the extent that the relative weight of the Cuban-born diminishes in the population as a whole, the share of those likely to send remittances declines.[42]

Though there are no accurate data on remittance patterns over time, extrapolating from the experience of other immigrant populations in the United States, in all likelihood there is an inverse relationship between length of residence in the United States and propensity to remit. There is some evidence that taking on U.S. citizenship also reduces inclination to send money home, an important indicator in the particular case of Cuban-Americans, who historically have a significantly higher rate of naturalization than other Hispanic groups. For the moment, these trends have been stanched by the post-1994–1995 entrants, but if the door is closed at some future date, the demographics at work in the early 1990s presumably would reassert themselves.

In theory at least, a political change in Cuba that justified shutting the door on immigration to the United States, while slowly closing off the flow of remittances, would at the same time open the floodgates of investment on the island by the more prosperous elements of the Cuban-American community. There has also been much talk of the possibility of large numbers of Cuban-Americans returning to their homeland for retirement. Such a move would have important economic implications for Cuba, just as the influx of American retirees has proven to be a major source of hard currency for Costa Rica, and to a lesser degree, parts of Mexico.

In fact, however, these happy prospects depend upon political imponderables. A flood of Cuban-American investment is likely to occur only if the government in Cuba decides to accept the active participation of the exile community in the island's reconstruction, an eventuality which in turn is mortgaged not only to the future character of the regime in Havana but the regime's own reading of the country's recent history. Nor is it at all certain that members of the Cuban-American elite will find the future government of the island sufficiently to their taste to want to invest large sums of money in the country or even to settle on the island in their declining years. This is a point to which we shall return in the next two chapters.

The Impact of Normalization

But assuming normalization of relations—for whatever reason—what form is the U.S.-Cuban immigration regime likely to assume? As a "normal" country, deprived of the special status provided by the Cuban Adjustment Act, Cuba may find itself in approximately the same situation as the Dominican Republic. Like Cuba, the latter was ruled for decades by a personalist dictator—in this case, Generalissimo Rafael Trujillo Molina—who generally prohibited his people from leaving the country without his permission.[43] After Trujillo's assassination in 1962 and the dismantling of his military-police apparatus, there was a sudden burst of legal migration to the United States—93,292 in the 1961–1970 period alone, more than *nine* times the figure for 1951–1960. In the 1971–1980 period, the number of Dominican immigrants was 148,135. After increasing to 252,035 between 1981 and 1990, the number of Dominican arrivals in the United States between 1991 and 1996 held relatively stable at 254,832.[44]

To be sure, several broader trends lie behind these numbers. The massive influx of Dominicans in the 1960s was similar to that of other Caribbean nationalities, all of whom benefited indirectly from the change in rules that had been biased in favor of countries already well represented in the U.S. population. At the same time, the subsequent leveling off since 1991 can be attributed to stricter immigration rules and more effective enforcement mechanisms, as well as means tests established in 1996 and 1998 for families who wish to sponsor relatives. The impact of the latter has been considerable, according to one study at least, which found that between 40 and 46 percent of Dominican families in the United States do not have enough income to qualify for an immigrant visa for a member of their families.[45] As a result, fully 72 percent of the applications at the U.S. consulate in Santo Domingo are rejected.[46] Admittedly, these statistics deal only with *legal* immigration. The sheer size of the Dominican community in the New York metropolitan area alone (more than a million persons) suggests that the flow has been stanched somewhat less effectively than the official numbers would suggest.

Another useful point of reference might well be Nicaragua, a country that underwent a revolutionary experience in the 1980s inspired by—and in many respects at least partially replicating—the Cuban example. When the ruling Sandinista Front was voted out of office in 1990, individual Nicaraguans were deprived of any reasonable claim for political asylum in the United States. One major difference between Cuba and Nicaragua bears emphasis here, however: there was never a Nicaraguan version of the Cuban Adjustment Act. Contrary to complaints at the time by human rights groups and church-related organizations, "anti-Communist" Nicaraguan entrants were not granted preference over Salvadorans, Guatemalans, or Hondurans, all of whom claimed to be fleeing from "right-wing governments, military establishments, or death squads" in their countries. Indeed, the sheer multiplicity of appeals for political asylum during that decade finally led the Immigration and Naturalization Service to create an Asylum Corps whose specific task was to sort out appeals on a case-by-case basis.

The failure to establish a clear route to immigrant status for Nicaraguans—and indeed, other Central Americans—meant that by the end of the Sandinista regime and the civil wars in Guatemala and El Salvador in the early 1990s, several hundred thousand citizens of these countries languished in legal limbo in the United States. The Nicaraguan and Central American Relief Act of 1997 (NACARA) provided relief from deportation and rendered eligible for adjustment to the status of "permanent resident alien" those who could establish that they had been continuously resident in the United States since December 1, 1995, and met other qualifications of the Immigration and Nationality Act.[47] Presumably most of these people were resident in the United States well before that date. Those who have entered since then are subject to deportation.

The Dominican and Nicaraguan precedents are of limited value for extrapolation in the Cuban case, but they are the only models currently available. Predicting future immigration policy toward Cuba is complicated yet further by the uncertain nature of its impending political transition. If it is peaceful and orderly, it will be possible to lift the special rules that apply to Cubans in good conscience and with minimum turmoil. If the transition is violent and chaotic, new pressures will arise within the United States and within the island itself to sustain or even broaden existing exceptionalities. This will be particularly true if there is no firm authority in Havana with whom the United States can effectively deal. Even in the best of cases, lifting the current authoritarian restraints is bound to encourage many Cubans to attempt to migrate precipitously to the United States, rather than wait out an economic and social reconstruction process that—even if successful—is likely to be protracted. It is also possible that there will be no transition in Cuba at all—none, at least, in qualitative political or economic terms.[48] Under those circumstances, one must assume that the existing migratory arrangements will be perpetuated.

Or perhaps the outcome will be neither full continuity nor complete rupture with the past. Following the death or incapacitation of President Fidel Castro, there might be an adjustment (as opposed to a change) in political leadership and a moderation in the tone of public discourse, combined with minimal economic changes and a modest opening to some elements of civil society. At that point, U.S. policymakers might well be tempted to measure migration policy against its contributions (or lack of them) to the island's overall political stability. In that sense, the issues posed by Cuban migration might well come to resemble those of Haiti, the Dominican Republic, or the Windward or Leeward islands—different from them only in Cuba's greater geographical proximity to the United States and the collective memory of a massive exchange of populations that will probably be slow to die.

7

Civil Society

Communist "Civil Society"

In 1958, Cuban civil society—judging by the number and variety of organizations normally associated with the term—was extremely dense. It included not merely business associations and labor federations, but tenants on the great sugar estates, as well as professional organizations *(colegios)* representing lawyers, physicians, engineers, architects, and so on. In addition, the island possessed myriad fraternal and mutual aid associations based on ties to different regions of Spain, from whence many Cubans or their parents or grandparents had emigrated in the early years of the twentieth century.

At the same time, however, Cuban civil society was not particularly coherent—which is to say that in many cases it did not effectively convey the sentiment of individuals and small groups to the structures of authority. Rather, Cuban civil society could be seen as a series of "ink blots," some overlapping, others completely unrelated, many holding entirely different visions of what the country was supposed to be. In some ways this was merely one more aspect of the crisis of political legitimacy that afflicted the old Cuba. With no agreement on who should govern or to what purpose, civil society was more an exercise in *sauve qui peut* than a common project to which different organizations could lend their support.

After 1959 the old civil society was replaced with a Communist version that was precisely the opposite—extremely coherent, fully inclusive, but at the same time very thin in real content and driven from the top down rather than the bottom up. Although far better organized than its predecessor, Communist civil society cannot be said to have—or to aspire to—much of a life of its own. Rather, the idea to is to group Cubans into organizations that, officially at least, all share the same vision and the same objective, broken down according to their group identity (youth, women) or occupation (farmers, laborers, intellectuals). With the onset of the "Special Period" in 1991, some space was opened up for genuine nongovernmental organizations in Cuba, but, as will be seen, the government's tolerance for them has been extremely limited. Indeed, one might say that as of today they have either ceased to exist as independent actors or operate semi-clandestinely.

Paradoxically, over the last decade some elements of Cuban civil society, in spite of their evident fragility and in some respects artificiality, have forged significant and growing links to groups within the United States. Given the extremely restricted range of independent activity permitted on the island, it is perhaps not surprising that so many of these U.S. organizations share wholly or in part the Cuban government's vision of what civil society should be (for Cuba, at any rate). Under those circumstances, it is intriguing to speculate what role they can and will play if and when what Latin Americans call the *fuerzas vivas* are ever allowed to find full, open, and independent expression. The same question can be posed, though in radically different ways, with respect to the Cuban-American community in the United States, which has thrust itself forward as a kind of Cuban civil society in absentia. This chapter identifies and analyzes those elements relevant to the reconstruction of some sort of civil society in Cuba and then speculates on their future role.

The Roman Catholic Church

One of Rome's oldest ecclesiastical provinces in Latin America, the Cuban church is also the only institutional survivor of the pre-1959 order. Indeed, it alone possesses "the organization, popular constituency, and external support system that could enable it to become a counterweight to Cuba's strong state."[1] This is somewhat ironic, given that prior to the Castro revolution the Catholic Church was one of the weakest of the major institutions buttressing the established order. Although most Cubans were formally Catholic in 1959, the church had not sunk very deep roots into the society, having associated a bit too conspicuously with Spanish rule during the struggle for independence in the late nineteenth century, and with the upper-middle and upper classes after the advent of the republic. Moreover, from the late nineteenth century onward, the church had to contend with the increasing secularization and Americanization of Cuban society, as well as competition from *Santería,* a syncretic Afro-Cuban cult that enjoyed a large following among Cuban blacks (and—to a perhaps surprising degree—among some whites as well), and also, particularly after the U.S. occupation in 1899–1901, from numerous Protestant denominations, many of which enjoyed close relations with parent synods or conventions in the United States. Moreover, whereas the totality of *Santero* "priests" and the near totality of Protestant pastors were native-born Cubans, much of the Cuban Catholic clergy was made up of expatriate Spaniards.

In what turned out to be a serious tactical error, the Cuban Catholic hierarchy confronted the Castro regime frontally on the subject of Communism very early on—even before the revolution had publicly announced its final ideological destination. This gave the new government the excuse it needed to launch a devastating counterattack. In 1961, all private and religious schools were ordered closed except for seminaries; more than 100 foreign priests were expelled from the country; and nearly 500 more (accused by Castro of being Falangists) would depart the following year, when the new Cuban constitution formally declared the country an atheist state. For nearly three decades, the Catholic Church in Cuba was barely tolerated, and those of its followers who chose to practice their faith were openly subject to serious political and social disabilities. The Vatican and the local hierarchy, recognizing the weakness of their position, sought to concentrate on mere survival.[2]

The patience of both was rewarded in 1991, when the collapse of the Soviet Union and the onset of the Special Period plunged the island into a crisis as much spiritual as economic. The Marxist faith for which so many Cubans had for decades sacrificed their well-being, and in some cases their lives, was revealed to be hollow. As a result, there was a sudden burst of interest in religious life, and—unusual in Latin America—a burst of vocations for the priesthood and for women's religious orders.[3] Monsignor Roberto González Nieves, archbishop of San Juan, Puerto Rico, visiting the island for the first time since 1989, told the *Catholic World News* (March 12, 2001) that whereas on his previous trip "the churches were all empty, . . . at present [they] are filled with Catholics, especially young people." There has also been an explosion of primitively produced church publications, small in print runs but eagerly sought.[4] Perhaps by way of response, in 1994 the Vatican awarded a red hat to Monsignor Jaime Ortega, archbishop of Havana.

Both the regime and the church have adjusted to this new reality with considerable circumspection. The Vatican and the Cuban hierarchy, taking a longer-range view, are more interested in consolidating and slowly expanding the gains the church has made among the population than confronting the government. Indeed, some observers claim to perceive a definite muting of Cardinal Ortega's criticisms of the regime since his elevation,[5] and according to one authoritative report, "The church keeps [political] dissidents at arm's length. . . . For now, the church is playing a waiting game, pushing when it can, retreating when it seems prudent."[6] Its current agenda is reasonably modest—to expand its social programs, gain greater access to media, and obtain permission to import as many priests as it wishes from dioceses overseas.

For its part, the government has at times chosen to bend slightly to accommodate the church. Thus, in 1991 the Communist Party for the first time dropped its ban on membership for professing Christians, and the following year amended the Cuban constitution, declaring the country a "secular" rather than an "atheist" state. In 1996, President Fidel Castro was formally received by Pope John Paul II at the Vatican, where he invited the pontiff to visit Cuba. That historic event, which took place in January of the following year, was also the occasion for Christmas to be celebrated on the island for the first time since the early 1960s.

The sudden improvement in church-state relations was also due to an abrupt economic necessity on the part of the Cuban government. During the first half of the 1990s, the government permitted the church—the only nongovernmental organization with access to significant overseas resources—to fill the growing gap in social services. But government-church relations have deteriorated since the legalization of the dollar in the second half of the 1990s and the opening of the island to tourism and foreign investment—all of which have increased the resources at the disposal of the government, if not the population at large. The apparent opening that culminated in the Pope's visit has slowly begun to close. On a visit to Miami in 2001, Archbishop Adolfo Rodríguez of Camagüey spoke of "a certain regress, a freeze, . . . a wintering of relations."[7] Conceivably he was referring to policies outlined in an internal Communist Party document leaked shortly before to the Italian press agency ANSA. Therein Cuban government authorities complained of "religious interference in the area that forms part of the conquests of the Revolution for the benefit of the population"—charitable work, for example—and reiterated their determination to place new obstacles in the way of the church. The document also cited such intolerable transgressions as the use of donated [illegal] computers.[8]

In recent times, the government has reportedly turned down requests to establish permanent feeding sites for the poor, to purchase food or supplies wholesale, or in some cases to bring in priests from abroad. "Money isn't the problem," one lay leader told an American Catholic journalist during the preparations for the Pope's visit. "The problem is that the government won't allow us to purchase the things we need: paper, printing equipment, and so forth."[9] There is an iron logic to these restrictions. As one source close to the hierarchy explained, "The government sees the church as the only real opposition party in the country. It's the only dangerous one."[10]

Central to the church's new role in providing social services is Caritas, a Catholic relief organization based in Rome with branches in more than one hundred countries. Established in Cuba in 1991, it has branches in each diocese. It renders services to the elderly, to infants, especially those affected by Down's syndrome, and to young people afflicted by HIV/AIDS. It also distributes much-needed medicines unavailable in Cuban public clinics. These benefits have been financed almost entirely by donations from abroad; as of 1999 Cuba's Caritas had received some $20 million in donations from U.S. and European donors, roughly half from the U.S. Catholic Relief Services.[11]

The relationship of Caritas-Cuba to the government has always been problematic. An American academic generally sympathetic to the Castro regime admits that Caritas is "uncomfortable" with the requirement that the Cuban government be the final distributor of donated products but rather sunnily concludes that "the charity seems satisfied that donations are generally used for their designated purposes. In fact," she goes on to say, "the Caritas monitoring network is acquiring such a solid reputation that other NGOs have asked it to evaluate end-use of their donations, too."[12] A delegation from the Dutch pacifist organization Pax Christi, which visited the island repeatedly in the 1990s, formed a very different impression. On its fifth visit in 2000, it reported that Caritas was "always forced to set aside for the State an ever-changing percentage of the foreign donations received (medicines, food)." And it added that "many goods are stolen as soon as they reach the airport or harbor," though by whom—government functionaries or private individuals—it did not specify.[13]

The relationship between the Cuban church and its U.S. counterpart has been unusually close for some time. As long ago as the 1980s, American Catholic bishops were permitted to visit the island, and some of their Cuban counterparts have likewise been allowed to come to the United States. These exchanges have often been marked by considerable candor. For example, on a visit to Miami in May 1995, Cardinal Ortega called upon the exile community there to put aside "old quarrels, their sad and painful memories, and practice forgiveness."[14] The United States Catholic Conference (now consolidated with the U.S. Conference of Catholic Bishops) has strongly opposed the U.S. trade embargo, arguing that "getting that issue off the table could clear the way for more constructive dialogue and negotiations that must take place." This is, of course, the view of the Vatican itself, and—conveniently enough—coincides with that of the Cuban government. However, the same document goes on to state that

> the Catholic Bishops of Cuba are under no illusion that the end of the sanctions imposed by our government will usher in a time of economic prosperity for their people. They do know, however, that retaining the sanctions continues to hurt only the most vulnerable sectors of that society, and provides the regime with propaganda advantages it does not deserve.

And it adds that "we should be clear that whatever motives others may have in ending the embargo, we are not advocating 'a softer stance' toward Castro, or looking for an illusory reconciliation with the present regime. . . . We are well aware of the many limitations on the freedom of the Church and other parts of civil society, [and] of the routine violations of human rights and limitations on freedom of speech and assembly."[15] A combination of prudence, discretion, incrementalism, and a clear focus on long-term goals (along with a refusal to surrender on basic matters of principle) positions the Catholic Church in Cuba advantageously for the future, whether its interlocutor turns out to be the present government or something quite different.

Other Religious Bodies

At the time of the Castro revolution, the Protestant churches on the island were numerous but small in size, divided, and relatively new to the country. They were also politically vulnerable since most were closely associated with denominations based in the United States. As a result, many of these churches thought it the better part of valor to accept the regime or even actively support it. These "accommodationist" denominations played a major role in founding the Cuban Ecumenical Council (now the Cuban Council of Churches), which includes the Salvation Army, Quakers, Free Baptists, Episcopalians, Methodists, and Reformed Presbyterians. A small number of charismatic and evangelical churches—basically neutral or apolitical—enjoy observer status on the Council, but most bodies of this persuasion remain outside of it. The Council churches jointly support a Protestant Theological Seminary in Matanzas, which over time has developed a full theology in favor of the revolution—ironically, a curriculum not very different from that taught in similar institutions in the United States.

The creation of a convention of Protestant churches favorable to the revolutionary regime was in some ways a hollow victory for the government. In the early days, some ministers refused to cooperate and served long terms in prison; many of the laity refused to follow the lead of the more tractable members of the clergy, and either went into exile or ceased to participate in the affairs of their denomination. The Baptist Convention of Western and Eastern Cuba, historically affiliated with the U.S. Southern Baptists, flatly refused to join the Cuban Ecumenical Council, though in traditional Leninist fashion, the revolutionary government succeeded in hiving off several pro-regime ministers in the late sixties who subsequently founded their own version of the denomination. The most publicly visible of these, Reverend Raúl Suárez, director of the Martin Luther King, Jr. Center in Havana (and also a deputy in the National Assembly) is frequently produced for the delectation of foreign visitors as an example of the regime's tolerance for religious activity.

Since 1991, all denominations in Cuba have experienced a large increase in membership, though precise figures are unavailable. In 1994 a poll published in the *Miami Herald* found that 20 percent of the Cuban population attended either a Protestant or Catholic service at least once a month. Estimates of the number of practicing Protestants vary widely—from 1 million to 2 million; in either case, the figure would be a historic high.[16] Much of this growth is probably among independent churches, since the Council embraces only twenty-five of fifty-four denominations active on the island. Evangelical or charismatic Christianity has taken a particular hold among Afro-Cubans, as well as the young and the poor generally. This version of Protestantism is appealing both for its chiliastic and deeply spiritual content, as well as its lack of interest—indeed, its very rejection—of all things political.

An even more interesting development is the growth of "home churches" (*casas culto*), small groups of individuals who meet for religious services in private residences. This phenomenon undoubtedly reflects both a deep spiritual need and at the same time a rejection of the compromised clerical establishment. According to one estimate, since 1990 some 10,000 home churches have sprung up across the country. If each had roughly a dozen members, several hundred thousand Cubans would be participating in these religious groups. The government has begun to monitor and in some cases disband such bodies, often for violation of fire codes or other apparently extraneous reasons.[17] They are now subject to new restrictions; for example, they cannot buy electrical goods such as fax machines or photocopiers, or even more practical items such as cribs, cooking utensils, or soap.

The Cuban Council of Churches (CCC) continues to enjoy the government's political favor in meaningful ways; for example, the Cuban government has designated it as the only agency allowed to import and distribute Bibles. Even more important, Council churches are often permitted to administer shipments of food aid from abroad. Conversely, in 1994, the government ousted several U.S.-based mission organizations that were not associated with the Council and had been bringing in not only religious literature but also clothes, medicine, soap, and even automobile parts.

The CCC also enjoys the full support of its U.S. affiliate, the National Council of Churches of Christ in the U.S.A. (NCC)—a body that unites thirty-six Protestant, Anglican, and Orthodox denominations. Since 1992, its charitable affiliate, the Church World Service, has provided more than $7 million in humanitarian aid to be funneled to the Cuban people under CCC auspices. Like the U.S. Catholic Church, the NCC has frequently called for an end to the economic embargo and a policy of "constructive engagement"; unlike the former, however, over the years the latter has consistently supported the Cuban government and refused to criticize the political treatment of its citizens. On a "fact-finding" mission in 1999, its delegation reported discussions on human rights issues thusly: "The question and definition of human rights came up in several conversations, particularly with the 'dissident' trial going on at that time. Comparisons were drawn to the number of political prisoners in the U.S., some with very long sentences. Concern about the continued arms race and nuclear capacity of the U.S. was also raised."[18] At least to judge by its report, the delegation saw no reason to question this line of argument. The placing of the word dissident in quotation marks is likewise telling.

Another Protestant religious organization in the United States warmly sympathetic to the Castro regime is of interest mainly for folkloric reasons. Pastors for Peace was founded in 1988 by Rev. Lucius Walker, an African-American minister and former official of the NCC who had been let go some years earlier due to involvement in financial irregularities. (He blamed his dismissal on the NCC's alleged "drift to the Right.") Since 1992, Walker has organized "Friendship Caravans" of humanitarian aid with a view to delivering them to government-friendly churches in Cuba. The confrontational nature of the Pastors for Peace arises not from the content of its shipments but its refusal to apply for a U.S. Treasury license (which would be readily granted). The ensuing scuffles on the Canadian and Mexican borders—often lavishly publicized by the media—have provided him (and the Cuban government) with valuable publicity and also helped to spread confusion in the United States about the precise dimensions of the embargo.[19]

In a different political context—which is to say, one far more open than presently exists—it is possible that Cuban religious life would be significantly changed by the entry of denominations currently proscribed from activity on the island. One religious publication in the United States reported that some American evangelicals have been making covert trips to Cuba. An evangelist from Jacksonville, Florida, was quoted to the effect that "as soon as freedom comes, I will move in a matter of days to set up outdoor crusades with various pastors." Similar plans are envisioned by Campus Crusade for Christ, Open Doors with Brother Andrew, and Youth with a Mission.[20] While it is difficult to predict what kind of a reception such groups could expect, their presence on the island would significantly broaden the lines of religious communication with the United States. At a minimum, the complaisant relationship that the National Council of Churches in the United States has maintained with the Castro regime could exact a rather high institutional price once Cubans are allowed to make freer choices.

The syncretic Afro-Cuban cults play a more ambiguous role. These religions have been a crucial part of national life since the eighteenth century, when African slaves began to practice them openly. The three major versions— Santería, Palo Monte, and the Abakua secret societies—were never extinguished by the revolution, even during its most militantly antireligious phase. By the 1980s, the government had no choice but to conclude a compromise arrangement that allowed these religions to be practiced in private. The dispatch of combat soldiers to Angola in the 1970s and 1980s is said to have led to a heightened interest in Afro-Cuban religions, particularly among black and mulatto military personnel. The collapse of the Soviet system and the onset of widespread scarcities on the island in the early 1990s even led many Cuban whites to seek solace in these cults.

So significant was this development that the Ministry of Interior set about penetrating them by assigning undercover agents. At the same time, the Religious Affairs Department of the Communist Party set aside economic benefits for individual priests prepared to be cooperative. Academic institutions and museums were ordered to mount a widespread public relations campaign emphasizing the important contribution of Afro-Cuban cults to the nation's culture—an "anthropological" approach intended to defuse any potential political implications such movements might otherwise pose. Meanwhile, Babalaos, a pro-government version of Santería, enjoys a relationship of privilege with the state similar to, say, Reverend Suárez's schismatic version of the Baptist Church.[21]

Race

As one of the three great slave societies of the Western Hemisphere, Cuba has inevitably faced a serious racial question throughout its history. The presence of a potential black majority of citizens was one of the principal factors causing the Cuban Creole elite to maintain its loyalty to metropolitan Spain well into the first decades of the nineteenth century. Fear of "another Haiti" drove many Creole planters to seek annexation to the United States as a slave state in the 1840s and 1850s. Indeed, even during Cuba's First War of Independence (1868–1878), the principal political figure of the day, Carlos Manuel de Céspedes, repeatedly urged U.S. intervention "as a means of impeding the influence of blacks in a future republic."[22]

During the Second War of Independence (1895–1898), some 75 percent of the ground forces fighting the Spaniards were black, though only 25 percent of their officers. The sudden entry of the U.S. Army into the fray in the last weeks of the conflict arguably upset the emerging balance of power within Cuban society. Two years of U.S. military occupation and the forced demobilization of the patriot army effectively neutered whatever political leverage Cuban blacks might have obtained from their role in the struggle. While all of the subsequent ills of Cuban society can hardly be attributed to U.S. intervention, in its absence the emerging political elite—faced with a victorious liberation army composed largely of blacks—would have been restrained from reducing Cubans of African origin to second-class citizenship. Instead, the new "professional" Cuban army formed after 1901 deliberately discriminated against blacks, particularly in the officer ranks.

As early as 1907, some black veterans of the independence war sought to redress their grievances by forming an Independent Party of Color (PIC). Among other things, this organization called for an end to discrimination in public accommodations and appointments in the army and diplomatic service, as well as an end to the ban on nonwhite emigration. At its peak the party boasted some 60,000 members. In retrospect its demands seem remarkably moderate. Like the early civil rights movement that emerged six decades later in the United States, it embraced an "integrationist" vision, which is to say, it did not advocate a separate Afro-Cuban culture.[23]

Even so, the white political establishment in Cuba viewed the party's rise with extreme foreboding. When the PIC called for a violent protest in 1910 against the refusal of an American hotel in Havana to admit blacks, Senator Martín Morúa Delgado, himself a black, was persuaded to sponsor legislation in the Cuban congress that prohibited racially based parties. Two years later another riot—this time specifically aimed at the Morúa Law—gave the government the excuse to send in the army, which massacred many blacks, including some not directly involved in the protest. The 1912 bloodletting effectively removed blacks as corporate political actors in Cuban politics until the 1930s, when the Communist Party made an open effort to recruit them on an explicitly racial basis.[24]

Unlike the United States of the same period, there was no official racial segregation in the old Cuban republic.[25] Blacks were not forced to recur, regardless of their economic situation, to separate (and inferior) systems of education, transportation, or medical care. But they did not have access to well-paying jobs in either the private or public sectors; they did not attain mid-level positions in the military until the mid-1930s; and they were never diplomats, ministers, or higher-level functionaries. Rather, they were largely "shoe-polishers, cooks, domestics, gardeners, newspapers vendors, or poorly paid musicians."[26] Some exclusive resort areas, as well as private clubs, were closed to blacks until 1959, a practice that was technically illegal but never corrected. After the revolution of 1933, however, the security forces were opened to Cubans of African origin, particularly the middle ranks of the police, but also some of the higher posts in the army. The most outstanding example was strongman General Fulgencio Batista himself, regarded with contempt by the Cuban upper class for his obviously nonwhite racial origins. Indeed, Enrique Patterson has observed that much of the early support for Fidel Castro came from wealthy (and white) Cuban businessmen and society leaders who resented the crude and brutal rule of a "black" dictator![27]

One of the proudest—and most controversial—claims of the 1959 revolution is that of having eliminated racism in Cuba altogether. Rather remarkably, however, race was one of the very few subjects not touched upon by Fidel Castro in his marathon speech ("History Will Absolve Me") at his trial in 1956, and the discourse of the regime since then has been broadly "integrationist." As historian Carlos Moore puts it, "Castro's exclusive emphasis on the goal of racial integration was entirely consistent with the Latin model of race relations." What set him apart from previous Cuban politicians, he adds, "was his determination to implement the ethnic code of that model to its fullest integrationist implications."[28] Although all segregated hotels and beaches were eliminated after Castro's triumph, blacks were the only people in Cuba—in contrast to the Chinese, Arabs, or Jews—that were not permitted to organize into corporate groups under Communist Party control.

"Again, as in the Republican era," Patterson observes, "blacks could only advocate their positions as students or farmers, but never as blacks, the social construct within which they found themselves being the one most vulnerable to discrimination."[29]

In this regard, the Castro regime has broadly resembled all preceding Cuban governments. As historian Alejandro de la Fuente of the University of Pittsburgh explains, "A candid discussion of race is generally unwelcome among white Cubans, who frequently claim that racism has never been a problem on the island, that its open discussion will only serve the divisionist purposes of the enemy, however defined."[30] One of the most remarkable aspects of this practice has been the tendency to underestimate drastically the actual size of Cuba's black population. The national censuses of 1907, 1919, and 1931 all placed it at roughly 28 percent, a figure presumably calculated in part by separating mulattoes from blacks. The combined black-mulatto result in the 1953 census, however, was 34 percent. Somewhat remarkably, the 1981 census increased the percentage of people of color by a mere 5 to 6 percentage points. The credibility of this finding is drastically undercut by the fact that between 1960 and 1970, some 500,000 Cubans (96.4 percent of whom were white) left the island, and another 125,000 (80 percent of whom were white) left in the 1980 Mariel exodus.[31] As two French journalists who resided in Cuba throughout the 1990s remark, "One need only step outside the door and take a stroll anywhere in Cuba to see that the reality is quite different. The tendency in fact would be exactly the reverse, two thirds of Cubans are people of color, roughly a third are white."[32]

In some ways, Cuba resembles the United States and Brazil, two other countries with large African-descended populations, while in other ways it differs from them markedly. A comparison in each case is illuminating. Like the United States, the revolutionary government has embraced the goal of "color blindness"; but unlike it, Cuba claims to have fully achieved its objective and therefore is not in need of "affirmative action."[33] In the United States, everyone is black who is perceived to have African blood, however much or however little. In Cuba, as in many Latin American countries, the criterion for determining blackness is very nearly the opposite. In fact, Cubans are allowed in the national census to pick their own racial identity, which leads people "to regard themselves as a shade or two lighter than they really are."[34] Such practices make it more difficult to determine who is, and who is not, a victim of racism.

In Brazil the ambiguity of *mestizaje* creates a large intermediate category (neither white nor black), which "neutralizes racial identification among non-whites"—and, in the opinion at least of one anthropologist, "promot[es] racial discrimination while simultaneously denying its existence." Many mulattoes (called *morenos* in Brazil) are reluctant to abandon their interme-diate identity for what appears to them the limiting exclusiveness of "black-ness." Presumably some of the same pressures are at work in Cuba. At the same time, however, it is difficult for black groups in Brazil "to establish dia-critical emblems of black culture because, under the canopy of racial democ-racy, many [national] cultural touchstones that can be traced back to Africa have become symbols of Brazilian nationality."[35] In the Brazilian case these include feijoada (a spicy stew), the samba, and a balletic martial art. Similar examples in the Cuban case could be derived from folklore, music, popular turns of speech, and, of course, syncretic religious practices.

In evaluating the status of blacks under the revolutionary government, it is essential to bear in mind the historical context. All social revolutions create new opportunities for previously submerged groups, particularly when, as in the Cuban case, they are accompanied by the massive emigration of the middle, upper-middle, and upper class. After 1959, an occupational vacuum in Cuba created by the departure of hundreds of thousands of Cuban professionals, administrators, and government officials inevitably opened avenues to groups that had been historically underrepresented in certain occupations. That—and a generalized tendency toward leveling social differences generally—produced a situation during the first three decades of the revolution where the racial divides in education and the labor market were dramatically smaller than those in the United States and Brazil. Somewhat surprisingly, however, one study produced in the 1990s found persistent inequalities in the racial dis-tribution of different occupations; for example, 13 percent of whites were found in managerial positions, compared with 7 percent of blacks and 9 per-cent of mulattoes. The study also found a strong correlation between race and the quality of housing stock. (Because so little new housing had been constructed over the years, most blacks remained in the inferior dwellings where they—or their parents or grandparents—resided in 1959.) Blacks and mulattoes were also overrepresented in the criminal population.[36] At the same time, only three of the thirty-six principal leaders of party and state were of recognizable African origin.[37]

To be sure, manifestations of racism became socially unacceptable after 1959—at least in public. On the presumption that Cuba's problem had been "solved," the very subject of race disappeared from public discourse altogether, except when invidious comparisons were drawn to other societies (e.g., the United States or South Africa). Simply to cease to talk about a problem does not necessarily mean, of course, that it no longer exists—a point that has not escaped certain African-American observers. One, for example, writing in the late 1980s, complained that in spite of official policy, "white supremacist values" had survived in Cuba, "propelled by an inner dynamic of their own." He cited continued stereotyping of blacks in popular references with regard to "sex, song, spree, sports, sloppiness, shiftlessness and sorcery," and the fact that black faces rarely appeared in the print media. As elsewhere in Latin America (and the United States as well), the educational system was European in orientation, which meant that "ballet is culture but we are folklore." Also, he asserted, African religions were given less toleration, respect, and status than the Roman Catholic or Protestant cults.[38] Another African-American journalist who visited the island thirteen years later voiced similar sentiments. "Unfortunately, prejudice and [antiblack] stereotypes are alive and well in today's Cuba," she wrote, citing in particular resistance on the part of many families to racial intermarriage and the tendency to assume automatically that if something is missing, the thief had to be black.[39]

Since the onset of the Special Period and the legalization of dollars on the island, the economic gap between white and black Cubans has widened significantly, inasmuch as the community from which remittances have been forthcoming (namely, the U.S.-based diaspora) is overwhelmingly white. Nonwhite Cubans appear to be drastically underrepresented in the only dynamic sector of the Cuban economy—tourism—where *buena presencia* (a good appearance) is a precondition to employment, particularly in those parts of the enterprise where a Cuban will be meeting foreigners. Blacks are at a serious disadvantage in one of the few areas of self-employment open to Cubans—the operation of home restaurants, or *paladares*—inasmuch as the quality of their housing is generally too poor to attract customers, particularly

CUBAN RACISM IN THE "SPECIAL PERIOD"

An American reporter who visited Cuba in the spring of 2001 was surprised to find that even a researcher in a state-run think tank admitted that hotel administrators there were using an old "Hollywood" standard of beauty (blond hair and white skin) in the hiring of employees dealing directly with tourists. During a visit to the Meliá Santiago, eastern Cuba's first five-star hotel (run by a Spanish chain), he found none of the employees in the lobby to be black. [Ron Howell, "Tourism Reviving Racism in Cuba", *Chicago Tribune,* 18 May 2001.] I had a similar experience at the Golden Tulip Parque Central in Havana a few months earlier, but given the racial demography of eastern Cuba, the reporter's experience is the more striking.

Prior to his visit to Cuba in 2002, African-American syndicated columnist William Raspberry had been assured that Castro had "entrusted the civil service, the military officer corps, and much of the middle class to blacks." Once there, however, he found no evidence whatever for this claim. He "saw hardly any brown-skinned or black Cubans running anything—not as managers or ministers or maitre d's, not even as cashiers, clerks, or hotel maids. Black Cubans are plentiful, as a stroll through the poor sections of Havana will make clear. But all the good jobs in this socialist paradise seemed to go to people we used to describe as 'light, bright, or damned near white.'" When he raised the subject with black Cubans, they "blink[ed] as though they've just noticed it for the first time. There's no color problem in Cuba, they'll insist." [William Raspberry, "Our Man in Havana—Me," *Washington Post,* February 4, 2002.]

foreigners. Nor have blacks been able to participate in the small but dynamic private agricultural sector because, having been denied land ownership historically, they are disproportionately urban.

The new economic realities in Cuba have forced many blacks into informal—often illegal—economic activities such as the black market and prostitution. At the same time, the parlous economic situation in eastern Cuba, where the population is overwhelmingly black, has led to a large migration toward Havana. The consequent increase in street violence and petty crime—almost unknown in the capital for three decades or more—has been frequently explained in "racial" terms, as were the riots—the first in the history of the regime—that took place on Havana's sea wall on August 5, 1994. As de la Fuente succinctly puts it,

> Racism is . . . a self-fulfilling prophecy. Blacks are denied opportunities on the grounds that they are unfit and inferior. Their subsequent strategies for adaptation and survival are perceived not as ways of coping with adversity, but as further proof of their inferiority, laziness, lack of morality, and propensity to commit criminal acts. The entire crisis and its many social ills have become, as a result, racialized.[40]

Not surprisingly perhaps, some blacks have begun to find their way into the ranks of political dissidence. Of the six leaders that called for a democratic transition in 1999, four were nonwhite. Afro-Cuban dissidents count among their number Oscar Elías Biscet, a physician sentenced to three years for staging peaceful protests (he had criticized what he called "tourism apartheid"); Jorge Luís García Pérez, a former cane cutter; and Félix Bonne, a lawyer and president of the Cuban Civic Mainstream. The most prominent personality in this group is Vladimiro Roca, son of a veteran Communist labor leader who subsequently became a fighter pilot trained in the Soviet Union. For founding a group favoring democratic socialism, he was condemned to solitary confinement and released only three years later on the eve of a visit by former U.S. President Jimmy Carter.[41] While this development is unsettling to the regime, it is probably less so than more anomic forms of social protest by younger blacks—whether expressed through criminality or laggardness in the fulfillment of their revolutionary duties—since blacks in particular are expected by the authorities to behave as "passive 'beneficiaries' of revolutionary gains, not as active protagonists of their own well-being and future."[42]

Although for many years race has been largely eliminated as a topic of official discussion in Cuba, it has frequently been deployed as a weapon in the regime's relationship with the United States, and particularly with regard to the African-American community. In the early days of the revolution, the Cuban government deliberately reached out to particularly radical elements of black America, offering shelter to self-proclaimed revolutionaries such as Robert Williams, Eldridge Cleaver, and Stokely Carmichael, and for a time even became a kind of "underground railroad" for such individuals on the run. But almost from the beginning, it successfully cultivated support from more mainstream elements of the U.S. black elite. As early as 1961, a group of prominent black intellectuals, entertainers, and other public figures took a full-page advertisement in the *New York Times* in support of the Castro government, which, it held, was under siege from Washington because it had supposedly freed blacks from oppression on the island. Beginning in the 1970s, Castro played host to personalities such as Angela Davis, Sidney Poitier, Harry Belafonte, and Congressman Ron Dellums (D-Cal.), as well as organizations such as the National Congress of Black Lawyers and the National Council of Black Churches.

Particularly since the end of the Cold War, the Cuban government has maintained something of a special relationship with the Black Caucus of the U.S. Congress, six members of which visited the island in 1999, heaping praise on its government and particularly upon its supreme leader.[43] The same year, Randall Robinson, president of Trans-Africa, went to Havana with a group of black celebrities, including Danny Glover, Camille Cosby, and Johnetta Cole. For his part, the Reverend Jesse Jackson, self-styled president of Black America, has warned that no one should suppose that when Fidel Castro leaves the scene, the revolution's handiwork will vanish with him. "The decades have formed a generation of Cubans," he declared, "through almost universal schooling, through doctors and teachers dispatched to desperate reaches of the world, through military missions against the likes of South Africa, through long moral purpose and conditionings—that will not easily be separated from that experience."[44]

In September 2000, President Fidel Castro went to Harlem while on a visit to New York to celebrate the fiftieth anniversary of the United Nations. Speaking at the Abyssinian Baptist Church, he launched a five-hour attack on (U.S.) racism, particularly denouncing opposition to—of all things—"affirmative action," while Rep. Maxine Waters (D-Cal.) sat on the platform nearby in rapt attention. At the end of his lengthy discourse, the overwhelmingly black crowd howled approval. "It is in Harlem," the Cuban dictator proclaimed, "that I have found my best friends."[45]

Castro's popularity with the American black community, and particularly its leadership, seems particularly paradoxical in light of the fact that black issues on the island have been rigorously subordinated to other considerations. Even more remarkable, the Castro regime has often been praised for having achieved a goal that the African-American leadership emphatically rejects for its own country—a "colorblind" approach to race relations. As Rep. James Clyburn (D-S.C.) declared after a visit in May-June 2000, "It's good living in a country where race is not an issue . . . , there's no separation by the color of your skin in Cuba."[46] Cuban ambiguity on the subject of racial identity (who is black and who is not) is ignored altogether, as if the island were identical in this respect to the United States. "In Cuba," declared Rep. Barbara Lee (D-Cal.), addressing a forum in Washington, D.C., "most people look like me—it's a black country."[47] The fact that most of the leadership is white seems not to bother either legislator, although Rep. Charles Rangel (D-N.Y.), normally one of Fidel Castro's most tireless apologists in the U.S. Congress, claims that he has persistently raised the issue of black underrepresentation in elite positions on the island, as well as the disproportionate number of blacks in the country's prison population.[48]

The curious relationship between the Castro regime and the leadership of the African-American community in the United States can be largely explained as a reaction on the part of the latter to stimuli that have little to do with Cuba. The U.S. exile community, particularly in Miami, is regarded (often rightly) as racist; at any rate, the community has made little attempt to disguise its contempt for blacks generally, whom it often holds responsible for the tragedy that has befallen its homeland. Some of Castro's most dedicated enemies in the United States—former Senator Jesse Helms (R-N.C.), for example—are regarded with horror and loathing by American blacks; the same goes for many American conservative politicians notable for their opposition to the Cuban government. This is true despite the fact that some conservatives have broken with the Cuban-American community on the subject of the trade embargo or even, in some cases, the normalization of relations; or that the exile community has made a special effort to call attention to the increasing black presence among dissidents.[49] Castro's interventions in Africa, anathema to white Americans and particularly those of a conservative bent, are appreciated by the more internationally oriented members of the black professional and intellectual classes. To a large degree, these same groups share Castro's anti-Americanism and derive vicarious satisfaction from his incendiary rhetoric. Finally, as Roger Wilkins succinctly puts it, "Castro talks a better game on race than Batista."[50]

The black community in the United States also fears that the end of the Castro regime will mean a return of the "white" exiles, and with it, a turning back of the clock to 1958—as if such a thing were possible, particularly given the current racial composition of the island. One commentator—a black Cuban living in U.S. exile but echoing views frequently heard in the African-American community—asserts that whether the island's future lies with former Communists-become-capitalists (as in Russia) or with the returning exiles, "Blacks can expect to be sent to the back of the bus." History will repeat itself in Cuba, he warns, with the United States playing the same role that it did in 1900, possibly even invading to preserve "stability," leaving only when a "cooperative" government is in place.[51]

While no one can say what form the next government of Cuba will assume, it is virtually certain that the issue of race will once again be put on the table, not only for demographic reasons but because the U.S. African-American community will be there to make sure that it is. (There are some signs that adversarial expressions of U.S. black culture—notably "hip hop" music—are already seeping into the island.)[52] Thanks to a fortuitous conjunction of domestic factors in the United States, the Castro regime has received a free pass from the African-American community on the subject of racial progress. Unless the next Cuban government succeeds in maintaining the same level of virulent hatred of the United States (and remains as solicitous of its black friends in the United States), race relations in Cuba will become a central and contentious part of the bilateral relationship.

To be sure, one would hope that Cuba would be permitted to address racial issues on its own terms, particularly in the event that a representative democracy emerges on the island. In an earlier period the influence of the civil rights movement in the United States might have provided a helpful model; however, the emergence of a new set of racial grievances in the United States, going well beyond affirmative action—for example, compensation for slavery—suggests that to the extent that the African-American community has anything to say about it, the racial kettle will be kept on high boil in

Cuba, without necessarily resolving any of the peculiar problems that ethnic differences pose for Cubans, black or white.

Nongovernmental Organizations

Until the onset of the Special Period, terms such as "civil society" and "nongovernmental organizations" (NGOs) were viewed with hostility and suspicion in official Cuba. In the early 1990s, in a general environment of widespread economic scarcity, the government suddenly grasped the point that many of its mass and front organizations—officially renamed NGOs—were capable of harnessing considerable foreign resources from private organizations and governments, particularly in Canada and Western Europe. At the same time, some genuinely independent groups decided to test the government's tolerance by applying for a license from the Ministry of Justice; supposedly some 2,200 groups were registered by 1994.[53] This sudden explosion of real or ostensibly private groups provoked much comment in the foreign press, as if they represented a significant innovation in the texture of Cuban life.[54]

A closer look reveals a very different picture. The only organizations with any political relevance that were allowed to register were either originally creatures of the state or party, or bodies that were specifically created by the state to attract external funding. The first category includes preexisting bodies that were simply declared to be independent or nongovernmental, such as the Federation of Cuban Women, headed by Vilma Espín, wife of General Raúl Castro; the National Association of Small Peasants (ANAP); and the Union of Artists and Writers of Cuba (UNEAC), headed by Abel Prieto, a member of the Politburo. Although their real nature should have been obvious to all and sundry, some sources of foreign funding have chosen to close their eyes to reality; for example, the Federation of Cuban Women has been receiving financial assistance from the United Nations Development Program (UNDP).

The second category is composed of organizations that were created out of whole cloth to act as magnets for external resources, inspiring the creation of a new term—"government-organized nongovernmental organization" (GONGOs). In Cuba they included think tanks such as the Center for the Study of the Americas (CEA) or the Center for European Studies; environmental organizations such as Pro-Natura; agencies to promote international cooperation such as the Félix Varela Center, or to promote Cuban culture, such as the Pablo Milanés Foundation; or groups aimed at absorbing potentially dissident elements of the black community, such as the Martin Luther King Center and the Yoruba Cultural Association. The Varela Center was particularly adept at attracting foreign assistance, not only from the various branches of OXFAM (UK, Canada, Belgium), but also the American Friends Service Committee.

During the mid-1990s, some observers of the Cuban scene were at considerable pains to insist that the NGO/GONGO dynamic was more complicated than it might first appear. Thus one frequent U.S.-based academic visitor to the island professed to find that "some top-down NGOs, such as Pro-Natura, have strong grassroots connections, and some bottom-up groups, like the Martin Luther King Center, have close relations with the state." The same author went on to say that while the state frequently attempted to convert what she called "bottom-up NGOs" into pliable instruments, citizens "occasionally try to reshape top-down NGOs into grass roots organizations." She also insisted that "the ideological lines between groups are . . . fluid. Bottom-up organizations are not necessarily anti-state, and top-down organizations are not necessarily anti-citizen empowerment."[55]

Seven years later, there is precious little evidence to substantiate this rather optimistic assessment. Rather, even pro-government organizations have often been shut down or taken over by the authorities. A case in point is the Pablo Milanés Foundation. Established in 1993 by a popular black singer—a self-described "proud Cuban socialist"[56]—its purpose was to support young Cuban artists and independent cultural institutions through the profits of record sales throughout Latin America, where Milanés is something of a cultural icon. Within two years of its creation, however, the organization was taken over by the Ministry of Culture. In an unusual public outburst, Milanés bitterly protested the action.[57] For its part, the government accused the singer of having fled after embezzling $25 million in foundation funds, a charge the singer heatedly denied. (He is still officially resident on the island but now spends most of his time in Spain.)[58] Presumably Milanés's access to large amounts of foreign currency provided him with a dangerous degree of potential independence.

A similar fate befell the CEA, described as "a cutting edge think tank devoted to studying political and economic developments from Alaska to

Argentina." For reasons yet to be explained, it came under public attack in mid-1996 by General Raúl Castro for allegedly "falling into the spider's web spun by Cuban experts abroad, in reality servants of the United States and its policy of fomenting a fifth column." The CEA's director, Luís Suárez, was asked to volunteer for agricultural work for a few months, and six of its other top researchers were either sent home or to work in the fields.[59] The CEA had in fact worked on some projects with the Washington-based Center for International Policy (CIP), but by the wildest stretch of the imagination, this could hardly represent collusion with the U.S. government, given the sharp adversarial position that the CEA's North American partner almost invariably assumes vis-à-vis U.S. policy worldwide.

Another troubling example is the Cuban Red Cross, established in 1909 by an act of the Cuban Congress. According to its own web site, it works closely with Cuban government agencies "in its daily tasks and during times of disaster." It also maintains "close interaction with the popular assemblies at the provincial and municipal level. The youth Red Cross keeps close working links with other Cuban youth associations, especially at the local level." This sounds as if it resembles similar bodies elsewhere in the world, and in fact it has received assistance from both the International Federation of Red Cross societies and the Norwegian and Netherlands affiliates. In times of disaster, it has also received grants from the United Kingdom and the European Union.

What the web page does not say is that the Red Cross has also acted as a cover for government security operations. During the Pope's visit to Cuba in early 1998, police operatives were permitted to dress in Red Cross uniforms and discipline the crowds; in one case, a man who had shouted a protest against the government was arrested and carried off in a Red Cross ambulance.[60] Apparently this incident was far from exceptional; during its most recent visit to Cuba, the delegation from Pax Christi Netherlands was told by the Justice and Peace Commission of the Catholic Church that the covert relationship between the security services and the Red Cross was of sufficient magnitude to merit denunciation by the International Committee of the organization.[61]

At this point, the only nongovernmental organizations worthy of the name are those operating outside the purview of official sanction. In this connection, three particular movements are worthy of mention—independent journalists, independent economists, and independent libraries. Despite censorship, employment sanctions, lack of access to the Internet, and political persecution, the island has seen a burgeoning of independent news agencies since the early 1990s. The best known of these is Cuba Press, founded in 1995 by Raúl Rivero, but his is only one of more than two dozen agencies, some of which are based in the provinces. Virtually all independent journalists are former employees of state outlets. Much of their work appears on the Cubanet.org web site or in foreign papers such as Miami's *Nuevo Herald*, transmitted either on (illegal) cell phones or through fax machines. (There is no clandestine press in Cuba.) Independent journalism is an extremely dangerous activity, since it contravenes the "88 Law" (February 1999), which threatens sanctions against "any person who collaborates, by any means whatsoever, with radio or television programs, magazines or any other foreign media" or "provides information likely to serve U.S. policy." The frequent arrest and confinement of independent journalists have been the targets of repeated campaigns by Amnesty International, Index on Censorship, and Reporters Sans Frontières.

Cuba's independent economists are likewise former functionaries of the regime. Their work consists of trying to decipher economic reality from official government statistics, a task for which they are particularly well suited. Their work circulates in manuscript or crude mimeograph form. One of their recent projects has been to compile a list of things Cubans are forbidden to do (own cell phones; rent cars; watch television programs from other countries; fish without authorization; use hospitals designated for foreign tourists, even if they can pay in dollars). The most outstanding personality of this movement, Marta Beatriz Roque, was sentenced to three years in prison for signing a statement entitled "The Fatherland Belongs to All" in 1997. Her adoption as a prisoner of conscience by Amnesty International and the wide publicity given to her case abroad have given her a certain immunity since her release, but as she told a group of American visitors in early 2001, "One gets up in the morning not knowing whether one will spend the night in the same bed or in some prison cell."[62] Her organization can hardly be regarded as the embryo of a future economic team, since so many of its members have opted for exile. As she told one American journalist, of the seventeen people with whom she went to prison, none were currently residing in Cuba.[63]

An independent library movement began in March 1998, when President Fidel Castro was widely quoted as saying that "in Cuba there are no prohibited books. Only those we do not have the money to buy." Various individuals around the island took the government at its word and began to assemble collections in private homes. The basic concept was to create "neutral spaces" free of ideological filters. As one American journalist reported from the island, "Getting your hands on a book that the government has decided you do not need to read can be difficult here." Though Cuba has an extensive network of state and school libraries and what is reportedly one of the Third World's best technical collections, "Admission is often restricted and access to certain volumes is determined by a need-to-know color code."[64]

As of mid-2001, eighty such libraries were reported to exist throughout the island.[65] Building collections has been difficult because some shipments, especially of political books from Europe and the United States, have been confiscated, and some libraries have been under surveillance or searched by authorities.[66] Some independent librarians have been arrested, others taunted by mobs, and entire collections have been confiscated.[67] These actions have drawn fire from Amnesty International (*Annual Report,* 2000),[68] the intellectual freedom committee of the International Federation of Library Associations, and the Friends of the Cuban Libraries in the United States.

Rather remarkably, however, a delegation dispatched to Cuba by the American Library Association found no fault with this state of affairs. To the contrary, its report, which consistently put the word "independent" in quotation marks, complained that the principals did not "have degrees or training in librarianship, nor do they even appear to be what we might call 'book oriented' people. They are not librarians by any definition that we would understand." Rather, the delegation protested, most of the independent librarians encountered by the group were "self-professed political dissidents, dedicated to the overthrow of the Cuban government. . . . Several had been arrested by the Cuban authorities, but they [the authorities] emphasized that these arrests had nothing to do with their 'independent' library activities." Rather, we are assured, the librarians were detained "in all cases . . . for subversive and clandestine activities carried out to undermine the Cuban government."[69]

There are, to be sure, independent groups in Cuba whose stated purpose is to change the political system. They are extremely numerous, but small, divided, and probably heavily infiltrated by government security agents. They include such groups as Oswaldo Payá's Varela Project, which has managed to acquire the 10,000 signatures needed to ask Cuba's National Assembly to call a plebiscite on the form of government that Cubans prefer;[70] the Christian Liberation Movement; Solidaridad Democrática, an artists' group; Movimiento Cívico Máximo Gómez; Universitarios sin Frontera; the Domestic Dissidents Working Group, led by Vladimiro Roca, Marta Beatriz Roque, Félix Bonne, and René Gómez Manzano; and tiny branches of international political communities such as Social Democrats, Christian Democrats, and Liberals. Perhaps the best known is the Cuban Commission for Human Rights and National Reconciliation led by Elizardo Sánchez, which has been described as "the most informed, organized, and articulate source of information about political prisoners and the domestic opposition."[71]

According to Cuban Foreign Minister Felipe Pérez Roque, these organizations are "small splinter groups which have resulted solely from U.S. financing. They have no authority. They are not legitimate."[72] This has not prevented them, however, from being treated as if they were a serious threat to the established order. A blanket of silence covers their very existence in the Cuban media, though most Cubans do not need to be reminded that anti-government activities invariably lead to loss of jobs, ration cards, or in some cases, personal freedom. Those courageous (or foolhardy) enough to soldier on face enormous obstacles. Paper is hard to come by in Cuba and access to a copying machine, the Internet, or a satellite dish is almost beyond imagining. The Cuban community in exile—equally divided, and with agendas of its own—does not generally provide dissidents with resources. Many who join these groups do so only to earn the title of "dissident," the faster to obtain a visa to emigrate to the United States. One report cited "long-term dissident" leaders as saying that "there may be no more than 500 genuine opposition activists" in the country as a whole.[73]

The Military

Since 1990, the Cuban military has been greatly reduced in size and in share of the budget, but paradoxically—by assuming a new economic role—has become the most important single institution of Communist civil society, or what passes for it in Cuba. "The reality of Cuba in 1995," a Latin American diplomat told a U.S. scholar, "is that the military is one of the few, if not the only, institution that really works. Revolutionary fervor has vanished, and with it, the credibility of the party, leaving the armed forces to fill the vacuum."[74]

Even before the collapse of the Soviet Union, the military was being conscripted to manage certain areas of the economy; with the onset of the Special Period, its writ widened to cover an astonishing range of activities—from sugar to the merchant marine, civil aviation, banking, cigars, electronics, and foreign trade.[75] Perhaps the best known of the military ventures is Gaviota, S.A., an organization that administers luxury hotels, restaurants, discotheques, hunting preserves, marinas, spas, bus tours, fishing expeditions, taxicab fleets, and charter air services. Since 1993, it has hived off a number of subsidiaries, including Texnotec (information technology and electronic equipment), Turcimex (cargo and mail delivery), Aerocaribe (air transport), and the "dollar stores" (Tiendas para la Recuperación de Divisas). As of 1999, the Cuban military was also operating twenty industrial companies, with roughly a third of their output destined for civilian sectors. Even more impressive is the fact that these same civilian enterprises obtain roughly 75 percent of their spare parts from military-run factories.[76]

The vigor of the military sector of the economy has meant that it is possible—and political considerations render it desirable—to make special provision for retirement, disability, and survivorship. Whereas the social security payments of most Cubans are based on their highest average salary for five of their last ten years of working life, officers retired from either the Ministry of the Armed Forces or the Ministry of Interior draw benefits "roughly equal to twice the salary increase rate of the averaging period."[77] Put more concretely, ordinary Cubans retiring under Law 24 (the standard social security law) receive benefits based on 100 percent of their annual salary up to $3,000 and 50 percent of the annual salary above that amount. Military and Interior Ministry personnel, however, retire under Laws 101 and 102, which recognize all pensionable salary at 100 percent. In effect, anyone earning more than $250 a month would receive benefits dramatically larger than those of ordinary workers. "The additional value ranges from a 5 percent greater pension for a captain who earns approximately $300 per month," according to one study, "to 29 percent greater pension for the Minister of Defense who earns approximately $450 a month."[78]

These benefits do not even take into account what one might call off-budget financial opportunities available to Cuban officers, active and retired, whose activities bring them into contact with foreign investors, particularly from countries such as Spain and Italy, where payoffs to government officials are the norm. (Corporations in these countries are even allowed to discount gratuities to foreign government officials from their earnings for tax purposes.)

In many ways, the Cuban military is thus beginning to approximate its counterparts in Central America. In Guatemala, for example, the military has its own pension system and its own bank, which is one of the largest financial institutions in the country. It is heavily involved as well in agriculture, fisheries, and real estate. As a result, although Guatemala returned to civilian rule in 1986 after a long hiatus, the military is probably the most influential actor in civil society, with privileged access to whoever the president may be, and the ability to exert a subtle but perceptible control over the entire political class.

The experience of Nicaragua is perhaps even more relevant to the Cuban case. Armies in both countries were products of nationalist movements that had their beginnings in the fight against patrimonial dictatorship; both subsequently embraced Marxism-Leninism as a political doctrine; most Nicaraguan officers received their training in East bloc countries (as well as from the Cubans); most of the military equipment used in Nicaragua—as in Cuba—came from the Soviet Union or Eastern Europe. Although the Sandinista Front (FSLN) was ousted from political power in the elections of 1990, it retained considerable influence within the military, so much so indeed that President Violeta Chamorro was forced to retain General Humberto Ortega, brother of the defeated dictator Daniel Ortega, as head of the armed forces. During the 1990s some efforts were made to normalize the status of the military, but the National Assembly was never able to gain control over the army's budget.

Moreover, during the final days of the Sandinista rule—which is to say, between the defeat of Ortega and the inauguration of Chamorro—an emergency decree enabled the military to establish and oversee businesses, construction companies, airlines, fisheries, and factories—many of which had been expropriated from their owners without compensation. At present the military even owns its own television and radio stations, as well as a daily newspaper.[79] During the Sandinista piñata,[80] numerous state enterprises were also made to conform to the army's pension system. While the relationship between the army and the Sandinista party has become more tenuous than it was formerly, a symbiotic relationship continues to exist, with the Sandinistas the strongest supporters of the armed forces in the National Assembly, and the army an unspoken guarantor that no government will strike at the heart of privileges doled out under the former dispensation.[81]

Presumably the involvement of Cuban military officers in economic activities has enhanced their interest in the regime's survival. Certainly that is one of the motives—if not indeed the principal one—for the economic "reforms" that have virtually militarized important sectors of the economy. One student has suggested that in so doing the regime runs the risk of "encouraging new entrepreneurial and corporate initiatives outside of the regime's control," which is to say, provoking unseemly appetites for privatization and genuine entrepreneurial freedom.[82] Although this was the case at times in the former Soviet Union and Eastern Europe, there is nothing inevitable about its replication in Cuba. It seems more prudent to assume that at a minimum, the Cuban military, like its counterparts elsewhere in the region, will have a stake in ensuring that any future transition will not threaten its interests.

The development of a military-entrepreneurial class presumably also strengthens the claim to political succession of General Raúl Castro, head of the armed forces ministry (MINFAR), since it was he—against the inclinations of his brother—who insisted on the pursuit of more pragmatic and results-oriented economic policies in the first place. At the same time, the military's central role in alleviating the country's most pressing economic problems "has provided it with a greater political profile and influence." One consequence has been an increasing representation of officers on the Central Committee of the Communist Party and in the Politburo, a development that points not "to extrication but direct involvement in any transition."[83]

The Cuban-American Community

One might think that the Cuban-American community would have no place in any discussion of the island's civil society inasmuch as it lives in another political jurisdiction. Indeed, its very presence abroad—largely in southern Florida—is the result of a concrete decision to emigrate, and as such represents a direct challenge and reproach to the revolutionary state. Not surprisingly, in official parlance, those who have chosen exile are regarded as having ceased to be Cuban at all.[84] According to journalistic accounts, this attitude is widely shared by the Cuban population as a whole. "Whatever mistakes we've made in the revolution," one professional in Santiago told the *Washington Post,* "we want to work out our own destiny after Fidel."

"We don't want them making our decision for us," a cab driver told the same source. "Those people are frozen in the 1950s. They don't have any idea what we've been through here. They've mostly become American citizens and made a lot of money. I don't blame them for that." But, he added, "they don't plan to come back and share our fate, whatever that is."[85]

This principled rejection masks several inconvenient facts—that remittances from the exile community now make up an important part of the budget of thousands of Cuban families; that frequent travel has broken down the wall of silence between communities divided by politics; that hundreds of thousands of Cubans have family in the United States and hope to rejoin their relatives at the earliest possible opportunity; that uncounted numbers aspire to emigrate to the United States; that the existence of "another Cuba" across the Florida straits—whose radio and even television transmissions in Cuban-accented Spanish are frequently picked up on the island—has caused the United States in many ways to cease to be a foreign country at all.

Likewise, there is something distinctive and *sui generis* about the Cuban community in the United States. All of the revolutions of modern history have produced sizable exile communities. But in no other case has the diaspora been so proportionately large, so wealthy, so geographically concentrated, so politically powerful in its country of adoption, and so physically proximate to its country of origin. The result is "a cultural hybrid—a community that is functionally American, but dwells spiritually in a cloud of imminence."[86] Although more than forty years have passed since the first exiles landed on American soil, two generations later many are still reluctant to bid farewell to their country of origin and accept the revolution and its detritus as the pitiless verdict of history.[87]

This anomalous situation is expressed in many ways. There has been a rigorous attempt to reconstruct the island's civil society on the U.S. mainland. Thus, in Miami there is a Cuban Bar Association (in exile), a Cuban Medical Association (in exile), a Ranchers' and Landowners' Association, a University of Havana Alumni Association, as well as *centros* or *círculos*, which unite natives of particular provinces or cities. (There is even a Havana *Social Register in*

Exile!) This replication of the old Cuban civil society is so completely articulated that it is possible for the life of a Cuban-American to begin "in the hands of a Cuban obstetrician and . . . end in the hands of a Cuban undertaker" without ever having to deal much with the outside (that is, non-Cuban) world.[88]

There have also been conscious efforts to preserve Cuban culture in exile, although what passes for "culture" is often superficial and deliberately outdated—for example, an exhibit entitled "Cuba Nostalgia" at the Coconut Grove Convention Center, which for three years running has been "showcasing Cuban life and traditions of a half-century ago."[89] And there have been efforts to encourage an artificial Cuban identity among young people who have never seen the island or left it at too early an age to have any memories. One Cuban-American recalls that his whole family always told him that he was "born in Miami by accident, that I really didn't belong there, that I was a victim of circumstance stripped of a glorious potential life by a Cuban revolution they were not a part of." In spite of the converging pressures of U.S. popular culture, "we were raised as Cuban kids, . . . we were taught to honor our grandparents, . . . we were taught to like Cuban food and celebrate all holidays Cuban-style."[90]

Not surprisingly, Cubans who return to the island after many years of absence are often in for something of a shock. As one Cuban exile put it, "You feel that you are in a changed, almost foreign country." Even the language and colloquialisms of everyday speech are almost incomprehensible.[91] Meanwhile, demographic changes in the United States are slowly eating away at the sources of Cuban identity. Cuban-Americans who move away from Miami or who are not Cuban-born or who do not have Cuban-born parents tend to consider themselves mainstream Americans. In 1997, of the approximately 1.6 million persons of Cuban origin in the United States, nearly 25 percent no longer identified themselves as Cubans. For those who live in metropolitan Miami, the predictors of identity—place of residence and Cuban-born with Cuban-born parents—are very nearly reversed. But even there, fully 88 percent of children raised in Spanish-speaking homes preferred to speak English (based on a 1995–1996 survey), a trend that has accelerated over time.[92]

The impact of demographics is also obvious in long-term political trends. Although the community as a whole has a (perhaps deserved) reputation for intransigence and revanchist rhetoric, it is also true that there are growing differences of opinion based on date of emigration or whether the individual was born in the United States. These differences are evident in the sixth of a series of public opinion polls conducted in October 2000 among Cuban and Cuban-American residents of Miami-Dade County, the epicenter of immigration.[93]

Taken as a whole, the results are far from surprising—strong support for continuing the U.S. economic embargo (64.2 percent), and even for military action by exile groups (69.6 percent) or a U.S. invasion of the island (61 percent). When the sample is broken down into generational cohorts, however, the picture that emerges is rather more complex. While only 43.3 percent of those who emigrated between 1959 and 1984 (the so-called historic emigration) favor dialogue with the Cuban government, 61.6 percent of those entering the U.S. after that date so favor, as do 67.9 of U.S.-born Cubans. Likewise, while all three groups advocate continuation of the U.S. economic embargo, support is significantly stronger in the 1959–1984 cohort (69.5 percent) and weakest among those who have entered since 1984 (46.9 percent), with U.S.-born Cubans slightly more favorable (51.5 percent).

The results are similar when respondents are asked whether the United States should permit unrestricted travel to Cuba. While only 43.8 percent of those who entered between 1959 and 1984 so favored, the number rose dramatically to 74.3 percent among those who entered after 1984, with U.S.-born Cubans again approaching the latter group at 58.3 percent. On the subject of a resumption of formal diplomatic relations with the island, only 17.9 percent of the 1959–1984 group replied in the affirmative, while 56.3 percent of those who entered after 1984 so favored, as did 55 percent of those born in the United States.

When asked whether it was "likely" or "somewhat likely" that they would eventually return to the island, 39.9 percent the 1959–1984 group answered in the affirmative, while 50.5 percent of the post-1984 did so—but a mere 19.6 percent of those born in the United States contemplated such a move. The relatively large share of Cubans in the first group who say they plan to return to the island to live may reflect nothing more than the fact that many of these people are at or fast approaching retirement age. In the second group, the sizable portion considering a return to the island is at least partly based on the fact that an overwhelming 95 percent of this group still has relatives in Cuba.

Significantly, only a fifth of those born in the United States express an interest in returning to Cuba on a permanent basis.[94]

These demographic differences may eventually produce important changes in the political stance of the Cuban-American community. At present its most representative, most politically organized, and best-funded expression is the Cuban American National Foundation (CANF), founded in 1980 by the late Jorge Mas Canosa, a Miami businessman. Deliberately copying the techniques of the Israel lobby in the United States (AIPAC), the Foundation established its own political action committee, contributing to the war chests of candidates of both parties. It is principally responsible for the Cuban Democracy Act (1992) and the Helms-Burton Law (1996), both of which tightened the trade embargo, the latter significantly so. It also has its own radio station in Miami (The Voice of the Foundation) whose broadcasts can be picked up at different locations on the island, and engages in philanthropic work, principally assisting the settlement and integration of new arrivals. Most recently, it has launched a plan to send humanitarian assistance to the island after natural disasters, to be distributed by human rights organizations, independent journalists, and other genuine nongovernmental organizations.[95] It is best known however, for its effective lobbying tools in Washington.

Although other groups have emerged in recent years to challenge the dominance of the CANF—the Cuban Committee for Democracy, Cambio Cubano, the Cuban-American Alliance Education Fund, as well as Cuban-American branches of Christian Democracy and the Liberal International—so far they have not gained a significant foothold in the community nor made a meaningful impact on the policy community in Washington. Most of these groups favor dialogue with the Cuban government; many favor lifting the embargo and initiating a policy of "constructive engagement." This places them in stark opposition to the Foundation, whose basic strategy has been to apply economic and political pressure on the island until the Castro regime falls. While all of these groups advocate some sort of change in Cuba, there is some difference of opinion on precisely what configuration the new republic should assume, and to what degree the revolution and its practices and institutions should be accepted as an accomplished fact. To be sure, much of this debate among Cuban-Americans is irrelevant to Cuba itself, since none of these groups has meaningful representation there, and current conditions do not allow for truly open debate on alternatives for the future.

For many years the standard caricature of Cuban-Americans retailed by the U.S., European, and Latin American media was that of a dispossessed wealthy elite continually plotting to recover their ill-gotten gains through the agency of the U.S. Marines. More recently—and somewhat more accurately—it has shifted to depicting a clutch of successful Miami émigré businessmen who plan to take over the island once Castro is gone. An American journalist was able to locate a number of examples for a major U.S. daily newspaper. "With Castro dead or deposed," he quoted a Cuban-American homebuilder as saying, "there won't be enough flights, enough hotels, enough anything in Cuba to accommodate us all." He also found the owner of a farm equipment company: "Sure we'll be there. I've been raised around it, raised in a town where it's always in your face." The journalist spoke with Miami businessman and civic leader Carlos Saldrigas, who has a more sober and realistic view. "I'm . . . careful about the term 'reconstruction' because it implies we want to return to what was there before. In a historical and practical sense, that's not possible." And he adds, "What's missing for us is a sense of reality about [what] it is to be in Cuba today. The exiles from the '60s have never been back. They have a view of things that's not subject to a reality check."[96]

Some Cuban-American businessmen have already made their reality check and are not waiting. This much was revealed in the course of an indictment of a high-ranking Cuban-American official of the Immigration and Naturalization Service in Miami in May 2000. The official was arrested for maintaining an illicit relationship with a firm specifically created in 1993 by a group of Cuban-American businessmen intent upon doing $60 million worth of business on the island as exclusive representatives of Procter and Gamble; the firm also contemplated buying land and warehouses in Cuba through third parties. People in the know in Miami were not surprised by the news—indeed, many thought these revelations were merely the tip of the iceberg. "In reality," affirmed economist Jorge Salazar of Florida International University, "there already is open trade between Cuba and South Florida," which he estimated at $20 million to $30 million a year. For his part, Jorge Sanguinetti, a consulting economist in Miami, remarked that "Cuba has very aggressively pursued contacts with Cuban businessmen in the U.S." since the end of Soviet subsidies.[97]

There is some evidence as well that in spite of ideological differences, the Cuban government is interested in establishing contact with selected members of this community. "For its size and dynamism," one Cuban academic told a Miami newspaper, "Cuban-American business in the United States could play an important role in a future normalization of relations with the U.S.," noting that the whole of the island's foreign trade (slightly more than $3 billion), scarcely amounted to 30 percent of the value added to the gross income of Cuban-American enterprises.[98] Exactly what political conditions each side would have to meet to effect complete economic engagement remained undefined.

Concluding Remarks

Cuba today is evidently far poorer in the elements of civil society than it was in 1959, which in and of itself limits options for the future. Like Guatemala or Honduras, the only strong institutions are the armed forces and the Roman Catholic Church. The latter maintains a close relationship with its U.S. analogue and, indeed, could be the only independent agency on the island with an effective international reach; as for the former, it is conceivable that at some future date, practical security reasons—drugs, border control, broad political stability—will lead the U.S. defense establishment to seek a close relationship with its Cuban counterpart. (Indeed, there is much evidence that such a desire already exists.) As in the case of Central America, the military-to-military relationship may be shaped by pragmatic necessity rather than political or ethical concerns; after decades of subscribing to a "hypothesis of conflict," both institutions may discover a wide commonality of interests. This in turn would reinforce what is already the strongest single element of Cuban civil society at the expense of other forces working for genuine democracy and pluralism.

Some elements of Communist civil society that presently maintain close relations with their U.S. counterparts—government-organized nongovernmental organizations such as Pro-Natura, universities, cultural institutions, the Cuban Council of Churches—have yet to expose themselves to the competition inherent in a truly open environment. Under such circumstances, some might transform themselves into genuinely independent organisms; others would be revealed for the hollow vessels—the instruments of government patronage—they have always been. To the extent that a more open environment develops in Cuba, new groups are bound to emerge and seek links with U.S. organizations of a wide variety of ideological flavors. At the same time, however, the liberation of Cuban institutions from government control or an end to official hostility in U.S.-Cuban relations might well deprive the island of the glamour that currently inspires groups in both the United States and Western Europe to work with what passes there for civil society.

8

The Prospect

History is infinitely complex; though continuous, it never moves in a straight line. Historical analysis makes clear, therefore, that no mere extrapolation of past experience will suffice as a guide to the future.

—Henry Wriston[1]

An Impending Succession Crisis?

Writing in the days when the Cuban revolution was still young, one American analyst confessed it difficult "to summon the scene of a gray-bearded Fidel Castro at the age of seventy-seven delivering five-hour speeches to an enthralled nationwide Cuban audience on the glories of the ninth five-year agrarian reform plan." One is tempted to conclude, he added, that "time in the long run is against Fidel, as it always is against the red-eyed zealot. . . . Eventually Castro will either be inspired to do something foolish that will lead to his violent destruction or will find himself forced to negotiate his way back into the Western Hemisphere at a considerable price."[2]

More than thirty-five years after those words were written, Fidel Castro at seventy-six remains in power in Cuba. Although perhaps in failing health and no longer given to making as many five-hour speeches, he continues to be the symbol and the substance of the regime he created, having outlived and out-maneuvered all his enemies, domestic and foreign, and even survived the collapse of the socialist world to which he attached his fledgling revolution. Unfortunately for him, for his associates and functionaries, perhaps even for a significant portion of the Cuban people, he cannot escape the law of human mortality. In all likelihood sometime in the present decade he will pass on, and in so doing raise the issue of his succession.

217

So central do outsiders regard the Maximum Leader to Cuba and to its revolution that a minor cottage industry has grown up speculating on what will happen once he has departed the scene or is physically and mentally incapacitated. Two French journalists who lived on the island in the mid-1990s have walked their readers through six different possibilities: a transition led by Castro himself (the so-called "Chilean" scenario); a palace revolution (the "Tunisian" scenario—"the simple replacement of one dictator by another, younger, who turns to good account the single party and the repressive apparatus of his predecessor to establish his personal power"); chaos (the "Haitian" scenario—"in . . . an ambience of anarchy and violence driven by want, nothing would prevent an explosion of crime of the most brutal sort, today barely contained by the repressive apparatus"—a possiblity which, in its most extreme form, the authors argue, could lead to U.S. military intervention, with the "most revanchist elements of the exile community" in its train; orderly transfer in accordance with Article 94 of the constitution; a pacted transition (the "Spanish scenario" in which the government and elements of the domestic opposition would reach an accord over the heads of the Miami exile community); or a political-military scenario in which a provisional government, probably a civil-military junta would join technocrats with ultra-orthodox elements of the Communist Party and the army to assure protection of both political stability and vested economic interests.[3] Presumably these scenarios do not exhaust the possibilities.

For many Cuban officials, all talk of a "succession crisis"—as opposed to the inevitable fact of succession itself—is sheer wishful thinking by the exile community and its allies in the United States. Indeed, according to Ricardo Alarcón, president of the Cuban National Assembly, a transition has already occurred. He points to the fact that there has been a far-reaching generational renewal of the major cadres of power—the Council of State, the Central Committee of the Communist Party, as well as provincial governing authorities—where the average age, he claims, ranges between thirty and forty years. Moreover, as Alarcón explained to a Mexican journalist, in the event of Fidel Castro's death, the constitution clearly establishes that his successor should be the vice-president of the Council of State, who happens to be General Raúl Castro. It is "an error to consider the subject of succession [to Fidel Castro] as if the revolution were a monarchy, a nineteenth century comic opera republic," he emphasized, apparently without irony. "Cuba has clear laws. At all levels of government, the first vice-president substitutes for the president when the latter disappears. In the absence of both, the Assembly decides."[4]

Is Castroism without Castro—or at least, without *Fidel* Castro—possible? Elizardo Sánchez, the island's best-known dissident, doubts it. "That phenomenon could happen," he told a reporter, "but it would be a very rare historical exception. It is a proven fact that when the days of charismatic caudillos are over, their ideologies are also over."[5]

"Fidel is a unique phenomenon in our history," writes Roberto Luque Escalona. "No one will be able to fill the void left by his death or disappearance. . . . His regime is an edifice constructed on one pillar. It cannot stand once the pillar has fallen."[6]

Huber Matos, one of Fidel Castro's original associates in the Sierra Maestra, who broke with him early on and spent more than two decade in his jails, agrees. He adds that Raúl Castro is not the man to control power after his brother's disappearance, not only because he lacks charisma but because he will inherit a multitude of insoluble problems. Moreover, he says, the Cuban people will "demand its rights and not accept an authoritarian succession."[7]

Vicky Huddleston, head of the U.S. Interests Section in Havana, puts it more baldly: "The whole system will be gone when [Fidel] Castro dies."[8]

The issue may not be so much a question of personality or popular expectations, however, as of concrete political and economic arrangements. Beyond constitutional formalities, General Raúl Castro, presumably with the approval of his brother, has summoned to life a new structure of power within the existing regime, by putting professionals and military men loyal to him in key positions, particularly in the few dynamic sectors of the economy such as biomedical products and tourism. "Men of Raúl"—most of them in their forties or fifties—are also in charge of key ministries (sugar, transport, communications, tourism, higher education, and basic industries) as well as the Central Bank. The same applies to the first secretaries of the Communist Party of the fourteen Cuban provinces, and the more than 400 military men in charge of municipal and provincial governments. Some twenty members of the National Assembly are *raulistas*, and many others reportedly loyal to the dictator's brother are in second-line positions waiting out the succession.[9]

THE CASTRO DYNASTY

Like many Cuban families, the Castros have been torn asunder by the revolution. The president's ex-wife Marta Díaz-Balart, his daughter Alina (by Natalia Revuelta) and his sister Juana all live in Spain, the latter two having spoken out vociferously against the regime and its leaders. In contrast, Fidel Castro's younger brother Raúl is minister of interior and chief of the Revolutionary Armed Forces, while another brother, Ramón, manages major agricultural enterprises and acts as a middleman in dealings with foreign investors. For some years, Fidel Castro Díaz-Balart, a Soviet-trained nuclear physicist and the dictator's only legitimate child, was head of the Cuban Atomic Energy Agency.

Fidel Castro is known to have fathered five other sons by Delia Soto del Valle, with whom he still lives, and possibly another son by another Cuban woman.

For most of the last four decades, the Castro children, legitimate and illegitimate, have remained outside of the public eye. In early 2002, however, three articles suddenly appeared in the Cuban press concerning two of the dictator's sons, Fidel Castro Díaz-Balart (who bears a stunning resemblance to his father in his younger days, right down to the beard) and Antonio Castro del Valle, an orthopedic surgeon. The profiles—which coyly omitted specific mention of the blood relationship of the subjects to the chief of state, unnecessary in any case—broke through a rigorous wall of silence concerning Fidel Castro's personal life that has prevailed for decades in Cuba. While Castro Díaz-Balart had formerly figured in the press in connection with his scientific duties, until very recently Cubans were in total ignorance of the existence of Castro Soto del Valle. Will the light of publicity suddenly settle on other Castro progeny? What could have prompted this sudden change in policy? The question suggests its own answer—and tantalizes us with a possible "Korean" succession scenario. [See "Se descorre el velo insondable de la intimidad de Castro," *El Nuevo Herald* (Miami), February 20, 2002.]

According to a recent report in the Spanish press, the Castro brothers and Raúl's son-in-law Luis Alberto Rodríguez "control an authentic economic empire in Cuba through a huge holding company (Grupo de Administración Empresarial) whose income—from tourism, arms manufacture, hotels, and transport services—does not "end up in the treasury but rather operates as a sort of parallel economy," representing $1 billion worth of transactions a year.[10] Many of these enterprises are joint ventures with foreign partners, including some of the most important companies in Spain, Italy, Canada, and Mexico. Presumably in good time, they will be joined by American concerns prepared to do business with whoever answers the telephone in Havana. With such immense resources—both political and economic— General Raúl Castro is not exaggerating when he says that "things are all arranged—but good (*todo es atado y bien atado*)."[11]

Nothing could be farther from this vision than the notions of Cuba's future found on the other side of the Florida straits, where the exile community firmly believes that Cubans want a very different form of economy and society and, given the chance, will jump at it. Or even if the Cubans don't want it, they will get it anyway. Its most extreme expression is found among exiles who speak openly of "retaking" their country, their properties, and their sense of self. One such exile recently called for "'unconditional surrender' of the anti-Western terrorist regime in Havana," including "the immediate turning over of Fidel Castro and the henchmen of his regime to international judicial authorities, together with a timetable for the democratization of Cuba over the short term."[12]

In a more moderate tone, successive administrations and both political parties in the United States have already announced their own plans for a peaceful and orderly democratic succession in Cuba. Unfortunately, all of these projects operate on the assumption that such a shift is in the natural order of things, so that the task of Cuba's foreign friends is merely to be able to facilitate the transition once it begins. For example, the International Republican Institute issued a transition guide in 1995 that covered a wide range of practical issues—from humanitarian relief to revival of the country's once vigorous small-business sector—without speculating excessively on how the necessary political preconditions might come about.[13] The Clinton White House report on the same subject, issued two years later, made the same logical leap. "A democratic government, a free press, an active civil society, and the rule of law [in Cuba]," it predicted, "will all help to ensure that a market economy emerges in Cuba." By the same token, "economic policies that lead to growth and broad dispersion of property ownership, while protecting vulnerable groups, will help guarantee political stability and the consolidation of democracy." While holding back from a specific promise of aid to a new Cuban government, the same document thought it

> reasonable to project that, during the six-year period following the establishment of a transition government, Cuba would receive from $4 billion to $8 billion in private assistance and loans, grants and guarantees from the international financial institutions, multilateral organizations, and individual countries. After this period, the economic transition should be well advanced, and private and commercial flows into Cuba ought to be sufficient to make the economy self-sustaining without significant further external official assistance. [14]

Early in the administration of President George W. Bush, a $1 million grant was announced to the Institute of Cuban and Cuban-American Studies at the University of Miami to examine the issues affecting a transition to democracy on the island. As project director Jaime Suchlicki explained, "The overriding concept of this project is that it would lead to a democratic, open-market economy. The idea is not to perpetuate the system that exists in Cuba." But he added in a pregnant coda, "The people in a free Cuba can accept our recommendations or ignore them." This begs the question altogether as to whether ordinary Cubans will be in a position to make such choices at any time in the foreseeable future.[15]

U.S. Constituencies for Post-Castro Cuba

When one speaks of "post-Castro Cuba," one may not be referring to a political and economic system very much different from the one that presently exists. Indeed, even without modifications, the current synthesis invites the interest and support of numerous constituencies within the United States. The oldest and best established of these is a grab-bag of civil rights activists, church people, educators, writers, artists, pacifists, and others of an adversarial temper for whom the Cuban revolution is one of the great achievements of mankind—a lesson from which Americans in particular have much to learn. These people advocate the lifting of the trade embargo and the normalization of relations as a way of both legitimizing the Castro regime and providing it with a crucial measure of economic oxygen. They are also, however, the least influential of all constituencies.

Far more important are elements of the U.S. business and farm communities, who believe that the current embargo prevents them from realizing huge profits from Cuba, extrapolating somewhat crudely from the size of its market for American products as existed in 1958. According to the Cuba Policy Foundation, an advocacy group specifically founded to fight the trade embargo, under "optimum conditions—a Cuban economy running at full throttle," U.S. agricultural exports to the island could generate up to $4.8 billion a year for American firms.[16] The same organization sponsored another study by two Rice University economists which claims that U.S. energy companies are losing $3 billion a year as a consequence of the embargo, which, they insist, "is blocking promising projects that would help to improve the energy security of the United States, diversify sources of energy for Florida, and relieve a projected lack of capacity by American refineries." They specifically assert that Cuba's territorial waters could be converted "into a rich source of natural gas which could be brought to the Florida mainland through a pipeline (yet to be constructed)."[17] These grandiose predictions have drawn skepticism not only from the exile community but even business-related organizations such as the U.S.-Cuba Trade and Economic Council in New York.

Nonetheless, Cuba fever appears to be catching. Here are some random indications. "Cuba Could Be the Next Emerging Markets Hotspot"—a headline in the *Financial Times* (November 7, 2001). Or "Silicon Island: A Cuban Fantasy?" (Wired News, June 6, 2001). "More Food on the Table Raises Expectations for Cuban Consumers and U.S. Food Companies" (press release, PROMAR International, May 30, 2001). In the year 2000 alone, some 3,400 American business leaders visited the island, including personnel from port authorities with a long history of commerce with Cuba—New Orleans, Houston, Jacksonville, and Baton Rouge. More than 700 U.S. companies have registered some 3,000 trademarks in Cuba.[18] In early 2002, U.S. businessmen and Cuban officials met for a three-day conference in Cancún,

Mexico, shortly after Washington and Havana had agreed to a one-time-only cash transaction to sell the island $35 million worth of food in the wake of Hurricane Michelle. At that meeting Americans were promised as much as $1 billion a year in future food sales ("to start"), increasing over time— 19 percent of total U.S. exports of rice, and 37 percent of total U.S. exports of milk products.[19] But, as National Assembly President Alarcón never tires of telling U.S. trade missions to Havana, "without substantial changes in U.S. policy"—beginning with a lifting of the embargo and an extension of "soft" credits—Americans can expect to do little or no business with Cuba.[20]

Precisely because so many business-related organizations have begun to lobby for a lifting of the embargo, in late 2000 the U.S. International Trade Commission was specifically tasked to investigate the potential size of the Cuban market. Its report, published in early 2001, produced figures far more modest. Based on trade data for 1996–1998, in the absence of the existing trade embargo, U.S. exports to Cuba from all sources would have ranged between $658 million to $1 billion, somewhat less than 0.5 percent of *all* U.S. exports.[21] Put in a regional perspective, these figures would make Cuba a significantly less interesting customer than either the Dominican Republic, which—with roughly a third of Cuba's population—takes more than $4.4 billion in goods and services each year from the United States, or Costa Rica, which—with less than a fifth of Cuba's population—takes nearly $2.5 billion.[22]

In its report, the International Trade Commission explained that production constraints in Cuba limited near-term export potential; that foreign exchange shortages limited its import purchasing power; and that its investment regime remained extremely restrictive. It also pointed out that Cuba tends to select its trading partners based on political considerations, taking extreme care not to become dependent on a single market or customer. Finally, it noted, systemic constraints would limit Cuba's near-term ability to increase production of its main export products.

Some highlights of the report are worth bringing forward. Lifting sanctions on tourism would account for no more than 1 percent of total passenger revenues for U.S. airlines. Cuba would remain a small market for banking and insurance because of existing restrictions. There would be a small impact on construction due to "the small size of the Cuban economy, limited business opportunities, and alternative opportunities elsewhere in Latin

America." Opportunities in telecommunications may be limited because of the prior entry of Italian and Canadian concerns into the Cuban market.

Even in agricultural products Cuba represents a small and insignificant market for U.S. exports. The most important sectors are wheat and rice (potentially 1 percent and 4–6 percent of total U.S. exports, respectively); other export lines (feed grains, animal feed, fats and oils, meat, and dairy) hover slightly below the former figure. Cuba might well take winter vegetables from the United States to supply the tourism sector (but this would amount to less than 0.5 percent of all exports). The same holds true for tropical fruits. Paradoxically, because Cuba has developed its own biomedical industry, it represents an insignificant market for U.S. pharmaceuticals. Other lines are cement (2 to 3 percent of total U.S. exports), plastics (0.5 percent), tires (1 percent), and sporting goods (less than 0.5 percent).[23]

Theoretically, of course, it is possible to construct models of Cuban economic growth and investment that would justify a far larger estimate of market size. But such predictions are based on stacking best-case scenarios against each other—drastic changes in economic policies that presuppose a radical alteration not merely in the nature of Cuban politics, but even in the texture of life on the island. From its very inception, the revolutionary government has subordinated economic performance to its political goals, so that barring a wholesale political upheaval or a radical turnaround in leadership style and objectives, the limits to economic growth are firm and fixed.[24] It seems likely, however, that as long as Americans are forbidden to do business with Cuba, they will feel a gnawing sense of deprivation. As one Silicon Valley entrepreneur told the Florida press, Cuban investment opportunities were like a "game of musical chairs. . . . [I] don't want to be caught without a seat when the music stops."[25] And of course, even if the numbers never exceed the lowest estimates in the ITC report, they will still represent a market large enough to justify trade with Cuba—for those actually engaged in it.

A far less dewy-eyed constituency for normalization is the U.S. military. It is an open secret in Washington that for some time now the Joint Chiefs of Staff have privately agonized over the prospects of a violent transition in Cuba, erupting into civil war. Under such circumstances, they fear that the U.S. exile community would intervene, forcing the U.S. military to invade the island and separate the contending forces.[26] For obvious reasons, no active duty officer has chosen to voice opposition to current U.S. policy, and particularly against the policy of limiting official contacts between the U.S. and Cuban militaries. But since their retirement, a number of high-ranking flag officers have made recent trips to Cuba under the auspices of the Center for Defense Information. These include General John Sheehan, U.S. Marine Corps (retired) and former commander of the U.S. Atlantic Command in Norfolk, as well as two former commanders-in-chief of the U.S. Southern Command—General Charles Wilhelm, U.S. Marine Corps (retired), and General Barry McCaffrey, U.S. Army (retired) and subsequently director of the Office of Drug Policy in the Clinton administration. All are impressed with the professionalism and good will evinced by their Cuban counterparts and are eager to improve communication with them.[27] As General Wilhelm put it, "I think we would profit greatly by better coordinating our mutual efforts, . . . working together more effectively in enterprises like search and rescue [missions] and curbing illegal immigration."[28]

General McCaffrey put it somewhat differently: "Cuba will not remain a collapsing Communist dictatorship with a goofy economic system much longer," he declared on his return. "Eventually it is going to be another economic center in the hemisphere, so we clearly don't want international drug crime dominating Cuba."[29]

There is in fact a striking coherence between the Cuban agenda of the U.S. military—stability, continuity, lack of violence, cooperation on outstanding bilateral issues—and that of its counterpart on the island. As one (unidentified) Spanish journalist put it, the younger Cuban leaders understand that "their own future is intimately mortgaged to the country's overall stability, which will be impossible without the cooperation of Washington in a scenario in which [Fidel] Castro may no longer be present." That explains, he adds, "why the Cuban military may be transforming itself into allies of the Americans, both determined to assume that the transition takes place with a minimum of trauma." He even speculates that the United States might be shopping around for a "General Spínola" (the Portuguese officer who initiated the dismantling of the Salazar-Caetano regime in Portugal in 1974) to carry out "reconciliation without vengeance, at the same time guaranteeing basic order."[30]

There may be no need to look for such a person at all: arguably General Raúl Castro is already advancing himself for the position. During 2001, he declared no less than three times that Cuba and the United States should widen their areas of cooperation "in spite of political differences." He specifically mentioned drugs, emigration, and the struggle against terrorism. As he put it,

> We can live together, they with their social system, we with ours, maintaining all the cooperation of which each side is capable, but within a framework of mutual respect and non-intervention in each other's internal affairs. We are ready to cooperate in any way possible, but without taking orders from anyone, much less accepting threats.[31]

As if to underscore the point, General Castro went out of his way in early 2002 to pledge his cooperation with U.S. forces at Guantánamo Naval Base, then being used as a place of confinement for Taliban fighters captured during combat in Afghanistan. This is all the more remarkable since return of the base to Cuban sovereignty has long been one of the primary demands of the Castro government. Moreover, in sharp contrast to Western European, Latin American, and U.S. liberal protests, General Castro "expressed Cuba's confidence that the U.S. government will fulfill its declarations regarding the humane treatment of prisoners." Should any Taliban fighter manage to escape to territorial Cuba, he emphasized, "I . . . say that they would be captured and returned."[32] A more emphatic wink to the United States could hardly be imagined.

To be sure, on paper the Helms-Burton Law precludes such an alliance. Indeed, it raises the bar for resumption of relations so high that one cannot help thinking that its purpose was to prevent such an eventuality rather than facilitate it. Concretely, its Title II, section 205 requires a radical transformation of Cuba, including free and fair elections; the release of all political prisoners; establishment of the right of free speech, assembly, press, and political activity; and progress toward compensating the owners of confiscated property. Even more remarkably, it specifically indicates that any future government of Cuba cannot include either Fidel or Raúl Castro, both of whom are specifically named in the legislation.

Nevertheless, no one who knows how the U.S. political process works can doubt that once there is evidence of a new kind of regime in Cuba—even one falling far short of the demands laid down in legislation—the political coalition behind Helms-Burton is bound to break up, as different elements of that constituency (along with many others) reposition themselves to take advantage of the new reality on the ground.[33] Exactly what changes might be required for the United States to perceive any Cuban regime as "new" is difficult to say—presumably almost any alteration but the most fundamental would provoke heated controversy in Washington, Miami, and elsewhere. Still, with so many interests waiting for an excuse to resume relations, it is likely that any credible movement in the right political direction would dissolve much of the glue that holds present U.S. policy together.

In such a situation, one cannot even exclude elements of the Cuban-American community. Its potential for rivalry, factionalism, and discord is always just beneath the surface; it is Fidel Castro alone who has created and maintained its cohesion. Once he is gone, thousands of Cuban-Americans would suddenly have an excuse to visit the island or admit that they have been doing so clandestinely. It may even become acceptable for them to publicly do business there (as some are already attempting to do so through third parties or third countries). For its part, the Cuban government seems ready to make its peace with individual Cuban-Americans, if not the community in its current organized expression. In an interview with the Venezuelan press, National Assembly President Alarcón has pointed piquantly to the fact that Miami is the foreign city that has the closest relations with Cuba (four flights daily) and that Cuban-Americans are the largest single group of visitors to the island (130,000 a year).[34] Foreign Minister Felipe Pérez Roque, speaking to a Miami Cuban radio station (of admittedly leftist tendencies), put it this way: "We defend normal migratory relations between both countries, we defend the right of Cubans to emigrate when they deem it necessary. . . . We do not consider an enemy of the country the Cuban who decides to emigrate for economic reasons, for personal reasons, for family reasons, in search of new opportunities."[35]

Perhaps the best metaphor for conceptualizing the possible evolution of the Cuban-American community can be drawn from the relatively recent history of its Chinese-American counterpart. For many years after the collapse of the Nationalist government in 1949, the U.S. Chinese community was firmly anti-Communist, often led by elderly exiles loyal to the Kuomintang party which had taken refuge on Taiwan. Following President Richard Nixon's visit to China in 1972, younger Chinese-Americans seized upon new opportunities offered by the prospect of normalization, exploiting to full advantage their U.S. citizenship; their knowledge of English and of Chinese dialects; and their potential importance to the business communities of San Francisco, Los Angeles, Seattle, Chicago, and New York. It is hard to believe that a group as rich in entrepreneurial skills as the Cuban-American will—at least in its totality—stand aside to allow others to exploit commercial openings between the island and the United States once they occur.

The Chinese precedent may also serve as a useful predictor for the future attitude of the U.S. conservative community. During the early years of the Cold War, no element of the U.S. political spectrum was more firmly opposed to normalization of relations with Beijing, even to the point of playing to the charade that Chiang Kai-shek's government on Taiwan was the only China, deserving not only an embassy in Washington but also a seat on the Security Council of the United Nations. Three decades after President Nixon's visit, Beijing has opened itself to trade and investment, and "powerful forces within the conservative movement no longer see China as a mortal enemy; they see it as an economic opportunity." The reason is that China, unlike the Soviet Union, "has opened itself to American corporate investment and the lure of the Chinese market has eroded the right's appetite for moral combat."[36] The Cuban market for U.S. products will probably never again be as large as it once was, and the potential for investment in Cuba is an almost invisible speck when compared with the potential in China. Yet Cuba does not represent the kind of strategic threat that Beijing arguably could (or does). Instead, under the stern hand of General Raúl Castro and his minions (perhaps with Alarcón or some other civilian as prime minister or president), it could embody an updated model of the cooperative, friendly, modestly profitable dictatorships that have been historically regarded by many American conservatives as the optimal system for small Caribbean countries.

Ironically, the one discordant note likely to be struck after normalization of relations with Cuba might well come from the group that has fought for normalization longer than any other—the aforementioned civil rights activists, church people, educators, writers, artists, and pacifists. To begin with, the very fact of normalization—that the United States no longer finds the Cuban government objectionable, indeed, grants it the legitimacy it has long craved through full diplomatic recognition—will deprive Cuba overnight of much of its adversarial mystique. (How *revolutionary*, really, can such a government be if it finally is acceptable to Washington?) Moreover, without the embargo to explain persistent poverty and growing inequality on the island, American liberals may cast a more critical glance at the way Cuba is ruled, all the more so when it appears that giant multinationals such as Archer-Daniels-Midland or Cargill are turning out to be the principal beneficiaries of the new state of affairs.

Here the Mexican experience may shed some light on what might be expected. For decades after the Mexican Revolution of 1910, successive governments in that country were regarded as "left wing" or even "revolutionary" by Americans of a progressive persuasion, thanks to an often vehemently anti-U.S. foreign policy and a political culture rich in anti-capitalist and "anti-imperialist" symbolism. Indeed, liberal American intellectuals visiting that country as late as the 1970s—provided they did not look beyond surface appearances—could come away with the notion, thrilling to them, that they had been to a revolutionary socialist republic. In point of fact, for nearly seventy years the prominent features of the Mexican system had been an immensely wealthy business elite closely tied to the ruling Institutional Revolutionary Party (PRI), a forcibly neutered labor movement, rigorous press censorship, a servile intelligentsia, and a sinister network of police agencies specializing in unexplained disappearances of political opponents and "uncooperative" community leaders (in effect, a system similar to, although significantly more sophisticated than, the frequently vilified Guatemalan regime to Mexico's immediate south). Paradoxically—a fact that American innocents usually failed to notice—at the very same time, Mexico was also the favorite Latin America country of Wall Street and the U.S. Department of State, both of which appreciated its stability and predictability.[37]

While Argentina, Chile, and Uruguay received intensive (and justified) scrutiny by the international human rights community throughout the 1970s, Mexico received no attention whatsoever. Then, suddenly, in the early 1980s, for the very first time, Amnesty International mentioned it in its report on torture. In 1986 it followed with a groundbreaking publication on human rights violations in rural areas.[38] Mexico did not earn a place in its annual review, however, until 1988.[39] The following year, Human Rights

Watch (formerly America's Watch) followed suit.[40] The Washington Office on Latin America finally caught up in 1993. From then on, the silence of decades was broken by a flood of Amnesty publications with such garish titles as *Unceasing Abuses* (1991) and *Brutality Unchecked* (1992). The emergence of a rural resistance movement in Chiapas in the mid-1990s purportedly spearheading a nationwide protest against globalization has transformed Mexico—once regarded as untouchable—into one of the chief targets of the international human rights movement.

What led to the change? Unquestionably the rise of a human rights movement in Mexico itself in the middle 1980s was partly responsible. But one cannot help being struck by the coincidence of dates. In 1988 the candidate of the left wing of the ruling Institutional Revolutionary Party (PRI), Cuauhtémoc Cárdenas, failed to obtain the presidential nomination of the PRI. Defeated in the backroom negotiations that perennially decided the outcome of Mexican elections even before they were held, Cárdenas broke with his party and launched an independent candidacy. In the subsequent elections, in all probability he defeated the ruling party's standard-bearer Carlos Salinas de Gortari but was denied the prize by electoral fraud. In the past the protests by the opposition PAN party against ballot manipulation in Mexico fell on deaf ears in the United States and elsewhere, largely because of its image as "right wing" or "Catholic." But as a man of the left and the son of a left-wing president, Cárdenas was ideally placed to shatter the myth of the Mexican Revolution, or at least of its "institutional" party.

More important still, 1988–1989 marks a crucial turning point in the history of Mexican economic policy. The country's government entered into negotiations with the United States for a free trade agreement. In the process, it reformed the Mexican economy, privatizing many government enterprises and changing property laws to make the country more attractive to foreign investors. At the same time, quietly but unmistakably, Mexico also shifted its foreign policies, particularly in Central America, where it had long favored Marxist guerrillas in El Salvador and a Marxist-guerrilla government in Nicaragua.[41] Cuba after Fidel Castro will have to tread a very narrow path between pragmatism and ideology, and take care not to veer too far from its historic "revolutionary" persona, lest it lose its oldest and firmest constituency in the United States.

A Question of Identity

If the present regime survives another seven years—by no means an impossible achievement—it will embrace more than half the country's independent existence. Indeed, one might even argue that the Cuban revolution, however one chooses to regard it, has become virtually coterminous with the Cuban national experience. This is so not only because of its longevity, but because the revolutionary government claims to carry forward (and in a certain way does carry forward) many pre-revolutionary nationalist themes common to Cubans of all political persuasions.[42] As Carlos Alberto Montaner puts it, Cuban history has always been rendered as "an epic tale in which the Cubans, always good and always selfless, suffered the attack and the cruelties of the enemies of their freedom and independence."[43] Expanding on this theme, another expatriate Cuban author points out that the main ideology of Cubans for virtually all of the nineteenth and twentieth centuries has been "revolutionism" of one form or another—against Spain, against different governments during the republican period (1901–1959), and subsequently against the United States. "Together with a faith in political violence as the proper method of gaining independence and consolidating the Cuban nationality," he adds, "another essential element of continuity is a belief in a particularly grandiose destiny which the Cuban people were called upon to fulfill, largely through emancipatory warfare."[44]

Curiously enough, in some ways this dimension of Cuban national identity has only been enhanced and enlarged since the collapse of the Soviet Union. Having survived the disappearance of its principal ally and trading partner, Cuba is more than ever a credible example to Latin Americans—and not only to those of a leftist persuasion—of "courage, imagination, liberation, a widening of horizons, above all a praiseworthy affirmation of Latin American identity against the Colossus of the North."[45] And not to Latin Americans alone. As a principal exemplar of the growing worldwide antiglobalization movement, Cuba benefits from new sources of emotional solidarity in Western Europe, Canada, Africa, and parts of Asia, as well as the elite media and the universities in the United States.[46] While good wishes from around the globe are no substitute for a six-billion-dollar annual subsidy from the Soviet Union, in terms meaningful to Cuba's elites—and for all one can know, substantial sections of the Cuban public—they nourish a pride and self-respect which, like all small countries, the island has always passionately sought. At the same time, Cuba's position as a kind of founding member of the hate-America club—an organization with a rapidly growing membership worldwide—raises its international stature and prestige far beyond what its concrete indices of wealth and power might otherwise justify.[47]

Moreover, countries have to explain their national experiences to themselves. In the Cuban case, much of this must be done in largely ideological terms, since the revolution itself has constructed so little in the way of houses, roads, or permanent infrastructure; the havoc it has visited upon important parts of the island's natural environment raises still higher the bar to full economic recovery. Even the much-vaunted achievements in education and health have suffered such serious deterioration since 1990 that one must increasingly speak of them in the past tense. The centerpiece of Cuba's revolutionary experience must be, therefore, resistance to U.S. "hegemonism." For this reason, the Museum of the Revolution in Havana gives pride of place to the defeat of the exile force at the Bay of Pigs and the alleged importation of a virus to destroy Cuban livestock.[48]

But the Cuban revolution is also "about" Cuba's global reach—aiding and training revolutionaries in Latin America, but also fighting the South Africans and their allies in Angola or the enemies of the pro-Soviet regime in Ethiopia. While North Americans or Westerners in general might regard Cuban activities in Africa as a sort of bizarre sideshow to the Cold War, Cubans themselves (and perhaps many Africans) see that role as crucial to breaking the back of white rule in Southern Africa, or in a larger regional sense, of destroying the nefarious "imperialist" pretensions of the United States and its European allies. For decades to come, Cuban children may be taught that one of their country's greatest achievements was helping to end more than two centuries of colonialism, racism, and other attendant evils in the Dark Continent. Whether what has replaced them is better or worse for the Africans themselves is another matter, as is the question of whether the thousands of Cubans who lie in unmarked graves thousands of miles from home might not have met a different and happier destiny.[49]

Since 1989, Cuba has emphasized its exportation of doctors, teachers, sports trainers, and other specialists to the Third World. The humanitarian dimension of this practice loses some of its luster, however, when examined more carefully. Cuba typically rents out its people in exchange for hard currency from host governments (or, in the case of Hugo Chávez's Venezuela, for oil at fire-sale prices). In recent times it has been reported that thousands of Cubans are working in Spain as construction workers (at salaries roughly a quarter to a third of those paid to local laborers); likewise, Cuban women are being exported to Italy, supposedly to work as hotel maids or dancers (but in the case of the latter, very possibly as prostitutes).[50]

To be sure, no one can say how normalization of relations with the United States will compromise Cuba's revolutionary identity, if indeed it does at all. If the case of Mexico offers any guidance, a Latin American revolutionary regime may be able to sustain significant cognitive dissidence for generations. From a substantive point of view, the Mexican revolution (1910–1940) ended its radical phase relatively early—in some interpretations at the very moment it gained diplomatic recognition from the United States in 1923.[51] Nonetheless, as late as the 1970s, school textbooks in that country were still being written in an extreme Marxist vein, even to the point of praising Asian Communist leaders like Mao Zedong and Ho Chi Minh.[52] Perhaps Cuba's revolutionary experience has been so searing and intense that it will continue to shape public discourse and national identity indefinitely. But even if it does, Cubans will still have to find a way of explaining to themselves and their children why the return to the island of American business and American tourists—the very vices that the revolution was presumably called upon to eradicate—should be regarded as its final (and greatest) victory.

The Riddle of Cuban Nationalism

The collapse of the Soviet Union and the end of the Cuban-Soviet alliance have shifted the ideological focus of the regime away from Marxist socialism toward an emphasis on sovereignty and anti-Americanism. Indeed, at this point one might almost say that these are the only elements that remain of the Cuban ideology. For some foreigners, particularly foreign academics, this seems eminently logical. Cubans *should* hate the United States, and it is the fault of the United States that they do.[53] But, as journalist David Rieff has observed, to depend so heavily on abstractions like sovereignty and anti-Americanism "could be seen as bespeaking a weak national identity rather than a strong one Cubans often boast of. . . . The emphasis on sovereignty and combat can be understood to express the fear that the United States will overwhelm Cuba's identity."[54] Perhaps indeed—despite the image the regime projects—the siren song of American culture is already doing so.

The curious fact is that despite forty years of anti-U.S. rhetoric in official propaganda outlets—not to mention morbid media attention to every incident in American society intended to emphasize its violence, racism, and fundamental economic inequality—the Cuban fascination for the United States is perhaps greater than it has ever been. "Like a pining ex-lover," writes a Canadian visitor, "being cut off from the United States has done nothing to dampen the Cubans' nostalgia for all that is North American—from old cars to movie stars."[55]

This observation is supported by much anecdotal evidence. Clandestine access to U.S. television by pirating signals has become the fashion in Cuba "for all ages, tastes, and economic means," challenging government control of the media. The most popular television program in the capital—for those who have access to it—is the same as in Miami, *Sábado Gigante*.[56] Any visitor to Havana is immediately struck by the number of young people wearing T-shirts from American colleges, or even—Heaven forfend!—with the American flag emblazoned on the front. As one Swiss journalist points out, the relationship between the island and the exile community "has grown into an actual obsession" on the part of the country's artistic elite. One recent film representing the experience of two disillusioned Miami expatriates who have returned to Cuba is intended to drive home the sterility and rootlessness of exile life in the United States. But, the same writer points out, "among younger audiences, even before they enter the cinema, the very idea of anyone returning to Cuba voluntarily causes them to shake their heads."[57]

Indeed, today just as in the days of the old Cuba, the mere presence of the United States nearby—a model that, for all its attractiveness, can never be fully replicated at home—continues to constitute a potentially destabilizing force in Cuban politics. This point, made in chapter 1, bears amplification here. Before the revolution, it was useless to point out to Cubans that they had very nearly the highest standard of living in Latin America, since it was not to Latin America but the United States that they compared themselves.

Two generations later, nothing appears to have changed. "I'm not saying I suffer like in Africa," one young Cuban recently told an American journalist, "but Africa did not have forty-two years of revolution. If you are comparing us for forty-two years with the United States only in bad things, why not the good also." And, he added tellingly, "Don't compare me with those children who die in Africa. Compare me with the children who go to school in Miami on motorcycles."

One of the island's leading dissidents considers this continuing and even deepening attraction to the United States "very dangerous." As he explains, "Here the culture is controlled. The worry is that when there is a change there could also be a transformation from the most anti-American place on earth to an invasion where people embrace a culture that is not theirs." One example he cited was the popularity of American gangster films. Although the government presumably approves their distribution on the grounds that they reveal the dark underside of American society, the actual reaction of viewers may not be what is anticipated. "You hear people say, 'You saw the car the bad guy had?'"[58]

In many ways this paradox is far from new. "Though some will point to the irony of so nationalist a regime unable to guarantee a satisfactory national synthesis," two Cuban-American scholars have written, "this is not the first time in Cuban history that this has occurred." Indeed, all three Cuban regimes since independence—the "old republic" (1901–1933) of soldiers and students, followed by the reign of Batista (1934–1958) and the Castro revolution (beginning in 1959) have failed "to generate a viable model of political and economic development accompanied by a solid cultural identity and authentic national self-confidence." Cuba, they conclude, closes the twentieth century "still struggling to define its national identity and sovereignty."[59]

The exile community in Florida—even when granted its often-exaggerated rhetoric, ideological intransigence, and capacity to polarize opinion—has contributed to the decline of nationalism on the island. Today Cubans of all classes and conditions *know,* both as a matter of fact and in their bones, that the United States has become the place where hundreds of thousands of their compatriots can and do realize many of their ambitions and live a more satisfying life, all the more so because, unlike other immigrant groups, they have refused to surrender their identity in the process. (To many Cubans, the

United States is not the fifty states at all, but a kind of ideal Cuba, a dreamland they frequently call "la Yuma," where all the promises of the revolution have been fulfilled.)

This is not to suggest that no important political and cultural differences remain to divide the two communities. The Cubans of southern Florida, at least those who belong to the more established first waves of immigration, practice a nationalism of their own, one that is far less racially inclusive and less socially liberal than the one that was common to Cuba before 1959. Indeed, one Cuban-American who went to the island for the first time since her infancy during the visit of Pope John II in 1998 cautioned her compatriots "to accept [the fact] that when a transition actually takes place, the Cuba that will be there will be far from the ideal we have struggled for." And, she adds, those in the exile community "will have to work with people who've lived under the current system all their lives and have idiosyncrasies and ideas very different from those of us who left. . . . This is the only possible answer to rescuing something from the ashes that injustice, hatred, antagonism, abuse, division, separation, exclusion, deprivation—indeed, a long trail of sufferings—have left behind."[60] If the exile community fails to heed this generous, well-founded counsel, it may succeed in rescuing from the ashbin of history the revolutionary nationalism discredited by a half-century of practice.

The United States and Cuba: The Question of Insertion

For many years, the Cuban government regarded the U.S. trade embargo as a futile gesture that in no way prevented the regime from functioning effectively. Indeed, one of the major achievements of the revolution was thought to be the ease and celerity with which it was circumvented. Since the collapse of the Soviet Union, however, the government has completely changed its tune: now the embargo—not the loss of a six-billion-dollar annual subsidy, much less an irrational economic system—is the sole and unique cause of all the island's ills. If children die in hospitals; if there are no books or pencils in schools; if cities are subject to repeated blackouts; if the ration stores have no rice or beans—it is all due to the U.S. "blockade."[61] Presumably, once the United States reverses its policy, milk and honey will flow. To the extent that ordinary Cubans believe this, they are pinning their hopes for the future on a very shaky proposition.

For the fact is that Cuba and the United States have both changed over the past half-century in ways that make it impossible to resume the kind of relationship that existed in the past, for good or for ill. To some extent, Cuban patriots of all persuasions can appreciate at least one achievement of the revolution—never again will the United States play the role on the island it once did. But the reverse holds true as well. Today Cuba has nothing the United States needs or wants. Sugar is a drug on the world market, and in any case, the Cuban industry is in ruins and there are few incentives to revive it. Cuba's geographical position is no longer of much strategic interest; the United States no longer controls the Panama Canal, and therefore need not trouble itself excessively about its seaborne approaches. Although there is some modest potential for tourism, it will be decades before Cuba is in a position to compete effectively with Mexico and the other Caribbean islands; indeed, much of its appeal to Americans at present is its forbidden quality. Once they are allowed to visit it, Cuba will lose its special draw, particularly when compared with more developed facilities elsewhere. In any case, one cannot speak of any particular tourist venue—as opposed, say, to oil—as something the United States, or for that matter anyone else, "needs."

Indeed, the principal concern of the United States down the line may be Cuba's lack of economic viability—not only because of changes in the world economy, but because of the destruction of the sugar industry and Cuba's loss of its formerly dominant place in the global sweetener market. To this must be added the inherent limitations of tourism as a source of revenue, not to mention bad habits inculcated by nearly a half-century of socialism—loss of respect for work; the assumption that free housing, education, and health care are a matter of right; a tendency to steal raw materials from factories and farms; the constant recurrence to black-market operations;[62] or the widespread practice of bribing officials to engage in illicit practices.[63] Even the supposed proliferation of scientists, technicians, and engineers—according to the Cuban government as numerous in the population as in the advanced industrial countries—may prove to be a burden rather than an asset, since the country is unlikely to ever possess the kind of infrastructure capable of absorbing such large amounts of sophisticated manpower. As it is, with some 7,000 veterinarians and 11,000 agronomists, Cuba is far from able to feed itself.[64]

These economic problems are bound to be complicated by three other factors. One is Cuba's curious demography: a birthrate that is below replacement level, a steady exodus of young people, and a growing elderly population of 1.5 million. By 2025, the country will have one of the oldest populations in the world.[65] Meanwhile, Cuba's pension system is virtually bankrupt. This portends a major social crisis that no government, regardless of its ideology, will find easy to resolve.[66] Another problem is the potential contagion of a more open people-to-people relationship with the United States. American tourists—unlike their Canadian, European, or Latin American counterparts—are intrusive and inquiring. At present, the American citizens Cubans have the opportunity to meet—with the exception, evidently, of Cuban-Americans returning to see their families—are for the most part supportive of the revolutionary regime or at any rate critical of their own country's policies toward it. (Many deliberately defy U.S. Treasury regulations to travel to the island in order to make a concrete political statement.) In an atmosphere of normal travel, the kind of Americans with whom ordinary Cubans regularly come in contact will be less self-selecting. And with a ratcheting up of the number of visitors by several orders of magnitude, the authoritarian apparatus may also find it far more difficult to meet its daily policing tasks. To the extent that this creates problems of public order, it may ultimately provide as much cause for concern in Washington as in Havana.

Finally, there is the question of immigration. For four decades U.S. willingness to take unhappy or dissatisfied Cubans off the revolution's hands has been one of the principal factors underpinning the country's fundamental stability. The same, of course, could be said to some extent of nonrevolutionary societies such as the Dominican Republic or Jamaica or even Mexico. The difference, however, is that the aforementioned have economic systems that at least permit some growth and diversification, particularly in the small business sector. Such cannot be permitted in Cuba without fundamentally endangering the political order, so that pressures to emigrate are bound to intensify in coming years. Will the United States be able—in the face of lobbying from other national and racial interest groups—to maintain its special entry regime for Cubans in an environment of détente and improved political relations? Will it even want to? And if it fails to do so, will it be prepared to pay the price in terms of disorder on the island?

HARD TIMES

Independent economist Oscar Espinosa Chepe points out that the average Cuban pension of 104 pesos a month (U.S. $4.73) is not enough to buy a gallon of cooking oil in government stores. Moreover, he adds, expenditures for social security are rising: in 1989, they consumed 7.8 percent of the total budget; ten years later, 13.0 percent, but without any significant increase in individual retirement pensions. At the same time, the deficit in the social security fund almost doubled—from 417.5 million pesos in 1989 to 700 million in 1999. ["Dismal Future," Cubanet.org, June 25, 2001.]

At the end of the day, then, Cuba and the United States are poised to end more than four decades of conflict in ways that neither could have anticipated in 1959. On one hand, in its revolutionary expression, Cuba has stood down all attempts to destroy it—by exile invasions, trade embargoes, radio broadcasts, strong-armed diplomacy, even the loss of its overseas patron and protector. On the other, having mortgaged its vision of the future to a fraudulent doctrine of economic and social organization, it has lost the vitality and resources—moral and material—that once made it an economic and cultural leader in Latin America. Indeed, in many ways the revolution has put an end to Cuba's *Sonderweg*, turning the island into just another Caribbean principality, dependent upon tourism, remittances from its overseas nationals, and a few specialty exports such as cigars, rum, or nickel, as well as one or two biomedical products. The primordial dependence on tourism in particular is ironic. It not only bespeaks a historic failure to develop a measure of self-sufficiency in agriculture and industry, but constitutes "an enthusiastic surrender to a foreign domination more subtle, but no less real, than the one Castro claims to have repulsed 40 years ago."[67] Such an outcome is a strange destiny for a country whose ambitions and aspirations have always outrun its possibilities.

Meanwhile, the United States has gone from strength to strength, emerging as the world's only superpower. It can draw no satisfaction, however, from Cuba's problematic status. Failed states typically become—like Haiti—platforms for the export of illicit substances, centers of international criminality, and vessels leaking illegal migrants. Perhaps, indeed, the island will somehow avoid this fate, but present indicators do not offer much encouragement. The only certainty that lies ahead is that Cuba—under whatever political guise—is bound to pose immense dilemmas for the United States, a country to which it is linked by history, geography, and imagination, whether either side wills it or not.

Notes

Chapter 1: The Shadow of the Past

1. Lowry Nelson, *Cuba: The Measure of a Revolution* (Minneapolis: University of Minnesota Press, 1972), 184–185.

2. In many ways, *Havana* was intended as a remake of the earlier Humphrey Bogart film, *Casablanca,* with the Cuban revolutionaries acting as a contemporary expression of the anti-Nazi resistance and Batista standing in as a rather pallid substitute for Adolf Hitler. For some idea of Redford's muddled political ideas about Cuba and Castro, see Merle Linda Wolin, "Hollywood Goes Havana: Fidel, Gabriel and the Sundance Kid," *New Republic*, 16 April 1990.

3. Arthur Schlesinger, Jr., *A Thousand Days: John F. Kennedy in the White House* (Boston: Houghton Mifflin, 1965), 173.

4. Compare the opening lines of Robert Redford's film: "I've been a lot of places since Pearl Harbor, . . . but there's only one city I miss. General Batista's been running the country for almost thirty years. But this is 1958 and we weren't paying attention to the rebels in the hills. All we knew about Havana was that the lights in the Prado never went out, and if you had a dame you had the chance for the time of your life."

5. Quotes taken from Episode 10, "Cuba," *The Cold War* (CNN).

6. "Unofficial Envoy: An Historic Report from Two Capitals," *New Republic,* 7 December 1963.

7. Quoted in Hugh Thomas, *Cuba: The Pursuit of Freedom* (New York: Harper and Row, 1971), 216.

8. Quoted in Robert F. Smith, *What Happened in Cuba: A Documentary History* (New York: Twayne Publishers, 1963), 33, 35.

9. Quoted in Thomas, *Cuba*, 101.

10. Spanish historians and some Cuban historians as well have traditionally argued that the United States purposely ignited the ship to provide it with an excuse to intervene. It appears, however, that the *Maine* blew up because it was carrying excessive quantities of a new kind of gunpowder that was needed for heavier guns but often caused explosions in its first years of use. See Thomas, *Cuba*, 361–364.

11. These points are explored with considerable sophistication in Robert Freeman Smith, *The United States and Cuba: Business and Diplomacy, 1917–1960* (New

243

Haven, Conn.: College and University Press, 1960), and in Marifeli Pérez-Stable, *The Cuban Revolution: Origins, Course, and Legacy* (New York: Oxford University Press, 1993).

12. Alistair Hennessy, "Cuba," in *The Spanish Civil War, 1936–39: American Hemispheric Perspectives,* ed. Mark Falcoff and F. B. Pike (Lincoln, Neb.: University of Nebraska Press, 1982), 105.

13. For two richly filigreed accounts of these complex events, see Luis Aguilar, *Cuba, 1933: Prologue to Revolution* (Ithaca, N.Y.: Cornell University Press, 1972) and Justo Carillo, *Cuba 1933: Students, Yankees, and Soldiers* (New Brunswick, N.J.: Transaction Publishers, 1994).

14. Roosevelt's innovations were actually the culmination of a long process inasmuch as a good deal of rethinking about the desirability of U.S. military and diplomatic intervention had taken place in both the Coolidge and Hoover administrations. See Bryce Wood, *The Making of the Good Neighbor Policy* (New York: Columbia University Press, 1961).

15. See Mark Falcoff, ed., *The Cuban Revolution and the United States, 1958–1960: A History in Documents* (Washington, D.C.: U.S. Cuba Press, 2001).

16. It is easy to lose sight of Cuba's uniqueness in this regard, since we are speaking here of the days before jet travel, satellite television broadcasts, inexpensive long distance service, low-cost tourism, massive Latin emigration, and the globalization of the world economy, all of which have greatly diminished the cultural and physical distance between the rest of Latin America and the United States.

17. See chap. 2.

18. For a fuller discussion, see Pérez-Stable, *The Cuban Revolution,* chaps. 1–2.

19. Henry Wriston, "A Historical Perspective," in *Cuba and the United States: Long-Range Perspectives,* ed. John Plank (Washington, D.C.: Brookings Institution, 1967), 28–29, and Boris Goldenberg, *The Cuban Revolution and the United States* (New York: Praeger, 1966), 121–122.

20. This is the argument of James O'Connor, *The Origins of Socialism in Cuba* (Ithaca, N.Y.: Cornell University Press, 1970).

21. Goldenberg, *The Cuban Revolution,* 136.

22. *Verde Olivo,* 30 July 1961, quoted in Theodore Draper, *Castro's Revolution: Myths and Realities* (New York: Praeger, 1962), 22n.

23. Ernesto Guevara, *Che Guevara on Guerrilla Warfare* (New York: Praeger, 1962). See also Luigi Einaudi, *Cuban Concepts of Revolution* (Santa Monica, Cal.: RAND, 1965). The American leftist expatriate Maurice Halperin, who went to Havana from Moscow in the early 1960s to work in a government agency, was at first astounded by Cuba's living standard, which was considerably higher than that of the Soviet Union, where he had already spent several years. "Later," he writes, "it became clear that Cuba's infant socialism was living off the fat of Cuban capitalism" rather than producing abundance on its own. See Maurice Halperin, *Return to Havana: The Decline of Cuban Society under Castro* (Nashville, Tenn.: Vanderbilt University Press, 1994), 23–24.

24. Goldenberg, *The Cuban Revolution*, 121; Nelson, *Cuba: The Measure of a Revolution*, 44–49; Vicente Echerri, "Cuba: autopsía de revolución" in *La isla a fin de siglo: Cuba y el futuro de su libertad*, ed. Julio A. Torrente (n.p., n.d.), 262–263; Draper, *Castro's Revolution*, 21–23; Manuel Sánchez Herrero and Arnaldo Ramos Lauzurique, *The So-called "Achievements" of the Cuban Revolution* (Miami: Cuban Dissidence Task Group, n.d.), n.p.; Jorge Salazar-Carillo, "Independence and Economic Performance in Cuba," in *Cuban Communism*, 7th ed., ed. Irving Louis Horowitz (New Brunswick, N.J.: Transaction Publishers, 1984), 227–234; Norman Luxenberg, "Social Conditions Before and After the Revolution," in *Cuban Communism*, 5th ed., ed. Irving Louis Horowitz (New Brunswick, N.J.: Transaction Publishers, 1983), 407–414. These sources utilize figures from the World Bank, World Health Organization, United Nations, Organization of American States, the *Statistical Abstract of Latin America*, and Cuba's own *Anuario Estadístico*.

25. Nelson, *Cuba: The Measure of a Revolution*, 189; Manuel Sánchez Herrero, "El 'igualitarismo' en Cuba," *ICEI Boletín del Instituto Cubano de Economistas Independientes* 1, no. 1 (January-February 1996).

26. Goldenberg, *The Cuban Revolution*, 126.

27. Ibid., 132–133.

28. A report by the International Bank for Reconstruction and Development (*Investment in Cuba*, 1950) put the matter succinctly. "Living levels of the farmers, agricultural laborers, industrial workers, storekeepers and others, are higher all along the line than for corresponding groups in other tropical countries and in nearly all other Latin American countries. This does not mean," it cautioned, "that there is no dire poverty in Cuba, but simply that in comparative terms Cubans are better off, *on the average*, than people of other areas." Emphasis added. Quoted in Goldenberg, *The Cuban Revolution*, 123.

29. Robert Freeman Smith, "Castro's Revolution: Domestic Sources and Consequences," in *Cuba and the United States*, ed. John Plank (Washington, D.C.: Brookings Institution, 1967), 58–59.

30. "Social revolution and the ensuing radical transformation of Cuban society were neither inevitable nor aberrational. The old Cuba sheltered these options as well as others that were never or only partially realized." Pérez-Stable, *The Cuban Revolution*, 7.

31. The term is Pérez-Stable's.

32. David Gonzalez, "To Have and Have Not: Cubans' Life with Castro," *New York Times*, 22 December 1999.

33. Kevin J. Whitelaw and Carey W. English, "World Poverty: Factoring in Healthy and Wise," *U.S. News and World Report*, 23 June 1997.

34. United Nations Development Program, *Human Development Report: 1999* (New York: Oxford University Press, 1999), 134–135.

35. Ibid., 146–147.

36. Since 1988, the Cuban government not only has refused to release data on its Gross Domestic Product, but has rigorously withheld information on the distribution

of income, wages in agricultural and nonagricultural activities, the incidence of poverty, even the actual occupational distribution of the labor force. See James Wilkie and José Guadalupe Ortega, eds., *Statistical Abstract of Latin America,* vol. 33 (Los Angeles: UCLA Latin American Center, 1997). Carmelo Mesa-Lago has written that it is "impossible to estimate the crucial economic indicator of the H[uman] D[evelopment] I[ndex] [for Cuba] because of the lack of essential statistics." Moreover, journalists and other commentators seem unaware of the fact that in the 1990s the United Nations covertly shifted its methodologies in ranking countries. As a result, in the 1999 edition of the *Report* (based on 1997 data), Cuba was inexplicably catapulted from 85th to 58th place in the world and from 11th to 9th in Latin America; in the 2000 edition, Cuba climbed to the 56th and 6th places, respectively. "This miraculous leap could not be justified," he finds, "based on the incomplete process of economic recovery on the island." For a fuller discussion of these points, see Carmelo Mesa-Lago, "Cuba in the Human Development Index in the 1990s: Decline, Rebound and Exclusion" in *Cuba in Transition,* vol. 12 (Washington, D.C.: Association for the Study of the Cuban Economy, 2002), 450–463. I am grateful to Professor Mesa-Lago for making available a prepublication copy of the manuscript.

37. United Nations, *Human Development Report: 1999,* 142–143.

38. How they disaggregate male and female incomes when both occupy the same household is not clear, since Cuba's national accounts do not separate out such data by gender.

39. Juan Tamayo, "La economía cubana fue 'abominable' en 1998," *El Nuevo Herald* (Miami), 9 July 1999. A French embassy report, which characterized Cuba's economy performance as "execrable," was available at www.dree.org/cuba/francais/infoeco/sit-fit.htm (accessed 2001).

40. Carmelo Mesa-Lago, "The Cuban Economy in 1999–2001: Evaluation of Performance and Debate on the Future," in *Cuba in Transition,* vol. 11 (Washington, D.C.: Association for the Study of the Cuban Economy, 2001), 5.

41. In fact, *all* Latin American countries have made dramatic improvements in literacy during the past forty years, including even Paraguay, where literacy increased from 68 to 92 percent. Is this an "achievement" to be credited to the dictatorship of the egregious General Alfredo Stroessner?

42. Jorge Pérez-López, "The Cuban Economy in an Unending Special Period" (paper prepared for Conference on Cuba, Colegio de México, 15 March 2002), Table 1.

43. Manuel Sánchez Herrero and Arnaldo Ramos Lauzurique, "El sector agropecuario cubano bajo el socialismo de estado," in *Cuba in Transition,* vol. 8 (Washington, D.C.: Association for the Study of the Cuban Economy, 1998), 439–459.

44. Mesa-Lago, "The Cuban Economy in 1999–2001," 8.

45. Agricultural Development Consultants, Inc., *Cuban Agriculture in the 1990s* (Arlington, Va.: U.S.-Cuba Business Council, 1999). The statistics in this report are

drawn from the United Nations Food and Agriculture Organization (FAO), the Economic Commission for Latin America, and Cuba's own official *Boletín Estadístico.*

46. Carlos Franqui, former editor of the official daily *Revolución,* cautions against excessive praise for the regime's "achievements" in the area of health services. "Communist medicine is not Western medicine," he writes. "Its quality is inferior, and the Cuban population accustomed to it is forced now to accept a kind of penicillin that produces horrendous side effects." Members of the ruling elite typically consume Western medicines, not Cuban products, and even during the days of the Soviet alliance, ailing members of the high nomenklatura were sent to Western medical centers, rather than Moscow, for treatment. He summarizes matters thusly: "Today in Cuba there are more doctors, nurses, and hospitals; less medicine; less quality in the pharmaceutical products, and a tremendous backwardness in surgery, science, and medical education." Carlos Franqui, *Vida, aventuras y desastres de un hombre llamado Castro* (Barcelona: Planeta, 1988), 428–430.

47. Wilkie and Ortega, *Statistical Abstract of Latin America.* See also Claudia Márquez, "Más de 3 milliones de abortos en 30 anos," *El Nuevo Herald,* 23 September 2000. According to a physician who recently defected to the United States, Cuban doctors are encouraged to forcibly terminate potentially problematic births. Dessy Mendoza Rivero (with Illeana Fuentes and Ena Curnow), *Cuban Doctor: Epidemics and Public Health Care in Revolutionary Cuba* (Washington, D.C.: Center for a Free Cuba, forthcoming). For a worm's eye view, so to speak, of health care in Cuba, see Prensa Independiente en Cuba, *Salud pública cubana: otro perfil* (Coral Gables, Fla.: Cubanet, 2000).

48. The rate in Cuba was so high in 1982 (23.2 per 100,000 persons—a record for the country) that a special commission was appointed to investigate the causes. It should be noted that Cuban émigrés in the United States also suffer from a high suicide rate—the highest, in fact, of all large Hispanic groups. Of course, Cubans are the only Hispanics that qualify as "exiles" rather than immigrants, and as such are subject to special emotional and identity problems. See Maida Donate-Armada and Zoila Macías, *Suicide in Miami and Cuba* (Miami: The Cuban American National Council, Inc., 1998), 24, 41.

49. David Rieff, "Cuba Refrozen," *Foreign Affairs* (July-August 1996): 69.

50. Human Rights Watch, *Cuba's Repressive Machinery* (New York, Washington, London, and Brussels: Human Rights Watch, 1999), 1.

51. A survey conducted between December 1998 and April 1999 of more than 1,000 Cubans who had been living in the United States for three months or less revealed that, even among a sample made up almost exclusively of regime opponents, fully 90 percent favored the retention of free education and 89 percent free medical care in a post-Castro Cuba. Presumably the figures on the part of regime supporters— that is, those who do not choose to leave the island—would be even higher. *Measuring Cuban Public Opinion: A Project Report* (Gainesville: University of Florida/U.S. Agency for International Development, 1999), Tables 8B and 12B.

Chapter 2: Sugar

1. These have been collected by Hugh Thomas, *Cuba: The Pursuit of Freedom* (New York: Harper and Row, 1971), 1151–1152, and by Philip Bonsal, *Castro, Cuba, and the United States* (Pittsburgh: University of Pittsburgh Press, 1971), 229–245. I have followed Thomas' narrative closely here.

2. Thomas, *Cuba,* 1152.

3. The moving forces behind this piece of legislation were W. R. Grace and Company, the Hershey Company, the Baltimore Association of Commerce, and the Revere Sugar Company. Hershey was, of course, a huge consumer of industrial sugars and also an important landowner in Cuba. Robert Freeman Smith, *The United States and Cuba: Business and Diplomacy, 1917–1960* (New Haven, Conn.: College and University Press, 1960), 160.

4. "The Cuban Economy," *International Affairs* (October 1964), reprinted in *Venceremos: The Speeches and Writings of Ernesto Che Guevara,* ed. John Gerassi (London: Weidenfeld and Nicolson, 1968), 350.

5. Smith puts it this way: "The Reciprocal Trade Agreement and the Jones-Costigan Act embodied the New Deal approach to reconciling the international economic interests of the country with its domestic economic interests. . . . With these programs the sugar industry entered the era of managed capitalism characterized by regulation of competition. The United States Government assumed the role of 'broker' in mediating between the various segments of the sugar industry." Smith, *The United States and Cuba,* 161.

6. Oscar A. Echevarría, "Cuba and the International Sugar Market," in *Cuba in Transition,* vol. 5 (Washington, D.C.: Association for the Study of the Cuban Economy, 1995). He goes on to explain that the arrangements with the United States also allowed Cuba to have available a substantial standby reserve of almost one million tons of sugar and a capacity to extend the crop season for an additional million tons when needed. Echevarría (364) writes, "This reserve—amounting to almost 20 percent of what at the time was the volume of the international sugar market—allowed Cuba to be a market leader that was very efficient and effective in controlling price and thus the cornerstone of the International Sugar Agreement."

7. This last was neutralized somewhat by the relatively cheap price of land and the high sugar content of Cuban cane—at between 13 and 15 percent, among the highest in the world.

8. Thomas, *Cuba,* 1155.

9. See Mark Falcoff, ed., *The Cuban Revolution and the United States: A History in Documents, 1958–1960* (Washington, D.C.: U.S. Cuba Press, 2001), especially chapters 5, 8, and 9.

10. Theodore Draper, *Castroism: Theory and Practice* (New York: Praeger, 1965), 147.

11. René Dumont, *Is Cuba Socialist?* trans. Stanley Hochman (New York: Viking Press, 1974), 29.

12. Ibid., 29–30.

13. Dumont could not help remarking upon the precipitous abandonment of cotton cultivation, leaving "dozens of Soviet cotton-picking machines . . . rusting in sheds." Further, he added, two factories for processing kenaf remained "very underutilized." Ibid., 31.

14. The Soviet Union actually converted some of its beet sugar lands to other crops and ordered bloc partners Bulgaria and the German Democratic Republic to follow suit to create a market for Cuba where none had existed before.

15. The "convertible ruble" did not exist as a real currency but was merely a measure used to clear trading accounts. It was not, in fact, universally convertible, inasmuch as it could be "used" only within the area of the CMEA and only in some years. Eventually some member countries of CMEA refused to use it at all. This information was provided by a Cuban economist who formerly worked on trade issues for the Castro government.

16. Certainly the relationship was *intended* to be favorable to the Cubans from the Soviet side. Indeed, Cuba was the only member of the Soviet family of nations west of Moscow that was ever treated as a privileged child rather than a colony to be exploited (except insofar as thousands of Cuban soldiers ended up in foreign graves fighting for pro-Soviet regimes in Africa and elsewhere).

17. This is the view, for example, of Maurice Halperin, who served as an economic adviser to the Castro government from 1962 to 1968. See Maurice Halperin, *Return to Havana: The Decline of Cuban Society under Castro* (Nashville, Tenn.: Vanderbilt University Press, 1994), 81.

18. Among other things, GSP excludes so-called nonproductive sectors—for example, education and housing, which are included in GNP—and differs even on the very concept of economic activity being measured. For example, GSP includes the value of intermediate outputs; GNP measures only value added.

19. Jorge F. Pérez-López, "Economic Policies and Their Effects on the Sugar Industry," in *Cuban Communism,* 7th ed., ed. Irving Louis Horowitz (New Brunswick, N.J.: Transaction Publishers, 1989), 382. I have relied heavily on this paper in this section.

20. One hectare is equivalent to 2.471 acres.

21. Lázaro Peña Castellanos and José Alvarez, "The Transformation of the State Extensive Growth Model in Cuba's Sugar Cane Agriculture," in *Cuba in Transition,* vol. 5 (Washington, D.C.: Association for the Study of the Cuban Economy, 1995), 348–361.

22. The hard currency thus earned was used to service the island's Western trading partners and Japan until Cuba unilaterally suspended service on these obligations in 1986.

23. Armando H. Portela, "Cuba va en camino a una zafra pobre," *El Nuevo Herald* (Miami), 13 April 2000; see also "Concluye otra zafra pobre," ibid., 28 May 2000.

24. G. B. Hagelberg in *F. O. Licht's International Sugar and Sweetener Report,* 13 July 2001, quoted in *U.S. Cuba Policy Report* 8, no. 7 (2001). Cuban officials announced in August 2001 that the monthly sugar ration allotted to citizens would

be reduced by a half kilogram, presumably "to improve the nutritional state of the population." "Reducirán la cuota de azúcar a la población," *El Nuevo Herald,* 15 August 2001.

25. Juan Pérez Varela, "Fue un duro batallar de los azucareros," *Granma* (Havana), 1 June 2002.

26. José F. Alonso and Ralph J. Galliano, "Russian Oil-for-Sugar Barter Deals, 1989–1999," in *Cuba in Transition,* vol. 9 (Washington, D.C.: Association for the Study of the Cuban Economy, 1999), 335–341.

27. Alfredo Blanco, Jr., "The 1995–96 Sugar Zafra: Results and Implications— The Machinery Sector," in *Cuba in Transition,* vol. 6 (Washington, D.C.: Association for the Study of the Cuban Economy, 1996), 257.

28. For example, in 1996, the Tinguaro Sugar Mill carried on its payroll some five engineers and one boiler technician, none of whom participated in the mill's operation.

29. G. B. Hagelberg, "Cuba's Sugar Industry: Fettered by Ideology," in *F. O. Licht's International Sugar and Sweetener Report* 132, no. 8 (2000).

30. *U.S. Cuba Policy Report* 7, no. 4 (2000).

31. Agricultural wages in Cuba in 1996 were 4 pesos a day (U.S. $.16), which compares very unfavorably with the wages paid by Nike to its workers in Vietnam (U.S. $.88). The same author calculates that in 1958, field workers in Cuba earned U.S. $3.16 a day. Juan Tomás Sánchez, "Cuba: An Unreliable Producer of Sugar," in *Cuba in Transition,* vol. 6 (Washington, D.C.: Association for the Study of the Cuban Economy, 1996), 260–261.

32. Blanco, "The 1995–1996 Sugar Zafra," 258.

33. Carmelo Mesa-Lago, "Short on Sweet," *Hemisfile* 8, no. 4 (July-August 1997).

34. Hagelberg, "Cuba's Sugar Industry," 128.

35. Mauricio Vincent, "Cuba cierra cerca de la mitad de sus plantas azucareras y despide 100,000 trabajadores," *El País* (Madrid), 9 June 2002; Marc Frank, "Castro desmantela la industria azucarera," *El Nuevo Herald,* 5 June 2002; Jose de Cordoba, "Cuba's Economy is Suffering," *Globetechnology.com,* 6 June 2002.

36. Ron Lord, *Sugar: Background for 1995 Farm Legislation,* Agricultural Economic Report #711 (Washington, D.C.: U.S. Department of Agriculture, 1995).

37. Peter Buzzanell, *Latin America's Big Three Sugar Producers in Transition: Cuba, Mexico, and Brazil,* Agricultural Information Bulletin No. 656 (Washington, D.C.: U.S. Department of Agriculture, 1992), iv.

38. Bruce Stokes, "Raising Cane Won't Help Sugar Growers," *National Journal,* 15 April 2000. "Mexico's growing access," the author writes, "is only one boot in the door. Other Third World sugar producers are already demanding similar treatment and are holding up global trade negotiations to get it." See also Stephen L. Haley, "Sugar in Mexico: Policy Environment and Production Trends," in *Sugar and Sweetener Situation and Outlook Report* (Washington, D.C.: U.S. Department of Agriculture, Economic Research Service, December 1998). Haley points out that in

the 1997–1998 harvest season, Mexico produced a record 5.5 million metric tons, and that 42 percent of Mexico's sixty-two factories have seen significant increases in sugar production per hectare, at performance rates that compare favorably with the Florida industry.

39. "Saccharine No Longer Suspected Carcinogen," *Washington Times,* 16 May 2000. See also Peter Buzzanell and Fred Gray, "Have High-Intensity Sweeteners Reached Their Peak?" *Food Review* 16, no. 3 (September-December 1993), 44–50.

40. Ron Lord and Robert D. Barry, *The World Sugar Market: Government Intervention and Multilateral Policy Reform,* Staff Report No. AGES 9062 (Washington, D.C.: U.S. Department of Agriculture, Economic Research Service, September 1990), 19.

41. Lazaro Peña Castellanos and José Alvarez, "The Cuban Sugar Agroindustry and the International Sweetener Market in the 1990s: Implications for the Future" (paper presented at Conference on Sweetener Markets in the Twenty-First Century, Miami, Fla., 14–16 November 1999).

42. *Sugar and Sweetener Yearbook, 1997,* Doc. no. SSS-222 (Washington, D.C.: U.S. Department of Agriculture, Economic Research Service, 1997).

43. Stokes, "Raising Cane." Here is Ben Goodwin of the California Beet Sugar Growers Association: "The United States must continue to protect domestic sugar producers from unfair trade practices around the sugar world. No one can produce sugar for the current world price unless they receive governmental help. I don't believe that U.S. trade policy can redirect EU sugar subsidies, convince the Mexican government to shut down inefficient plants, influence Brazil's ethanol program, or make Third World producers meet U.S. standards in labor and environment." Ben Goodwin, "The Future of the U.S. Sugar Industry in a Changing Policy Environment," *Agricultural Outlook Forum 2000* (Washington, D.C.: U.S. Department of Agriculture, 2000), n.p.

44. David Swafford, "Cuban Sugar a Concern Equal to NAFTA, GATT," *South Florida Business Journal,* 9 July 1993.

45. Nicolás Rivero, "U.S. Policy Options on Cuban Sugar in a Post-Castro Period," unpublished manuscript. Under Sugar Minister General Rosales del Toro, much emphasis has been given to the development of sugar byproducts, particularly alcohol, animal feed, cane fiberboard, and inputs for its biotech industry. Except for the last, none of these has much potential as an earner of hard currency.

46. Coleen K. Nissl, vice-president and assistant general counsel of Borden, Inc. (address delivered at Fourth Annual Meeting of the Sugar Industry of Cuba Institute, Miami, Fla., 1997).

47. To be precise, as of 2000, Borden's claims were worth $1,121,143,000.

48. See chap. 3.

49. In 2000, citrus production was from 6 to 12 percent below its 1989 level, depending on the estimator. Compare Carmelo Mesa-Lago, "The Cuban Economy in 1999–2001: Evaluation of Performance and Debate on the Future," in *Cuba in Transition,* vol. 11 (Washington, D.C.: Association for the Study of the Cuban

Economy, 2001), 1–15, with Jorge Pérez-López, "The Cuban Economy in an Unending Special Period" (paper prepared for Conference on Cuba, Colegio de México, 15 March 2002), Table 1.

50. Pérez-López, "The Cuban Economy."

51. Mesa-Lago, "The Cuban Economy in 1999–2001."

52. William A. Messina, Jr., Thomas H. Spreen, Anne E. Moseley, and Charles M. Adams, "Cuba's Non-Sugar Agriculture: Current Situation and Prospects," in *Cuba in Transition,* vol. 6 (Washington, D.C.: Association for the Study of the Cuban Economy, 1996), 16–19.

53. James Suckling, "The Treasure of the Vuelta Abajo," *Cigar Aficionado,* Winter 1992.

54. The cigar boom has also led to a rise in clandestine production by farmers and cigar rollers who can make more money working on their own than for the government. So extensive has this practice become that the Cuban government has created a special task force of police officers (the Response Group to Tobacco Traffic) to track down and arrest anyone illegally producing cigars. Jay Amberg, "Cuban Counterfeit Cigar Production Purported to Be on the Rise," Bloomberg.com, 25 June 2001.

55. "Customs Nabs Second Record Illegal Cuban Cigar Shipment," U.S. Treasury Department press release, 3 September 1997. On this occasion, 108 cases of 2,700 cigars could have brought as much as $162,000 on the black market. The previous record seizure a few weeks before netted 81 cases (2,025 cigars), valued at as much as $121,500.

56. Joseph M. Perry, Louis A. Woods, Stephen L. Shapiro, and Jeffrey W. Steagall, "The Cuban Cigar Industry as the Transition Approaches," in *Cuba in Transition,* vol. 8 (Washington, D.C.: Association for the Study of the Cuban Economy, 1998), 414–425.

57. U.S. Federal Trade Commission, *Consumer Alert: Cigars—There's No Such Thing as a Safe Smoke*; Press release, "FTC Announces Settlements Requiring Disclosure of Cigar Health Risks"; Surgeon General's Report on Reducing Tobacco Use, *Warning Label Fact Sheet.*

58. Chuck Adams, "Recent Changes in Management Structure and Strategies of the Cuban Fishing Industry," in *Cuba in Transition,* vol. 10 (Washington, D.C.: Association for the Study of the Cuban Economy, 2000), 121–126. The last year for which official Cuban statistics are available is 1999.

59. Pérez-López, "The Cuban Economy," Table 1.

60. Messina, Jr., et al., "Cuba's Non-Sugar Agriculture," 19–22. The Venezuelan government of President Hugo Chávez has been offering Cuba oil at concessionary prices, but given that country's own ongoing political and economic crisis, the advantage could disappear at any time.

61. Gerardo González Núñez, "The Growth of Cuba's Mining Industry," *Cuba Today* 2, no. 4 (2002).

62. República de Cuba, *Anuario Estadístico* (La Habana, 2000), 140–141.

63. David Pilling, "Cuba's Medical Revolution," *Financial Times* (London), 13 January 2001.

64. Leonard Zehr, "Biotech Builds on Cuban Innovation," Globetechnology.com, 2 May 2001. This company is a successor to York Medical, Inc., which formerly retained the late former Canadian Prime Minister Pierre Trudeau as a "consultant."

65. Julie Feinsilver, "Cuban Biotechnology: A First World Approach to Development," in *Cuba at the Crossroads: Politics and Economics after the Fourth Party Congress,* ed. Jorge Pérez-López (Gainesville, Fla.: University Press of Florida, 1994), 184.

66. Ibid., 181.

67. Ibid., 183.

68. "Wine into Vinegar—The Fall of Cuba's Biotechnology," *Financial Times* (London) 28 November 2001.

69. "La biotecnología aumentó sus exportaciones en 42% en el 2001," *Granma Internacional* (Havana), 18 March 2002.

Chapter 3: Property

1. Emilio Cueto, "Property Claims of Cuban Nationals" (paper presented at Cuba Transition Workshop on Resolution of Property Claims, sponsored by Shaw, Pittman, Potts, and Trowbridge, Washington, D.C., January 1995).

2. Kern Alexander and Jon Mills, "Resolving Property Claims in Post-Socialist Cuba," *Law and Policy in International Business* 27, no. 1 (1995): 145.

3. Paul Sigmund, *Multinationals in Latin America: The Politics of Nationalization* (Madison, Wisc.: University of Wisconsin Press, 1980).

4. Ibid., 36–39.

5. Embassy of Spain, Washington, D.C.

6. Michael W. Gordon, "The Settlement of Claims for Expropriated Property between Cuba and Foreign Nations Other Than the United States," *Lawyer of the Americas* 5 (1973): 461.

7. Ibid., 466.

8. Pedro Monreal, "Las reclamaciones del sector privado de Estados Unidos contra Cuba: una perspectiva académica" (paper presented at the Cuba Transition Workshop cited in note 1 above). Señor Monreal was formerly a research associate of the Centro de Estudios de América in Havana.

9. For its part, the Foreign Claims Settlement Commission found that "no provision was made by the Cuban government for the payment of compensation for such property as required under the generally accepted rules of international law." *Annual Report* (Washington, D.C., 1972), 69.

10. Joseph Kahn, "Cuba May Be Ready to Talk about Expropriation Claims," *New York Times,* 3 June 2000.

11. George Gedda, "Private Entrepreneurs in Cuba Will Visit U.S., Chamber Official Says," *New York Times,* 2 June 2000. Lately the Cuban government,

through Foreign Minister Felipe Pérez Roque, has offered to pay "just and honorable" compensation to U.S.-certified claimants in exchange for a lifting of the embargo. But, he added, such an arrangement would have to take into full account the economic damages caused by U.S. policy since 1959. "Cuba ofrece compensar a compañíes de EE.UU. si levantan embargo," AFP dispatch, 28 November 2001.

12. These include a determination that Cuba has legalized all political activity; released all political prisoners "and allowed for investigations of Cuban prisons by appropriate international human rights organizations"; held internationally supervised elections in a timely manner within a period not exceeding eighteen months; made progress toward an independent judiciary; and most of all, that the existing authorities do not include either Fidel or Raúl Castro (sec. 205 of Helms-Burton Act). See the critique of Jorge Domínguez, "U.S.-Cuban Relations: From the Cold War to the Colder War," *Journal of Inter-American Studies and World Affairs* 39, no. 3 (1997); see also Mark Falcoff, "Response to Jorge Domínguez," *Journal of Inter-American Studies and World Affairs* 40, no. 2 (1998).

13. The actual size of Cuba's Soviet-era debt is difficult to calculate because it was drawn in rubles in a period when there was no reliable exchange rate. The $20 billion figure is the one used by President Vladimir Putin on his visit to Cuba in December 2000.

14. Matías F. Travieso-Díaz, *The Laws and Legal System of a Free Market Cuba* (Westport, Conn.: Quorum Books, 1997), 75. I have followed his argument closely here.

15. Ibid., 95n.

16. See chap. 5.

17. Travieso-Díaz, *Laws and Legal System,* 78. See also Nicolás Gutiérrez, Jr., "Righting Old Wrongs: A Summary of Restitution Schemes for Possible Application to a Democratic Cuba," in *Cuba in Transition,* vol. 6 (Washington, D.C.: Institute for the Study of the Cuban Economy, 1996).

18. Text was available at www.usia.gov/regional/ar/us-cuba/eu18.htm (accessed 2001). See also Stuart E. Eizenstat, "A Multilateral Approach to Property Rights," *Wall Street Journal,* 21 April 1997.

19. Daniel W. Fisk, "The EU-U.S. Agreement and Protection of American Property Rights in Cuba," *Occasional Papers Series* 2, no. 2 (Washington, D.C.: Institute for U.S.-Cuba Relations, 1998), 8.

20. David Wallace, "Certified Claimants and the EU-US Understanding" (remarks at Institute for U.S.-Cuba Relations Policy Forum, Washington, D.C., 23 July 1998).

21. "Dan garantías a los inversionistas de EU más allá de FC," *El Nuevo Herald* (Miami), 24 May 1999.

22. *Financial Times* (London), 6 February 1998.

23. "EU to Appeal against Cuban Rum Ruling," *Financial Times* (London), 6 August 2001. See also "Cuba Files Rum and Cigar Trademark Challenges in the U.S.," *New York Times*, 15 March 1997, and Jerome R. Stockfisch, "Cigar Brands Grow Into Smoldering Topic," *Winston-Salem Journal,* 19 August 2001.

24. "Cuba Files," *New York Times.*

25. Emphasis added.

26. Emphasis added.

27. Quoted in Robert Meese, Esq., *The Libertad Act: Implementation and International Law,* testimony before the Subcommittee on Western Hemisphere and Peace Corps Affairs of the Senate Committee on Foreign Relations, 104th Cong., 2d sess., 1996 (Washington, D.C.: Government Printing Office, 1996) 60.

28. Gutiérrez, "Righting Old Wrongs," 424.

29. Juan O. Tamayo, "Registro para las propiedades confiscadas por Castro," *El Nuevo Herald,* 4 August 1999. See also "Pay Back Time," *Miami Business,* March 2000.

30. "Nicaragua considera 'inaceptable' nuevas condiciones de ayuda de EU," *El Nuevo Herald,* 19 June 2000.

31. "Alemán alza la voz a los reclamos de EU," ibid., 15 June 2000.

32. A somewhat more systematic estimate by two exile economists put the figure at slightly more than $20 billion as of 1993. See Rolando H. Castañeda and George Plinio Montálvan, "Economic Factors in Selecting an Approach to Confiscation Claims in Cuba," in *Cuba in Transition,* vol. 5 (Washington, D.C.: Association for the Study of the Cuban Economy, 1995), 228.

33. U. S. Department of State, Bureau of Public Affairs, "Settlement of Outstanding United States Claims to Confiscated Property in Cuba" (Washington, D.C., 1996).

34. Travieso-Díaz, *Laws and Legal System,* 78.

35. It is true that in April 1952, Batista's Constitutional Act repealed the 1940 charter. The dictator later repromulgated parts of it, without provisions protecting private property. Since he did not follow the indicated amendment procedure, however, it can be argued that his constitutional innovations were null and void. This was certainly the view of important Cuban jurists at the time, including Castro's first president, Manuel Urrutia, and his first prime minister, José Miró Cardona. It should also be noted that from 1956 on, Castro's own program called for restoration of the 1940 Constitution. It was probably the one banner that united all elements of the anti-Batista opposition.

36. Alexander and Mills, "Resolving Property Claims," 148.

37. Juan C. Consuegra-Barquín, "Cuba's Residential Property Ownership Dilemma: A Human Rights Issue under International Law," *Rutgers Law Review* 46, no. 2 (1994).

38. Cueto, "Property Claims of Cuban Nationals," 13.

39. Ibid., 16.

40. In early 2000, the Cuban government suddenly ordered a census of all real estate on the island. According to one source, "everything seems to indicate that the Cuban government is preparing a legal framework to forestall future claims by their former owners or their families." See "Confiscated Real Estate to Be Registered in Camagüey," Cubanet.org, 11 April 2001.

41. Alexander and Mills, "Resolving Property Claims," 183.

42. Castañeda and Montálvan, "Economic Factors," 237.

43. Cueto, "Property Claims of Cuban Nationals," 12.

44. "Registry of Lost Properties Drawing Entries, Criticisms," Associated Press dispatch, 12 August 1990.

45. As part of a "compromise" brokered by former President Jimmy Carter between President-elect Violeta Chamorro and outgoing President Daniel Ortega, the Sandinista party was allowed to keep control of both the army and the police.

46. Castañeda and Montálvan, "Economic Factors," 235–236. See also David González, "Among Unpaid Wages of a Revolution: Competing Claims on Land in Nicaragua," *New York Times,* 10 September 2000.

47. Alexander and Mills, "Resolving Property Claims," 189. I have relied heavily on this article throughout this section.

48. Ibid., 183.

49. The United States is on record as being willing to negotiate this eventuality. See chap. 4.

50. "What Do Cubans Want?" *Miami Herald,* 14 August 2000.

Chapter 4: Security

1. See Mark Falcoff, ed., *The Cuban Revolution and the United States, 1958–1960: A History in Documents* (Washington, D.C.: U.S. Cuba Press, 2001), especially chap. 5.

2. When asked to comment on the Cuban claim that "it was their own idea to intervene in Africa," former Secretary of State Henry Kissinger offered this piquant reply: "I think that is possible but not probable. I am sure there are a lot of Caribbean islands that have a dream of global significance. But without Soviet logistics, transportation, and subvention, the Cubans could not have implemented it." *For the Record: Selected Statements, 1977–1980* (Boston: Little, Brown, 1981), 138.

3. Jorge Domínguez, *To Make a World Safe for Revolution: Cuba's Foreign Policy* (Cambridge, Mass.: Harvard University Press, 1989).

4. For example, compare *Cuba: Assessing the Threat to U.S. Security,* ed. Adolfo Leyva de Varona (Miami: Endowment for Cuban American Studies, 2001) with Center for International Policy, *Cuba Policy Should Be Reviewed in New International Context* (Washington, D.C., 2001).

5. U.S. Department of Defense, *The Cuban Threat to U.S. National Security* (Washington, D.C., 1998). See also "Secretary Cohen Forwards Cuban Threat Assessment to Congress," News Release, Office of Assistant Secretary of Defense, 6 May 1998.

6. William J. Casey Institute, *Perspective,* no. 98-C 54 (Washington, D.C.: Center for Security Policy, March 1998).

7. *Congressional Record,* 106th Cong., 1st sess. (25 March 1998): 1529. The broad thrust of the document had been leaked by the *Miami Herald* some weeks before its actual release, inspiring Rep. Díaz-Balart's remarks.

8. "No Cuban Threat," *Voice of America,* 1 April 1998.

9. Tim Golden, "Pentagon's Top Cuba Expert Pleads Guilty to Espionage," *New York Times,* 20 March 2002.

10. In a May 2001 survey of more than 1,500 American adults, the Pew Research Center for the People and the Press found that 20 percent considered the existence of the Castro regime in Cuba to be a "major threat," while 43 percent regarded it as a "minor threat." Another 26 percent opted for "not a threat."

11. Irving Louis Horowitz, "Military Origins and Outcomes of the Cuban Revolution," in *Cuban Communism,* 7th ed., ed. Irving Louis Horowitz (New Brunswick, N.J.: Transaction Publishers, 1989), 562.

12. A dramatic show trial in which General Arnaldo Ochoa and two high-ranking security officers, the De la Guardia brothers, were accused of drug trafficking and corruption. Some observers believe that General Ochoa's real crime was favoring Gorbachev-type reforms. This is the point of view advanced by the son-in-law of one of the De la Guardia brothers (and a former Cuban intelligence officer) in Jorge Masetti, *El furor y el delirio: itinerario de un hijo de la Revolución cubana* (Barcelona: Tusquets, 1999).

13. Phyllis Greene Walker, "The Cuban Military Service System: Organization, Objectives and Pressures," in *Cuban Communism,* 7th ed., 599–623.

14. Phyllis Greene Walker, "Cuba's Revolutionary Armed Forces: Adapting in a New Environment," *Cuban Studies,* no. 26 (1996), 71–72.

15. Jim Burns, "Castro's Brother Says U.S. Might Invade Cuba," *CNS News,* 16 April 2001.

16. Edward Atkeson, "Why Cuba Fired," *Washington Post,* 13 March 1996. See also his "Nine Hours with Fidel," *Army Magazine,* January 2000. See also "Amenazan con reventar a EU con 'minazos,'" *El Nuevo Herald* (Miami), 16 April 2001, where General Raúl Castro is quoted as saying that the United States has not abandoned the idea of invading Cuba. "The day I think otherwise," he added, "I will resign as minister of defense and advocate dissolving the army, leaving a few policemen on the street."

17. Bill Bertz and Rowan Scarborough, "Notes from the Pentagon," *Washington Times,* 8 December 2000. This article, which describes the program in considerable detail, cites as its source a classified report from the U.S. Defense Intelligence Agency.

18. Richard Millett, "Cuba's Armed Forces: From Triumph to Survival," Georgetown University Center for Latin American Studies, Caribbean Project, no. 4 (September 1993).

19. Ibid.

20. See chap. 5.

21. Phyllis Greene Walker, "Challenges Facing the Cuban Military," Georgetown University Center for Latin American Studies, Cuba Briefing Paper, no. 12 (October 1996).

22. Cuba and the United States, for all their differences, are the only Western states that have refused to sign the international treaty banning land mines.

23. Andrés Oppenheimer, "EU podría entregar a Guantánamo?" *El Nuevo Herald,* 19 January 1998.

24. U.S. Department of Defense daily news briefing, 2 May 1995.

25. Mark Falcoff, *Panama's Canal: What Happens When the United States Gives a Small Country What It Wants* (Washington, D.C.: AEI Press, 1998), 93–96.

26. Oppenheimer, "EU podría entregar a Guantánamo?"

27. Brian Donohue, "Questions Abound Regarding Al-Qaida Captives at Guantánamo Bay," Newhousenews.com, 2 April 2002. See also Warren Richey, "How Long Can Guantánamo Prisoners Be Held?" *Christian Science Monitor,* 9 April 2002. For a fuller discussion of the legal issues, see Jeremy Rabkin, "After Guantánamo: The War over the Geneva Convention," *National Interest* (Summer 2002).

28. Carol Rosenberg, "Cuba Base Faces Double Duty," *Miami Herald,* 30 March 2002.

29. Susan B. Glasser, "Russia to Dismantle Spy Facility in Cuba," *Washington Post,* 18 October 2001. See also Kevin Sullivan, "Cuba Upset by Closure of Russian Spy Base: Decision Is Viewed as 'Gift' to U.S.," ibid., 29 October 2001.

30. I am grateful to Dave Ewing, a retired telecommunications engineer, for explaining all of this to me in an e-mail (3 December 2000). Mr. Ewing went on to affirm that "most of what goes on at Lourdes is interception of primarily military HF and VHF-UHF radio traffic from the East Coast and Caribbean areas and South America, and most important interception of downlinks from all the U.S. domestic and international communication satellites visible from Cuba. One suspects that beyond this there is rather little there, though with all the satellites serving North America it is hardly a little stream of information to be searched through, especially with aging and less sophisticated gear than the N[ational] S[ecurity] A[gency] uses for the same task."

31. See "Cuba's Role in Russia's New Foreign Policy" in *The Military and the Transition in Cuba: Reference Guide for Policy and Crisis Management,* ed. Néstor Sánchez and Jay Mallin, Sr. (Washington, D.C.: International Research 2000 Inc., 1997), III-16-3, and Henry Goethals, "The Military Relationship Between Russia and Cuba," ibid., III-11-8. As late as June 2000, the official foreign policy of the Russian Federation referred to it as "a great power . . . , one of the most influential centers in the modern world [with a] responsibility for maintaining security in the world both on a global and regional level." Robert Levgold, "Russia's Unformed Foreign Policy," *Foreign Affairs* (September-October 2001).

32. *Izvestia* (Moscow), 24 May 2002. Cuban authorities are reported to have denied permission to transport the equipment back to Russia until Moscow settles a debt allegedly owed to Cuba for use of Lourdes. I am grateful to Dr. Leon Aron, my colleague at the American Enterprise Institute, for verifying that the resumés in the Spanish-language press corresponded to the original Russian text.

33. "Proliferation Risks and Non-Proliferation Opportunities in Cuba: An Assessment of Nuclear, Biological and Chemical Weapons Capabilities," in *The Military and the Transition in Cuba,* III-2-6.

34. Roberto Fabrizio, "Castro con armas bacteriológicas," *El Nuevo Herald,* 20 June 1999.

35. Patty Reinert and Michael Hedges, "Officials Contradict Remarks by Carter,"

Houston Chronicle, 13 May 2002, and David Adams, "So Is Cuba Biowar Threat or Not?" *St. Petersburg Times,* 29 May 2002.

36. Richard Wolfe, "Worries over Cuba Weapons Played Down," *Financial Times* (London), 5 June 2002. A 1998 U.S. Defense Department report wholly devoted to biological weaponry professed agnosticism on the subject of the Cuban threat. It limited itself to the observation that, given its advanced biotech industry, "Cuba *could* have a program of biological weapons of a defensive nature at least in the research and development stage." *The Menace of Biological Warfare* (Washington, D.C.: U.S. Department of Defense, May 1998). Emphasis added.

37. "Castro con armas biológicas," supra. Actually what Castro asked for was a missile attack on the American mainland in the event of a U.S. invasion of Cuba.

38. Ken Alibeck, *Biohazard: The Chilling True Story of the Largest Covert Biological Weapons Program in the World* (New York: Random House, 2000), especially 273–277.

39. Roberto Fabricio, "Las instalaciones cubanas de biotecnología 'estan llenas de zonas cerradas y secretas,'" *El Nuevo Herald,* 20 June 1999.

40. Roberto Fabricio, "Ex-oficial cubano confirma la posesión de armas bacteriológicas," ibid., 12 July 1999.

41. In 1988, the Centers for Disease Control in Atlanta donated a standard culture of St. Louis encephalitis (ESP)—similar to, but more powerful than, the West Nile virus—to studies on encephalitis being developed by Cuba's Pedro Korn Institute of Tropical Medicine. Pablo Alfonso, "Cuba experimenta con aves con fines de guerra biológica," *El Nuevo Herald,* 18 October 1999.

42. Pablo Alfonso, "Brote de encefalitis en Nueva York levanta suspicacia hacia La Habana," ibid., 20 October 1999.

43. The year before Prendes's allegations were published in the U.S. press, the Cuban government had announced ratification of the Chemical Weapons Convention.

44. A wild-card scenario would go further and suggest that Castro is not particularly interested in the future of Cuba, merely in destroying the United States. While this is wholly consonant with everything that is known about the man, and also in some measure replicates the unconfessed desires of Cuban nationalists of the most extreme sort (including non-Communists), to seriously consider this possibility requires a degree of political imagination that the leadership class in the United States, citizens of a successful and basically satisfied country, cannot easily grasp.

45. Nancy San Martin, "Cuba Forced to Sell Technology," *Miami Herald,* 10 October 2001.

46. Pablo Alfonso, "Crecen los vínculos en biotecnología con Irán," *El Nuevo Herald,* 11 October 2000.

47. *Financial Times* (London), 5 November 2001.

48. "Inició visita vicepresidente sirio," *Granma* (Havana), 17 June 2002.

49. John Hughes, "West Nile Virus: Part of Hussein's Plan via Cuba?" *Christian Science Monitor,* 18 September 2002.

50. William J. Casey Institute, "How to Respond to the Cuban KAL 007: Shut Down the Cuban Chernobyl," *Brief* no. 96-D19 (Washington, D.C.: Center for Security Policy, February 1996). See also Roger Robinson and Frank J. Gaffney, "Will Moscow Be Allowed to Recreate in Cuba the Nuclear Nightmare It Has Bequeathed to Bulgaria?" *Perspective,* 2 July 1997; "Cuba Plant Raises Fear of Disaster," *Orlando Sentinel,* 7 June 1995; Larry Rohter, "Cuba A-Plant Worries U.S. over Safety," *New York Times,* 25 February 1996.

51. The quote is from Rear Admiral (retired) Eugene Carroll, Jr., vice president of the Center for Defense Information, who led a delegation of retired flag officers to Cuba to inspect the reactor and talk to Cuban officials. "The Question of the Week," Show No. 315, Center for Defense Information, 3 May 1996. See also Jonathan Benjamín-Alvarado, "Proliferation Risks and Non-Proliferation Opportunities in Cuba," in *The Military and the Transition in Cuba,* as well as his "Cuba's Nuclear Program: A Hollow Threat?" Georgetown University Center for Latin American Studies, Caribbean Project, no. 19 (October 1998); Jack Mendelsohn, "Huddling with the Honchos in Havana," *Bulletin of Atomic Scientists* (September 1993). At the time, Mr. Mendelsohn was president of the Arms Control Association.

52. Wayne Smith, "Help Cuba with Nuclear Power," *Bulletin of Atomic Scientists* (September-October 1995). Mr. Smith was formerly chief of the U.S. Interests Section in Havana.

53. U.S. Government Accounting Office, *Nuclear Safety: Concerns about the Nuclear Power Reactors in Cuba,* Doc. no. RCED-92-262 (September 1992).

54. Patrick E. Tyler, "Cuba and Russia Abandon Nuclear Plant, an Unfinished Vestige of the Soviet Era," *New York Times,* 18 December 2000.

55. Joseph Albright, "Russians Announce Cuban Visit to Work Out Nuclear Plant Deal," *Miami Herald,* 6 October 1995. See also "Moscow Hails New 'Strategic Partnership' with Cuba: Pushes to Complete Jaraguá Nuclear Plant Begun by Soviets," *Russian Reform Monitor,* no. 59 (16 October 1995).

56. "Agreement Signed with EdF on Jaraguá Society," *Nuclear News,* April 1995.

57. This was the view presented by Coast Guard Captain Randy Beardsworth, who told the Washington chapter of the Council on Foreign Relations that insofar as narcotics interdiction is concerned, "Cuba is as good as any country in the Caribbean within its capability, although its resources are poor." Randy Beardsworth, "Practical Security Issues: Migration, Counternarcotics and the Environment," 9 March 2000.

58. Vivian Sequera, "U.S. Ex-Drug Czar Talks with Castro," *Washington Times,* 4 March 2002.

59. John C. Varrone, *Drug Trafficking in the Caribbean: Do Traffickers Use Cuba and Puerto Rico as Major Transit Locations for U.S.-Bound Narcotics?* Testimony before Committee on Government Reform, U.S. House of Representatives, 106th Cong., 2d sess., 3–4 January 2000.

60. William E. Ledwith, testimony before Committee on Government Reform, U.S. House of Representatives, 106th Cong., 2d sess., 3–4 January 2000.

61. Atkeson, "Nine Hours with Fidel." To such accounts, Rep. Bob Menendez (D-N.J.), one of three Cuban-American members of the U.S. Congress at the time, ripostes: "The idea that in a country where every human rights activist, political dissident, or journalist is followed . . . that drug traffickers could meet and the Cuban secret police know nothing about it—this is a tale out of *Alice in Wonderland!*" Gerardo Reyes, "Un punto vital en el mapa de narcotráfico," *El Nuevo Herald,* 18 October 1999.

62. Dan Burton and Benjamin Gilman, "Cocaine Trail Leads to Cuba, Despite Castro's 'Spin,'" *Miami Herald,* 28 June 1999.

63. Ibid.

64. Jeff Leen, "Traffickers Tie Castro to Drug Run," *Miami Herald,* 25 July 1996.

65. Comisión Económica para América Latina y el Caribe, *La economía cubana: reformas estructurales y desempeño en los noventa* (Mexico, D.F.: Fondo de Cultura Económica, 1997).

66. Somewhat surprisingly, this number has been accepted—even as a minimum—by the Institute of Independent Economists in Cuba, a dissident organization. "Remesas familiares a la isla superan los $1,000 milliones," *El Nuevo Herald,* 1 March 2001.

67. Ernesto F. Betancourt, "Cuba's Balance of Payments Gap, the Remittances Scam, Drug Trafficking, and Money Laundering," in *Cuba in Transition,* vol. 10 (Washington, D.C.: Association for the Study of the Cuban Economy, 2000), 149–161.

68. Comisión Económica para América Latina y el Caribe, *La economía cubana: reformas estructurales y desempeño en los noventa,* 2d ed. (Mexico, D.F.: Fondo de Cultura Económica, 2000), Table A30.

69. Gil Klein and Mark Johnson, "Cuba, U.S., Remain Locked in War of Spies," *Tampa Tribune,* 17 October 1998.

70. See Select Committee to Study Government Operations with Respect to Intelligence Activities, *Alleged Assassination Plots Involving Foreign Leaders,* 94th Cong., 1st sess. (Washington, D.C.: Government Printing Office, 1975), 91–180.

71. Brothers to the Rescue is an exile organization whose stated purpose is to patrol the international waters between Cuba and the United States on the lookout for rafters in need. They have also been known to drop antigovernment leaflets over Cuba itself. The shoot-down of four planes belonging to the group was the principal reason why President Clinton reversed himself and signed the Helms-Burton Law in 1996.

72. Rui Ferreira, "La infiltración de un espía cubano empezó a planearse en los años 80," *El Nuevo Herald,* 13 December 2000.

73. Rui Ferreira, "A la cárcel dos espías de la 'Red Avispa'," *El Nuevo Herald,* 3 February 2000.

74. Rui Ferreira, "Tribunal federal condena a dos espías cubanos confesos," *El Nuevo Herald,* 24 February 2000.

75. Rui Ferreira, "Dudan de capacidad el red de espionaje," *El Nuevo Herald,* 17 September 1998.

76. "Ejercito de EU sabía de red de espías," *El Nuevo Herald*, 18 September 1998.

77. Juan O. Tamayo, "Nuevos espías no operaban como antes," *El Nuevo Herald*, 17 September 1998.

78. "Castro Admits Cuba Has Spies in the U.S.," *Washington Times*, 20 October 1998.

79. Rui Ferreira, "Testigo de la fiscalía sirve a la defense en el juicio de los espías," *El Nuevo Herald*, 17 January 2001, and "Afirman que Cuba no necesita espiar al ejército de EU," *El Nuevo Herald*, 18 April 2001.

80. Gail Epstein Nieves, "Investigator From Cuba Takes Stand in Spy Trial," *Miami Herald*, 30 March 2001.

81. Gail Epstein Nieves, "Admiral: Cuba Hinted of Attack on Brothers," *Miami Herald*, 7 March 2001.

82. Tim Golden, "Pentagon's Top Cuba Expert Pleads Guilty to Espionage," *New York Times*, 20 March 2002.

83. For a taste of the controversy, see Center for International Policy, "Cuba Policy Should Be Reviewed in the New International Context" (Press Release, 25 September 2001); "Castro's Cuba: Continuing Sponsor of Terrorism: A Response to the Center for International Policy," Cuban American National Foundation *Issue Brief* (October 2001); and Philip Peters, "Cuba, the Terrorism List, and What the United States Should Do," *Issue Brief* (Alexandria, Va.: Lexington Institute), 20 November 2001.

84. *U.S. Cuba Policy Report* 7, no. 6 (1997).

85. Peters, "Cuba, the Terrorism List."

86. Isidoro Gilbert, "Cuba mira al islam en busca de nuevo orden mundial," Nueva Mayoría.com, 20 June 2001. Available at http://www.nuevamayoria.com (accessed 2001).

87. AFP dispatch, 10 May 2001.

88. See chaps. 2 and 5.

89. Phyllis Greene Walker, "Cuba and U.S. National Security: Rapporteur's Report" (paper presented at conference convened by Inter-American Dialogue, Washington, D.C., September 1997).

90. Brian Latell, "The United States and Cuba: Future Security Issues," unpublished manuscript, 1999. Prior to his retirement, Dr. Latell was national intelligence officer for Latin America at the Central Intelligence Agency. He is now an adjunct professor of government at Georgetown University.

91. Compared with 32 tons for Bahamas, 16.2 tons for Jamaica, and just short of 6 tons for the Dominican Republic. Figures from William Ledwith of the DEA, congressional testimony cited in note 60.

Chapter 5: Tourism and Environment

1. María Dolores Espino, "International Tourism in Cuba: An Economic Development Strategy?" in *Cuba in Transition*, vol. 1 (Washington, D.C.: Association for the Study of the Cuban Economy, 1991), 193–195.

2. María Dolores Espino, "Cuban Tourism during the Special Period," in *Cuba in Transition,* vol. 10 (Washington, D.C.: Association for the Study of the Cuban Economy, 2000), 360.

3. Francisco Vega W., "Los paraísos turísticos en América Latina," *El Mercurio* (Santiago de Chile), 15 July 2000.

4. Charles Suddahy, "Cuba's Tourism Industry," in *Cuba in Transition,* vol. 7 (Washington, D.C.: Association for the Study of the Cuban Economy, 1997), 123.

5. Nicolás Crespo, "Forty Years After: A Candid Account of Experiences at Tourism Destinations in Cuba" in *Cuba in Transition,* vol. 9 (Washington, D.C.: Association for the Study of the Cuban Economy, 1999), 378–385.

6. "Cuba's Tourist Industry: An Update," *La Sociedad Económica* (Paris), 15 January 1996.

7. Marie Sanz, "Proyectan un ferrocarril de lujo para los turistas," *El Nuevo Herald* (Miami), 7 July 2000. Tourism from Japan seems to be one of the fastest growing markets, and there have been moves to open a direct air link between Havana and Tokyo. The Cuban foreign minister on a visit to Japan expressed the hope that the number of Japanese visitors to his country would reach 20,000 in 2001, which would double the figure of the previous year. *News* (Kyoto, Japan), 6 March 2001.

8. Linda Robinson, "A Vacation in Havana: Sun, Fun, and Surgery," *U.S. News and World Report,* 5 May 1997.

9. It even maintained a web page until human rights activists in the United States gave wide circulation to its activities, which—evidently—were largely responsible for diverting doctors, medicines, and technical equipment away from the popular clinics. At that point, the web page was shut down.

10. Anita Snow, "Cuba Creeping toward Economic Recovery," *Miami Herald,* 11 January 2001.

11. It follows Puerto Rico, Cancún, the Dominican Republic, and the Bahamas.

12. ""El complejo mundo de la locomotora," *Granma* (Havana), 1 January 2001.

13. The bombing of the World Trade Center in New York curtailed air travel all over the world, but particularly long-haul flights. Since much of Cuba's tourism comes from Western Europe, it was bound to be disproportionately affected. "Cuba reconoce el fracaso de su metas para el turismo," *El Nuevo Herald,* 23 October 2001.

14. Espino, "International Tourism in Cuba," Table 2.

15. The U.S. travel ban is not absolute. Under current regulations Cuban-Americans are allowed to visit their families once a year. There is also a growing amount of illegal travel through third countries. The Cuban government claims to have received 140,000 visitors from the United States in 2000. Since the Cubans do not regard U.S. tourism as illegal, they make no effort to break down the numbers of licensed versus unlicensed visitors. Minister of Tourism Ibrahim Ferradaz, interview by author, Havana, 15 February 2001.

16. Nicolás Crespo and Charles Suddahy, "A Comparison of Cuba's Tourism Industry with the Dominican Republic and Cancún, 1988–1999," in *Cuba in Transition,* vol. 10 (Washington, D.C.: Association for the Study of the Cuban Economy, 2000), 352–359.

17. U.S.-Cuba Business Council, *Issue Brief,* no. 28 (22 January 1996); Jay Amberg, "Cuba Will Expand Island's Cruise Ship Capacity for 2001," Bloomberg.com, 2 May 2001.

18. "Cuba espera recibir hasta 100 mil turistas en escala de cruceros," *El Nuevo Herald,* 21 May 2001.

19. For its connections to the military, see chaps. 4 and 7.

20. Espino, "International Tourism in Cuba," 210.

21. Vice Minister of Tourism Eduardo Rodríguez de la Vega claims that in certain cases "the foreign investment law offers the possibility of acquiring 100 percent of the shares." Radio Havana, *Foreign Broadcast Information Service: Latin America,* 26 June 1997. He did not specify, however, whether anyone had yet been permitted to take advantage of the possibility.

22. Félix Blanco Godínez, "Cuba's Tourism Industry: Sol Meliá as a Case Study," in *Cuba in Transition,* vol. 8 (Washington, D.C.: Association for the Study of the Cuban Economy, 1998), 51.

23. See chap. 3.

24. These commissions must be very large indeed. While sitting in a travel agency in Buenos Aires in early 2000, I happened to compare the prices of a week in Havana-Varadero, Miami, and Cancún. Surprisingly, the cost of six days in Cuba was roughly the same as that of the other two destinations, even though the Miami package included an additional incentive of four free days of a rental car.

25. Saturnino E. Lucio II and Nicolás Crespo, "Impact of the Helms-Burton Law (The Cuban Liberty Act) on Cuban Tourism," in *Cuba in Transition,* vol. 7 (Washington, D.C.: Association for the Study of the Cuban Economy, 1997), 135.

26. Workers tend to pool their tips, and they have elaborate formulas for dividing them up so that workers who do not come into direct contact with foreigners—say, the people in a hotel laundry—get their share.

27. Joseph M. Perry, Jeffrey W. Steagall, and Louis A. Woods, "Cuban Tourism, Economic Growth, and the Welfare of the Cuban Worker," in *Cuba in Transition,* vol. 7 (Washington, D.C.: Association for the Study of the Cuban Economy, 1997), 144.

28. María C. Werlau, "Foreign Investment in Cuba: The Limits of Commercial Engagement," in *Cuba in Transition,* vol. 6 (Washington, D.C.: Association for the Study of the Cuban Economy, 1996), 471.

29. Quoted in "Los temores de los españoles," *El Nuevo Herald,* 4 June 1999.

30. Radio Havana, *Foreign Broadcast Information Service: Latin America,* 3 June 1997.

31. Havana Cubavision Network, ibid., 5 February 1997.

32. "El complejo mundo de la locomotora."

33. Quoted in David Rieff, "Cuba Refrozen," *Foreign Affairs* (July-August 1996): 65.

34. Espino, "Cuban Tourism during the Special Period," 370.

35. Perry, Steagall, and Woods, "Cuban Tourism," 142.

36. Espino, "Cuban Tourism during the Special Period," 370–371.

37. Ted Henken, "Last Resort or Bridge to the Future? Tourism and Workers in Cuba's Second Economy," in *Cuba in Transition,* vol. 10 (Washington, D.C.: Association for the Study of the Cuban Economy, 2000), 321–336. For what it may be worth, at the Havana paladar I visited in February 2001, the employees were friends, not relatives, of the owner.

38. The joint ventures and government tourist enterprises do not typically employ these people in areas where their skills might be needed.

39. I owe this story to a former official of the U.S. Interests Section in Havana.

40. Orlando Bordón Gálvez, "Blame the State Run Economy, Blame Tourism," *Cuba Free Press,* 19 March 1998. The strange syntax is due to an imperfect English translation of the original.

41. Robert Benson, "An Island on the Way to Ectopia," *Los Angeles Times,* 29 March 1992. In the same article, Professor Benson goes on to suggest that U.S. hostility to the Castro government is driven by a desperate need to "snuff out" so exemplary an environmental alternative.

42. Quoted in Sergio Díaz-Briquets and Jorge Pérez-López, *Conquering Nature: The Environmental Legacy of Socialism in Cuba* (Pittsburgh: University of Pittsburgh Press, 2000), 3.

43. Philip Peters, *Rescuing Old Havana* (Alexandria, Va.: Lexington Institute, 2001).

44. Amparo E. Avella, "The Process of Environmental Impact Assessment in Cuba," in *Cuba in Transition,* vol. 5 (Washington, D.C.: Association for the Study of the Cuban Economy, 1995).

45. David S. Collins, "Environmental Implications of Cuba's Economic Crisis," Georgetown University, Center for Latin American Studies, Caribbean Project, no. 8 (July 1995).

46. Carlos Wotzkow, "SOS para la naturaleza cubana," *Encuentro de la Cultura Cubana,* nos. 8–9 (Spring-Summer 1998): 16–23.

47. See note 40.

48. *The Environment in U.S.-Cuban Relations: Recommendations for Cooperation* (Washington, D.C.: Inter-American Dialogue, 1997), 8–9. The conference report went on to say (9) that it hoped that "uncertainty surrounding the nature of Cuban NGOs may pose a challenge to promoting contact between U.S. and Cuban NGOs" but would not prevent either government from allowing NGOs "to take advantage of these opportunities so long as they conform to the laws of each country."

49. Sergio Díaz-Briquets and Jorge Pérez-López, "Socialism and Environmental Disruption: Implications for Cuba," in *Cuba in Transition,* vol. 8 (Washington, D.C.: Association for the Study of the Cuban Economy, 1998), 154–172.

50. Sergio Díaz-Briquets, "Forestry Policies of Cuba's Socialist Government: An Appraisal," in *Cuba in Transition,* vol. 6 (Washington, D.C.: Association for the Study of the Cuban Economy, 1996), 428.

51. See René Dumont, *Is Cuba Socialist?* trans. Stanley Hochman (New York: Viking Press, 1974), 106–111.

52. Díaz-Briquets, "Forestry Policies," 430.

53. Quoted in Díaz-Briquets and Pérez-López, *Conquering Nature,* 433.

54. Díaz-Briquets, "Forestry Policies," 429. Compare with Carlos Wotzkow, *Natumaleza Cubana* (Miami: Ediciones Universal, 1998), 147–157.

55. James E. Ross, "Factors Affecting the Potential Market in Cuba for Selected U.S. Forest Products," in *Cuba in Transition,* vol. 9 (Washington, D.C.: Association for the Study of the Cuban Economy, 1999), 107.

56. Díaz-Briquets and Pérez-López, *Conquering Nature,* 434–435. See also René Costales, "Comments on 'Forestry Policies of Cuba's Socialist Government,'" in *Cuba in Transition,* vol. 6 (Washington, D.C.: Association for the Study of the Cuban Economy, 1996), 428.

57. Wotzkow, *Natumaleza Cubana,* 79–95.

58. Díaz-Briquets and Pérez-López, *Conquering Nature,* 94.

59. Ibid., 105.

60. Cited in ibid., 107.

61. Ibid., 137.

62. Ibid., 164–202.

63. Maurice Halperin, *Return to Havana: The Decline of Cuban Society under Castro* (Nashville, Tenn.: Vanderbilt University Press, 1994), 36–37.

64. Díaz-Briquets and Pérez-López, *Conquering Nature,* 245.

65. Ibid., 248.

66. Ibid., 254.

67. See, for example, *The Environment in U.S.-Cuban Relations,* 2.

68. Wotzkow, *Natumaleza Cubana,* 264.

69. See chap. 8.

70. Alberto Vega and Federico Poey, "Preliminary Environmental Action Plan for a Post-Castro Cuba," in *Cuba in Transition,* vol. 10 (Washington, D.C.: Association for the Study of the Cuban Economy, 2000), 190–206

71. *The Environment in U.S.-Cuban Relations,* 1.

72. See, for example, the interesting paper by Lt. Cmdr. Victoria Huyck, U.S. Coast Guard, "Protecting U.S. National Interests in the Event of a Major Oil Spill in the Straits of Florida," Cuba Briefing Paper, no. 27 (2001).

73. Matías F. Travieso-Díaz, "Key Environmental Legislation for Cuba's Transition Period," in *Cuba in Transition,* vol. 9 (Washington, D.C.: Association for the Study of the Cuban Economy, 1999), 386–408. See also Aldo M. Leiva, "Environmental Technology Transfer and Foreign Investment: Factors Impacting Environmental Protection in a Transition Era Cuba," *University of Miami Occasional*

Papers 4, no. 1 (Miami, Fla.: University of Miami, Institute of Cuban and Cuban-American Studies, 1999).

Chapter 6: Immigration

1. For further discussion of the émigré community, see chap. 7.

2. On that occasion, several thousand Cubans managed to wedge themselves into the grounds and buildings of the Peruvian embassy residence in Havana, all demanding political asylum. The Cuban government eventually resolved the crisis by inviting those who wished to leave to report to the port of Mariel, where they were picked up by small and medium-sized craft from the United States. More than 100,000 Cubans eventually took advantage of the opportunity.

3. According to the U.S. Coast Guard, interdictions at sea from Cuba dropped drastically, from 37,191 in 1994 to 617 in 1995. Between 1995 and 2000, they averaged slightly less than 1,000 a year.

4. Contrary to a widespread misconception, Cubans are not the only nationality allowed to adjust from parole to immigrant status. Other legislation exists for Soviets (now Russians) paroled out of Moscow, as well as Laotians, Vietnamese, and Cambodians. In the past, such exceptions existed for Hungarians and Poles.

5. See, for example, U.S. House of Representatives, Committee on the Judiciary, Subcommittee on International Law, Immigration, and Refugees, *Cuban and Haitian Immigration* (Hearings), 102nd Cong., 1st sess. (Washington, D.C.: Government Printing Office, 1992).

6. The departures also represent a modest financial windfall for the Cuban government, since every Cuban who leaves must pay a stiff departure fee, ranging between $400 and $600. Based on a floor of 20,000 émigrés, this means roughly $10,000,000 a year, several times the costs of processing.

7. This is still the case with Cubans who touch ground in third countries. The Cuban government commits itself not to prosecute only those returned by the United States.

8. Presumably the Democratic presidential candidate, Vice President Al Gore, was even more acutely aware of the prospect, inasmuch as he dramatically broke with his own administration to support the claims of the boy's Miami relatives.

9. It is perhaps worth noting that at the time of the Mariel crisis, President Clinton was governor of Arkansas, where a significant number of criminals from Cuba were temporarily incarcerated. Several ugly incidents at Fort Chafee, where they were confined, are supposed to have had a negative impact on his unsuccessful bid for re-election—a potential dress rehearsal for what might have happened if Elián González were not returned.

10. A somewhat similar agreement was reached in 1991 with the Duvalier regime in Haiti. Many congressional critics of the Bush administration found the policy immoral and intolerable, employing many of the same arguments as critics of the Clinton administration used four years later. See U.S. House of Representatives, *Cuban and Haitian Immigration.*

11. This was once true but is no longer. Today most Cuban illegals enter in fast boats operated by smugglers, come across the Mexican border on foot, or arrive at U.S. airports with fraudulent documentation.

12. U.S. House of Representatives, *Cuban and Haitian Immigration*, 3.

13. Ibid., 7.

14. Ibid., 27.

15. U.S. House of Representatives, Committee on International Relations, Subcommittee on the Western Hemisphere, *The Clinton Administration's Reversal of U.S. Policy Toward Cuba* (Hearings), 104th Cong., 1st sess. (Washington, D.C.: Government Printing Office, 1995), 6.

16. Ibid., 9

17. Ibid., 22–23.

18. Silvia Pedraza, "Cuba's Refugees: Manifold Migrations," in *Cuba in Transition*, vol. 5 (Washington, D.C.: Association for the Study of the Cuban Economy, 1995), 312.

19. U.S. Bureau of the Census, *Current Population Survey* (March 1999, March 2000).

20. Rubén G. Rumbaut and Lisandro Pérez, "Pinos Nuevos? Growing up American in Cuban Miami," *Cuban Affairs/Asuntos Cubanos* 5, nos. 1–2 (1999).

21. "In or near poverty" is defined here as having an income below 200 percent of the U.S. Department of Labor's poverty threshold.

22. Center for Immigration Studies, *Without Coverage: Immigration's Impact on the Size and Growth of the Population Lacking Health Insurance* (Washington, D.C.: Center for Immigration Studies, 2000), 29.

23. U.S. House of Representatives, *The Clinton Administration's Reversal of U.S. Policy*, 117.

24. Ibid., 123.

25. Interviews with INS officials, Washington, D.C., 25 May 2001.

26. U.S. House of Representatives, *Cuban and Haitian Immigration*, 75.

27. Ibid., 75–76.

28. John Lantigua and Stephen Doig, "Limit Cuban Immigration? Yes, Most on Survey Agree," *Miami Herald*, 15 May 1995. It is possible, of course, that the tepid enthusiasm of many Cuban-Americans for new arrivals is political; in the view of the former, the latter "stayed too long" on the island, and therefore do not "deserve" to be rescued. I have actually heard such sentiments expressed privately by some members of the Miami Cuban elite. On the other hand, the Cuban-American National Foundation continues to lobby on behalf of new arrivals, real or potential, without imposing any political tests.

29. Pedraza, "Cuba's Refugees," 324.

30. Steven A. Camarota, "Immigrants in the United States—2002: A Snapshot of America's Foreign-Born Population," Center for Immigration Studies *Backgrounder* (November 2002). See also Steven A. Camarota, "Immigrants in the United States—1998: A Snapshot of America's Foreign-Born Population," Center for

Immigration Studies *Backgrounder* (January 1999). Much of the data in these studies came from the *Current Population Survey,* published monthly by the U.S. Bureau of the Census.

31. Steven A. Camarota, *The Slowing Progress of Immigrants: An Examination of Income, Home Ownership, and Citizenship* (Washington, D.C.: Center for Immigration Studies, 2001).

32 Rep. Tom Lewis in U.S. House of Representatives, *Cuban and Haitian Immigration,* 43.

33. Alfonso Chardy, "Miami se vuelve una Meca del tráfico internacional de ilegales," *El Nuevo Herald* (Miami), 24 January 2001. The same officer reported that in a recent operation, INS officials discovered that Chinese illegals had paid about $60,000 each for a package that included Japanese passports and air tickets from China directly to Miami. Smuggling illegals has become a major industry in the Miami area, currently estimated in the CIA's *Global Trends 2015* to represent $7 billion a year.

34. This calculation is based on the assumption that the United States will be taking 27,000 Cubans a year, which is actually slightly less than the number (roughly 30,000) that entered under the various categories during 2000.

35. Daniel Shoer Roth, "Las remesas, un puntal de las economías de América Latina," *El Nuevo Herald,* 18 March 2001.

36. B. Lindsey Lowell and Rodolfo de la Garza, *The Developmental Role of Remittances in U.S. Latino Communities and in Latin American Countries: A Final Project Report* (Washington, D.C.: Inter-American Dialogue–Tomas Rivera Policy Institute, 2000). See also Manuel Orozco, "Globalization and Migration: The Impact of Family Remittances in Latin America," unpublished manuscript, July 2001. Mr. Orozco is project director for Central America, Inter-American Dialogue, Washington, D.C.

37. Sam Quinones, "Mexican Emigrants Spin a Bold Idea," *San Francisco Examiner,* 20 June 1999.

38. José Roberto López and Mitchell A. Seligson, "Small Business Development in El Salvador: The Impact of Remittances," in *Migration, Remittances, and Small Business Development: Mexico and the Caribbean Basin Countries,* ed. Sergio Díaz-Briquets and Sidney Weintraub (Boulder, Col.: Westview, 1991), 189. In Mexico, the figure ranged from 9 to 16 percent.

39. Sergio Díaz-Briquets, "Emigrant Remittances in the Cuban Economy: Their Significance during and after the Castro Regime," in *Cuba in Transition,* vol. 4 (Washington, D.C.: Association for the Study of the Cuban Economy, 1994), 219.

40. Pablo Alfonso, "Las remesas familiares sostienen la economía," *El Nuevo Herald,* 18 March 2001.

41. For a discussion of the implications of this factor for Cuba itself, see chap. 8.

42. Díaz-Briquets, "Emigrant Remittances," 220–221.

43. "On the surface there are no public restrictions [on freedom of movement in the Dominican Republic] except those which pertain to entering or leaving the country; in both cases, great difficulty is experienced. . . . Not even the Office of

Foreign Relations issues a passport without a previous investigation, that is often delayed indefinitely; the airports are closely watched." Jesús de Galíndez, *The Era of Trujillo: Dominican Dictator,* trans. Russell Fitzgibbon (Tucson: University of Arizona Press, 1973), 127. This volume, which originally appeared in Spanish in 1956, repays rereading in light of Cuba's experience with forty years of dictatorship, since—conceding the obvious differences in economic systems—some of the similarities are striking.

44. Bernardo Vega and Roberto Despradel, *Tendencias migratorias hacia los Estados Unidos de dominicanos y otros ciudadanos caribeños* (Santo Domingo: IOM–FLACSO, 2000), 14.

45. Ibid., 31–32. Not surprisingly, the same is true for other Caribbean nationalities.

46. Ibid., 34.

47. Those from Salvador and Guatemala had to meet an additional set of requirements. They were eligible only if they were party to a class-action suit dating back to the 1980s, if they were of "good moral character," and if they could prove that leaving the United States would cause them "extreme hardship." "The Path to a Green Card," *Washingtonian* (May 2001).

48. For a fuller discussion, see the scenarios reviewed in chap. 8.

Chapter 7: Civil Society

1. Edward González, *Cuba: Clearing Perilous Waters?* (Santa Monica, Cal.: RAND, 1996), 55.

2. That quest sometimes took the church rather far. As early as 1969, the Catholic bishops denounced the U.S. trade embargo, and a conference of laity urged Catholics to remain on the island "and participate in the revolutionary process." In 1979, the first year that exiles resident in the United States were permitted to visit the country, the church warned ordinary Cubans not to associate excessively with them "lest they become contaminated by greed and materialism." Again in the 1980 Mariel migration crisis, the church urged Cubans to remain on the island rather than take advantage of the opportunity to move to the United States. Shawn Malone, "Conflict, Coexistence, and Cooperation: Church-State Relations in Cuba," Georgetown University, Center for Latin American Studies, Caribbean Project, no. 10 (1996).

3. Cardinal Jaime Ortega, the archbishop of Havana, told *L'Osservatore Romano* (2 March 2001) that there were eighty seminarians in Cuba (as opposed to only twenty-five about five years earlier). The number of women in religious orders was now 600, he said, compared with 250 at most fifteen years earlier.

4. Dalia Acosta, "Cuba: Catholic Intellectuals Resist Intolerance," Inter Press Service, 22 January 1998.

5. A "liberal" Catholic publication put it this way: "Recently, the government has dramatically improved its treatment of religious believers. As a result, church officials are not eager to criticize the current system publicly. In fact, they are more likely to criticize the customary journalistic focus on the conflict, which often sets

church authority off against the state. They don't wish to jeopardize progress, thus their reticence with the media." Thomas Garofolo, "Letter from Cuba," *Commonweal,* 16 January 1998. A similar finding comes from Juanita Darling, "Cuba, Vatican, Have Faith in Improving Relations," *Los Angeles Times,* December 1, 1996.

6. Karen DeYoung, "Small Band of Dissidents Wages Lonely Battle in Cuba," *Washington Post,* 16 July 2000.

7. "Church-State Ties Souring in Cuba, Bishop Says," Zenit.org, 24 May 2001. See also Juan Clark, "The Pope's Visit to Cuba and Its Aftermath," University of Miami, Institute of Cuban and Cuban-American Studies, *Occasional Paper Series* (July 1999).

8. "Declaraciones de Cardinal Ortega: el partido comunista cubano quiere obstacularizar la expansión de la iglesia," Zenit.org, 12 March 2001.

9. Garofolo, "Letter from Cuba."

10. DeYoung, "Small Band of Dissidents."

11. Clark, "Pope's Visit to Cuba."

12. Gillian Gunn Clissold, "Cuba's NGOs: Government Puppets or Seeds of Civil Society?" Georgetown University, Center for Latin American Studies, Caribbean Project, no. 7 (1995).

13. Pax Christi, *Report on the Fifth Visit to Cuba* (Rotterdam: Pax Christi Netherlands, 2000).

14. Jack Wintz, OFM, "The Church in Cuba: Is a New Day Dawning?" *St. Anthony Messenger,* May 1996.

15. "Cuba Update," United States Catholic Conference, May 2001.

16. John W. Kennedy, "Cuba's Next Revolution," *Christianity Today,* 12 January 1998.

17. Malone, *Conflict, Coexistence, and Cooperation.*

18. "Fact-Finding Group Calls for an End to the Embargo of Cuba," National Council of Churches, press release, 16 March 1999.

19. Mark Tooley, "Pastors for Castro," *Heterodoxy* (April-May 1999), and Ross Douthat, "Pastors for Castro," *NROnLine,* 16 July 2000.

20. Kennedy, "Cuba's Next Revolution."

21. González, *Cuba: Clearing Perilous Waters?* 58.

22. Enrique Patterson, "The Role of Race Relations in U.S.-Cuban Relations: Implications of an Evolving Dynamic" (paper presented at Council on Foreign Relations, Washington, D.C., 28 June 2001).

23. Aline Helg, "Afro-Cuban Protest: The Partido Independiente de Color, 1908–1912," *Cuban Studies/Estudios Cubanos,* no. 21 (1991).

24. The U.S. Communist Party of the day followed a similar ploy, advocating "autonomy for the black belt"—as it then was—in the American South. For a fuller account of the 1912 rebellion, see Luis Aguilar, "Cuba, 1860–1930" in *Cuba: A Short History,* ed. Leslie Bethell (New York: Cambridge University Press, 1993), 42–43.

25. For a remarkably sophisticated study of the subject, see Alejandro de la Fuente, *Una nación para todos: raza, desigualdad, y política en Cuba, 1900–2000* (Madrid: Editorial Colibrí, 2001).

26. Patterson, "The Role of Race."

27. Ibid. During the final days of the Batista regime, the dictator's henchmen even put it out that Castro was leading a "white" revolution, setting back the "gains" Cuban blacks had made since the 1930s! See Carlos Moore, *Castro, the Blacks, and Africa* (Los Angeles: UCLA Center for Afro-American Studies, 1988), 12.

28. Moore, *Castro, the Blacks, and Africa*, 21.

29. Patterson, "The Role of Race."

30. "Recreating Racism: Race and Discrimination in Cuba's 'Special Period,'" Georgetown University, Center for Latin American Studies, Caribbean Project, no. 18 (July 1998).

31. Moore, *Castro, the Blacks, and Africa*, 359.

32. Corinne Cumerlato and Dennis Rousseau, *L'île du Docteur Castro: la transition confisquée* (Paris: Stock, 2000), 121.

33. To be sure, "affirmative action" remains a controversial subject in the United States, rejected by one of its two major political parties and beyond discussion by the other.

34. Cumerlato and Rousseau, *L'île du Docteur Castro*, 121.

35. Peter Fry, "Politics, Nationality, and the Meanings of 'Race' in Brazil," *Daedalus* (Spring 2000).

36. De la Fuente, *Recreating Racism.*

37. Tom Carter, "Cuban Racial Equality Termed a Myth," *Washington Times*, 24 October 2000. Carter's source for this estimate is Wayne Smith, former head of the U.S. Interests Section in Havana and a tireless critic of U.S. policy since his retirement from the Foreign Service.

38. Frank F. Taylor, "Revolution, Race, and Some Aspects of Foreign Relations in Cuba Since 1959," *Cuban Studies/Estudios Cubanos*, no. 18 (1988).

39. Patricia Grogg, "Cuba: Prejudice Prevails Despite Laws Against Discrimination," *The Black World Today*, 13 September 2001. In an opinion survey of white Cubans carried out by Havana's Centro de Antropología in 1995, fully 58 percent of those polled considered blacks less intelligent; 69 percent responded that blacks do not have the same values or "decency," and only 38 percent expressed no racial preferences concerning the composition of their neighborhood. Alejandro de la Fuente, "Silence, Race, and the 'Special Period': An Update," *Cuban Affairs/Asuntos Cubanos* 5, nos. 1–2 (1999).

40. De la Fuente, *Recreating Racism.*

41. Gerardo Tena, "Los 'no blancos' irrumpen en las filas de la dissidencia," *El Nuevo Herald* (Miami), 2 October 1999, and Liz Balmaseda, "The Color of Dissidence," *Miami Herald*, 7 May 2001.

42. De la Fuente, *Recreating Racism.*

43. "Castro Meets U.S. Legislators Visiting Cuba," *CNN News*, 20 February 1999.

44. Quoted in Jay Nordlinger, "In Castro's Corner," *National Review*, 6 March 2000.

45. Anita Snow, "Audience in Harlem Cheers Castro," *Washington Post,* 10 September 2000.

46. Rep. James Clyburn, press conference, 6 June 2000.

47. Patterson, "The Role of Race."

48. Carter, "Cuban Racial Equality Termed a Myth."

49. Rafael Lorente, "Exiles Try to Convince Black Caucus That Cuba Is Racist," *Chicago Tribune,* 1 August 2001.

50. Quoted in Nordlinger, "In Castro's Corner."

51. Pedro Dupré, "Cuba: A Nation, Many Governments; No Blacks Allowed Please," *Black World Today,* 23 July 2001.

52. Jordan Levin, "Hip Hop Beginning to Make Some Noise in Cuba," *Miami Herald,* 7 November 2001.

53. Clissold, *Cuba's NGOs.*

54. Juanita Darling, "From Dog Owners to Dancers, Cubans Are Getting Organized," *Los Angeles Times,* 9 August 1996.

55. Clissold, *Cuba's NGOs.*

56. Daniel Feist, "Passion Is Unifying Source in Songs of Cuba's Pablo Milanés," *Gazette* (Montreal), 5 December 1994.

57. "Prominent Singer Blasts Cuban Culture Ministry," *Orlando Sentinel,* 11 June 1995.

58. Gillian Walker, "Castro's Law Crumbles as Havana Turns Back into Caribbean Sin City," *Sunday Times* (London), 20 August 1995.

59. Roberto Fabricio, "Cuba Shows Old Form by Closing Think Tank," *Sun-Sentinel* (Ft. Lauderdale), 7 April 1996. See also Alberto Alvarez García and Gerardo González Núñez, *Intelectuales vs. Revolución? El caso del Centro de Estudios sobre América* (Montreal: Ediciones Arte DT, 2001).

60. *AAP News,* 27 January 1998.

61. Pax Christi, *Report on the Fifth Visit to Cuba.*

62. Marta Beatriz Roque, statement to a delegation from the Council on Foreign Relations, Havana, 16 February 2001.

63. DeYoung, "Cuban Dissidents."

64. Karen DeYoung, "Independent Libraries Mix Politics, Culture in Cuba," *Washington Post,* 3 August 2000.

65. Marion Lloyd, "Dissent by the Book," *Houston Chronicle,* 27 May 2001.

66. David Gonzalez, "In Book-Starved Cuba, Little Feasts for the Hungry," *New York Times,* 6 June 2001.

67. David Hemlock, "Cuba Tries to Shush Librarians," *Sun-Sentinel* (Ft. Lauderdale), 23 January 2000.

68. "Amnesty Asks 'Urgent Action' for Jailed Librarian," Amnesty International, press release, 12 September 2001.

69. "Testimony of U.S. Librarians Visiting Cuba," report to Charles Harmon, chair, and members of the American Library Association Committee on Professional Ethics, drafted by Larry R. Oberg, librarian, Willamette University, Salem, Oregon

(May 2000). See also Marion Lloyd, "Independent Libraries in Cuba Defy Government's Lock on Information," *Chronicle of Higher Education,* 8 June 2001, and the debate between Robert Kent of the New York Public Library and Ann Sparanese of the Englewood (N.J.) Public Library in *American Libraries* (April 2001).

70. This extraordinary feat led to a rapid counterattack by the Cuban government. A counterpetition reportedly signed by more than 98 percent of the adult population demanded that the National Assembly declare Cuba's form of government (socialism) "untouchable." "Sepulta Castro el intento de reforma," *El Nuevo Herald,* 28 June 2002.

71. DeYoung, "Cuban Dissidents."

72. Laurie Goering, "Freed Cuban Dissident Remains True to Her Cause," *Chicago Tribune,* 6 July 2001.

73. DeYoung, "Cuban Dissidents."

74. Frank Mora, "Raulismo and the Technocrat Soldier: The Economic Role of the FAR and Its Implications for the Transition in Cuba" (paper presented at Conference on the Politics of Military Extrication: The Case of Cuba, Monastery of Arrabida, Setúbal, Portugal, October 2000). See also Armando Mastrapa III, "Soldiers and Businessmen: The FAR during the Special Period," in *Cuba in Transition,* vol. 10 (Washington, D.C.: Association for the Study of the Cuban Economy, 2000), 428–432.

75. Domingo Amuchástegui, "FAR: Mastering Reforms," in *Cuba in Transition,* vol. 10 (Washington, D.C.: Association for the Study of the Cuban Economy, 2000), 433–441.

76. Mora, "Raulismo and the Technocrat-Soldier."

77. Ricardo Donate-Armada, "Preliminary Analysis of Retirement Programs for Personnel in the Ministry of the Armed Forces and Ministry of the Interior of the Republic of Cuba," in *Cuba in Transition,* vol. 5 (Washington, D.C.: Association for the Study of the Cuban Economy, 1995), 451.

78. Ibid., 452.

79. *Barricada,* which is, however, near bankruptcy.

80. A piñata is a papier-mâché animal filled with small toys, candy, and party favors, which children are invited to attack, blindfolded, to culminate birthday celebrations. In this context, it refers to the Sandinista practice of dividing up the wealth of Nicaragua among its followers, including key military personnel in their last days in power. See Jorge Castañeda, *Utopia Unarmed: The Latin American Left after the Cold War* (New York: Knopf, 1993).

81. J. C. Espinosa and Robert C. Harding II, "Olive Green Parachutes and Slow Motion Piñatas: The Cuban Armed Forces in Comparative Perspective" (paper presented at Conference on the Politics of Military Extrication: The Case of Cuba, Monastery of Arrabida, Setúbal, Portugal, October 2000).

82. Josep M. Colomer, "Hard-Line Military and the Prospects of a Transition in Cuba," ibid.

83. Mora, "Raulismo and the Technocrat-Soldier." Amuchástegui goes much further: "Their role is not simply determined . . . by how many high-ranking officers we find in the Central Committee and in the Politboro compared with earlier years, . . . but by the overwhelming centrality of the FAR in every single area of policy making. . . . The truth is that [their] frequent policy designs and recommendations can play a more influential and decisive role than those coming from other quarters in the party or the Government." Amuchástegui, "FAR: Mastering Reforms," 438.

84. This was, for example, the most devastating charge that occurred to Ricardo Alarcón, president of the National Assembly, in his effort to discredit the late Jorge Mas Canosa, leader of the Miami Cuban community, whom he debated in an extraordinary television broadcast on *CNN-Spanish,* 5 September 1996.

85. Ken Ringle, "The Autumn of Their Discontent," *Washington Post,* 13 August 2001.

86. Mark Falcoff, "The Other Cuba," *National Review,* 12 June 1995.

87. For a particularly moving account of one Cuban family, see Gustavo Pérez-Firmat, *Next Year in Cuba: A Cubano's Coming-of-Age in America* (New York: Anchor, 1995).

88. Gustavo Pérez-Firmat, *Life on the Hyphen: The Cuban-American Way* (Austin: University of Texas Press, 1994), 8.

89. Keny Feijoo, "Old Cuba Lives On at Cuba Nostalgia," *Miami Herald,* 19 May 2001. A distinguished Cuban artist in Miami complains that for most Cubans who settled in Miami, exile "has become defined solely in economic and political terms, and the most urgent and basic expressions of these to boot . . . a diasporic mind set has yet to dawn among the Cubans of *el exilio.*" Ricardo Pau-Llosa, "The Tasks of Exile," Cuban Studies Association *Occasional Papers* 2, no. 9 (1997)

90. Emilio San Pedro, "Exile, Twice Removed," *South Florida,* May 1996.

91. Nicolás Crespo, "Forty Years After: A Candid Recount of Experiences at Tourism Destinations in Cuba," in *Cuba in Transition,* vol. 9 (Washington, D.C.: Association for the Study of the Cuban Economy, 1999), 384.

92. Rubén G. Rumbaut and Lisandro Pérez, "Pinos Nuevos? Growing Up Cuban in Miami," *Cuban Affairs/Asuntos Cubanos* 5, nos. 1–2 (Spring-Summer, 1999).

93. Cuban Research Institute/Institute for Public Opinion Research/Center for Labor Research and Studies, Florida International University, *FIU/Cuba Poll,* Miami, October 2000.

94. A more recent poll conducted in April 2002 among 800 Cuban-American adults by the Bendixen Company shows a slight decline in support for the embargo (61 percent in favor; 28 percent opposed), and an almost even divide on whether the United States should allow unrestricted travel to Cuba by its citizens—that is, non–Cuban-Americans (46 percent in favor; 47 percent opposed). Perhaps its most important finding was that 50 percent support the Catholic church's call for "forgiveness and reconciliation" as the most important basis for a process of transition (39 percent against). While 52 percent think "change is impossible while Fidel

Castro is alive," fully 42 percent believe it is a mistake to wait for his death. At the same time, there is a continued refusal to "let go" of the country; 76 percent favor exile leaders taking part in the process of transition, with only 15 percent opposed.

95. Wilfredo Cancio Isla, "La Fundación lanza plan de ayuda directa a la isla," *El Nuevo Herald,* 9 November 2001.

96. James Cox, "Hungry Eyes Look towards Cuba as Sun Sets on Castro," *USA Today,* 10 May 2001.

97. Wilfredo Cancio Isla, "El juicio de Faget popne al descubierto intereses de empresarios en Cuba," *El Nuevo Herald,* 30 May 2000.

98. Pablo Alfonso, "Cuba ve a Miami como un factor decisivo para 'el día después,'" ibid., 12 March 2000.

Chapter 8: The Prospect

1. Henry Wriston, "A Historical Perspective," in *Cuba and the United States: Long-Range Perspectives,* ed. John Plank (Washington, D.C.: Brookings Institution, 1967), 2.

2. Bayless Manning, "An Overall Perspective," in *Cuba and the United States,* 68.

3. Corinne Cumerlato and Dennis Rousseau, *L'île du Docteur Castro: la transition confisquée* (Paris: Stock, 2000), 279–301.

4. Blanche Petrich, "Ricardo Alarcón, Presidente de la Asamblea Nacional: La transición cubana ya occurió; la sucesión, sin fórmulas inamoviles," *La Jornada* (Mexico City), 4 July 2001.

5. "Dissident Skeptical of 'Castroism without Castro,'" *Miami Herald,* 28 June 2001.

6. Roberto Luque Escalona, *The Tiger and the Children: Fidel Castro and the Judgment of History,* trans. Manuel A. Tellechea (New Brunswick, N.J.: Transaction Publishers, 1992), 199.

7. Jorge José Rodríguez, "Destaca líder la agudización de la crisis," *El Nuevo Herald* (Miami), 13 August 2001.

8. Max Boot, "To Have and Have Not in Havana," *Wall Street Journal,* 12 March 2002.

9. Pablo Alfonso, "El organograma de la sucesión: los hombres de Raúl," *El Nuevo Herald,* 12 August 2001.

10. G. Fernández and M. A. Menéndez, "GAESA: el poder económico de los hermanos Castro," *Diario* 16 (Madrid), 24 June 2001.

11. "La transición cubana," *Diario* 16 (Madrid), 8 July 2001.

12. Roberto Weill, "Cuba, rendición incondicional," *El Nuevo Herald,* 22 October 2001.

13. *Cuba Transition Guide: Preparing for Freedom* (Washington, D.C.: International Republican Institute, 1995).

14. Executive Office of the President, *Support for Democratic Transition in Cuba* (Washington, D.C.: U.S. Agency for International Development, 1997).

15. Elaine De Valle, "UM Receives Grant to Study a Post-Castro Cuba," *Miami Herald,* 22 February 2002.

16. Juan O. Tamayo, "Report Cites U.S. Benefits of Cuba Trade," *Miami Herald,* 28 January 2002.

17. Wilfredo Cancio Isla, "Sugieren crear un gaseoducto hacia la Florida," *El Nuevo Herald,* 18 December 2001.

18. Jonathan G. Clarke and William Ratliff, *Report from Havana: Time for a Reality Check on U.S. Policy toward Cuba,* Policy Analysis no. 418 (Washington, D.C.: Cato Institute, October 2001).

19. Pablo Alfonso, "La política y los negocios se dan la mano en Cancún," *El Nuevo Herald,* 3 February 2002.

20. Anita Snow, "Rechaza Cuba comercio con los Estados Unidos," ibid., 9 June 2001.

21. *The Economic Impact of U.S. Sanctions with Respect to Cuba* (Washington, D.C.: U.S. International Trade Commission, Publication no. 3398, Investigation no. 332-413, February 2001). The report admitted that this figure would "increase marginally" (from $684 million to $1.2 billion) if U.S. exports were to increase by the amount of estimated additional net foreign exchange inflows from telecommunications service payments, travel and tourism payments, and U.S. foreign direct investment.

22. U.S. Bureau of the Census.

23. For a sophisticated discussion of the methodology used by the commission, see the following articles in *Cuba in Transition,* vol. 11 (Washington, D.C.: Association for the Study of the Cuban Economy, 2001): Jonathan R. Coleman, "The Economic Impact of U.S. Sanctions with Respect to Cuba," 86–96; Gary H. Maybarduk, "Comments and Observations on the U.S. International Trade Commission Report," 97–101; William A. Messina, Jr., "Comments on the U.S. International Trade Commission Report," 102–104; William N. Trumbull, "Imperfect Methodology but the Right Results? The USITC Report on the Economic Impact of U.S. Sanctions with Respect to Cuba," 105–109.

24. See, for example, Archibald R. M. Ritter, "Cuba's Economic Performance and the Challenges Ahead," *FOCAL Research on Cuba Background Paper* (Ottawa: Cuban Foundation for the Americas, 2002). Ritter, the leading Canadian specialist on the Cuban economy, concludes that "Cuba still has its major process of economic reform, not to mention political reform, ahead of it." For an example of the kind of optimistic projections common among exile economists in the United States, see Sergio Díaz-Briquets, "Medicare: A Potential Income-Generating Activity for Cuba in the Future," in *Cuba in Transition,* vol. 11 (Washington, D.C.: Association for the Study of the Cuban Economy, 2001), 185–194.

25. Vanessa Bauzá, "U.S. Execs in Havana to Explore Future Trade," *Sun-Sentinel* (Ft. Lauderdale), 8 June 2001.

26. Significantly, Fidel Castro's fainting spell in June 2001 led Miami–Dade County officials to review their contingency plans, which include limiting boat traffic in and out of Florida, enlisting members of the clergy and Latin American leaders to call for

calm, and increasing the presence of Coast Guard cutters and aircraft in and around the waterborne access routes to Cuba. Dana Canedy, "Miami Officials Plan for Turmoil at Castro's Death," *Miami Herald,* 2 July 2001.

27. Retired Cuban Major General Jesús Bermúdez Cutiño, former chief of counterintelligence of the Armed Forces Ministry, has been appointed head of a new think tank (Centro de Estudios de Información de la Defensa) whose major purpose is to liaise with its U.S. military counterparts. Pablo Alfonso, "Hombre de Raúl en un organismo clave para la comunicación entre Cuba y EU," *El Nuevo Herald,* 6 September 2001.

28. Center for Defense Information, press release.

29. Carol Rosenberg, "Former Southcom Chief on Tour in Cuba," *Miami Herald,* 14 February 2001.

30. Petrich, "La transición cubana."

31. Pablo Alfonso, "R.C. desea más colaboración con Washington," *El Nuevo Herald,* 23 January 2002.

32. "Cuba's Raúl Castro Confident of 'Humane Treatment' of Taliban at Guantánamo," *BBC News On Line,* 22 January 2002.

33. For two different views on Helms-Burton and its implications for Cuba's future, see Jorge Domínguez, "U.S.-Cuban Relations: From the Cold War to the Colder War," *Journal of Inter-American Studies* 34, no. 3 (1997), and Mark Falcoff, "Response to Jorge Domínguez," *Journal of Inter-American Studies* 40, no. 2 (1998).

34. Pablo Alfonso, "Alarcón, el exilio y los vuelos a Cuba," *El Nuevo Herald,* 15 July 2001.

35. Felipe Pérez Roque, Radio Progreso, 4 May 2001.

36. John Judis, "Sullied Heritage: The Decline of Principled Conservative Hostility to China," *New Republic,* 23 April 2001.

37. Sergio Aguayo, *Myths and (Mis)perceptions: Clarifying U.S. Elite Visions of Mexico* (La Jolla, Cal.: University of California San Diego, Center for U.S.-Mexican Studies, 1998).

38. Amnesty International, *Los derechos humanos en zonas rurales* (1986), n.p.

39. *Annual Report, 1988* (London: Amnesty International, 1988), 123–125.

40. *World Report, 1989* (New York: Human Rights Watch, 1989), 185–186.

41. I was personally present at a breakfast meeting with the Mexican foreign minister in Washington early in 1990, when a prominent human rights personality actively threatened to "open the human rights dossier" on Mexico if that country did not resume its hostility to U.S. policy in Central America forthwith.

42. Enrico Mario Santí, "José Martí and the Cuban Revolution," *Cuban Studies* 16 (1986). See also Jeannine Verdès-Leroux, *La lune et le caudillo: le rêve des intellectuels et le régime cubain, 1959–71* (Paris: Gallimard, 1989), especially 31–86, and Duvon C. Corbitt, "Cuban Revisionist Interpretations of Cuba's Struggle for Independence," *Hispanic American Historical Review* 43 (August 1963).

43. Introduction to Julián B. Sorel [pseud.], *Nacionalismo y revolución en Cuba, 1823–1998* (Miami: Fundación Liberal José Martí, 1998), 11.

44. Ibid., 27.

45. Jorge Domínguez, "Cuba en las Américas: ancla y viraje (paper presented at Conference on Cuba, Colegio de México, Mexico City, 15 March 2002). I advanced a somewhat similar argument in "Why the Latins Still Love Fidel," *The American Enterprise,* November-December 1990.

46. Mark Frank, "Castro Lauds Anti-Globalization Protests," Reuters, 5 August 2001. Cuban flags were much in evidence at the protests against the G-8 leaders meeting in Genoa the same year. "Des milliers de manifestants anti-G8 défilent a Gênes," *Le Monde* (Paris), 29 July 2001.

47. Again, while such a position does not normally translate into economic benefits, it does position Cuba very advantageously with the international organizations and in the world media.

48. As recently as February 2002, Fidel Castro claimed that Cubans had suffered "dozens of biological attacks," even blaming the United States for destroying 16,000 beehives, causing an estimated $2 million in lost honey output since 1996. Andrew Cawthorne, "Cuba Accuses U.S. of Dozens of 'Biological Attacks,'" Reuters, 25 February 2002.

49. Cubans have never been able to openly discuss and evaluate the meaning and costs, human or otherwise, of their African wars. There are, obviously, no independent veterans organizations. Moreover, a Cuban friend of mine has called my attention to two interesting facts. One never sees *mutilados de guerra*—that is, seriously disabled veterans—in the streets of Havana or other Cuban cities. And the remains of Cubans in Africa brought home in small boxes were sealed in such a way that it was impossible to open them to verify their contents. A curtain of silence appears to have been drawn over the entire episode, even though it consumed the better part of a decade.

50. Luis Manuel García, "Trata de Cubanos," *Encuentro en la red* (Madrid), 30 January 2002.

51. Enrique Florescano, *El nuevo pasado mexicano* (Mexico, D.F.: Cal y Arena, 1991), especially 69–152.

52. Enrique Krauze, "PRI-Occupied," *New Republic,* 25 April 1994.

53. This is the argument of Elizabeth Katharyn Markovits, "The Enemy Makes the Man: U.S. Foreign Policy, Cuban Nationalism, and Regime Survival," *Problems of Post-Communism* (November-December 2001). "Cubans are born into a world in which the United States is a threatening enemy," she writes, "and the regime provides the *only* possible means of resistance." And she adds, "Washington, not Castro, is a primary obstacle to change in Cuba." This article is so anti-American that one can only imagine an American writing it.

54. David Rieff, "Cuba Refrozen," *Foreign Affairs* (July-August 1996).

55. Robyn Swanson, "Unraveling the Layers of Cuban Culture," *North Shore News* (Vancouver, B.C.), 4 February 2002.

56. Manuel Somoza, "Los cubanos saborean la televisión norteamericana," *El Nuevo Herald,* 18 February 2002.

57. Richard Bauer, "Cuba: Eine Gesellschaft ohne Elian," *Neue Zürcher Zeitung* (Zurich), 10 January 2002.

58. David Gonzalez, "In Castro's Changing World, Clashing Voices," *New York Times*, 30 May 2001.

59. Eusebio Mujál-León and Jorge Saavedra, "The International Dimensions of Regime Change: Cuba in the 1990s" (paper delivered at the Twenty-First International Conference of the Latin American Studies Association, Chicago, 24–26 September 1998). See also the discussion of Irving Louis Horowitz, "One Hundred Years of Ambiguity: U.S.-Cuban Relations in the Twentieth Century," *National Interest* (Spring 2002).

60. Maria C. Werlau, "Impressions on the Visit of Pope John Paul II to Cuba," University of Miami, Institute for Cuban and Cuban-American Studies, *Occasional Paper Series* (September 1998).

61. Despite its obvious flaws, this argument has won widespread acceptance among the clergy and intellectual classes in the United States. I once even heard it put by Bernard Cardinal Law, former archbishop of Boston.

62. Jorge Pérez-López, *Cuba's Second Economy: From Behind the Scenes to Center Stage* (New Brunswick, N.J.: Transaction, 1995).

63. Gillian Walker, "Castro's Law Crumbles as Havana Turns Back into a Caribbean Sin City," *Times* (London), 20 August 1995. Among other things, this journalist reported that hundreds of corpses supposedly buried by Havana's state-owned funeral parlors over the past fifteen years never existed, and corrupt officials were billing the state for flowers and coffins for imaginary burials.

64. Claudia Márquez Linares, "Loafing Legacy," Cubanet.org, 8 August 2001.

65. Tania Díaz Castro, "Elderly Cubans Are Suffering," Cubanet.org, 8 August 2001.

66. Ricardo A. Donate-Armada, "The Aging of the Cuban Population," in *Cuba in Transition*, vol. 11 (Washington, D.C.: Association for the Study of the Cuban Economy, 2001), 481–488.

67. Edward Wasserman, "Cuba: Bangkok of the Americas," *Miami Herald*, 7 May 2001.

Index

About the Author

Mark Falcoff is a resident scholar at the American Enterprise Institute, where he writes the monthly *Latin American Outlook*. He has taught at the Universities of Illinois, Oregon, and California at Los Angeles, as well as the U.S. Foreign Service Institute. He has served as a professional staff member on the Senate Committee on Foreign Relations, a senior consultant to the National Bipartisan Commission on Central America, and a visiting fellow at the Council on Foreign Relations. He is a member of the Council on Foreign Relations Task Force on U.S.-Cuban Relations.

Mr. Falcoff is editor of *The Cuban Revolution and the United States, 1958–1960: A History in Documents* (2001) and author of numerous books, including *A Culture of Its Own: Taking Latin America Seriously* (1998) and *Panama's Canal: What Happens When the United States Gives a Small Country What It Wants* (1998).

He received his M.A. and Ph.D. from Princeton University.

A Note on the Book

Juyne Linger of the AEI Press edited this book.

*Jennifer Morretta designed the book and
Amber Wilhelm set it in the typeface AGaramond.*

Nancy Rosenberg prepared the index.

*Edwards Brothers of Lillington, North Carolina,
printed the book on permanent acid-free paper.*